FOUR HUNDRED MILLION ACRES

FOUR HUNDRED MILLION ACRES
THE PUBLIC LANDS AND RESOURCES

CHARLES E. WINTER

ARNO PRESS
A New York Times Company
New York • 1979

Editorial Supervision: ANDREA HICKS

—————•————

Reprint Edition 1979 by Arno Press Inc.

Reprinted from a copy in The University
    of Illinois Library

THE DEVELOPMENT OF PUBLIC LAND LAW
IN THE UNITED STATES
ISBN for complete set: 0-405-11363-3
See last pages of this volume for titles.

Manufactured in the United States of America

—————•————

Library of Congress Cataloging in Publication Data

Winter, Charles Edwin, 1870-
    Four hundred million acres.

    (The Development of public land law in the United
States)
    Reprint of the ed. published by Overland Pub. Co.,
Casper, Wyo.
    Includes index.
    1. United States--Public lands--History. I. Title.
II. Series.
HD216.W5 1979   333.1'0973   78-53543
ISBN 0-405-11392-7

FOUR HUNDRED MILLION ACRES
THE PUBLIC LANDS AND RESOURCES

—By—

CHARLES E. WINTER

Author of
"Grandon of Sierra"
"Ben Warman"
"Wyoming"

History, Acquisition, Disposition,
Proposals, Memorials,
Briefs, Status.

A CHRONOLOGICAL RECORD
AND A
PROGRESSIVE STUDY

CONSERVATION
FEDERAL OR STATE?

Overland Publishing Company
Casper, Wyoming.

Printed in the United States

Press of
S. E. Boyer & Company
Casper, Wyoming.

DEDICATED

To the heroic pioneers who, beginning with the migration of the forefathers to America, started at the Atlantic shore and against inconceivable difficulties advanced the western border line of civilization and American dominion across the forests, prairies, plains and mountains to join the equally brave and indomitable settlers of the Pacific coast.

CONTENTS

INTRODUCTION

A Committee on Conservation and Administration of the Public Domain, appointed by President Hoover, has made its report. Congress will have under consideration a Bill embodying the recommendations which have been made. It is a subject of vast importance to all the people. This volume is presented primarily as a source of information. It is frankly declared that as a whole it supports the cession of all the remaining lands and their resources, excepting the National Parks, by the Federal Government to the States in which they are situated.

CHARLES E. WINTER.

From an Address by President Hoover, Lincoln Day, February 12, 1931

"The Federal Government has assumed many new responsibilities since Lincoln's time, and will probably assume more in the future when the States and local communities can not alone cure abuse or bear the entire cost of national programs, but there is an essential principle that should be maintained in these matters. I am convinced that where Federal action is essential then in most cases it should limit its responsibilities to supplement the States and local communities, and that it should not assume the major role or the entire responsibility, in replacement of the States or local government. To do otherwise threatens the whole foundation of local government, which is the very basis of self-government.

"The moment responsibilities of any community, particularly in economic and social questions, are shifted from any part of the Nation to Washington, then that community has subjected itself to a remote bureaucracy with its minimum of understanding and of sympathy. It has lost a large part of its voice and its control of its own destiny. Under Federal control the varied conditions of life in our country are forced into standard molds, with all their limitations upon life, either of the individual or the community. Where people divest themselves of local government responsibilities they at once lay the foundation for the destruction of their liberties.

"And buried in this problem lies something even deeper. The whole of our governmental machinery was devised for the purpose that through ordered liberty we give incentive and equality of opportunity to every individual to rise to that highest achievement of which he is capable. At once when government is centralized there arises a limitation upon the liberty of the individual and a restriction of individual opportunity."

From an Address by President Coolidge, Congress
Daughters of the American Revolution,
April 17, 1928

"There are always those who are willing to surrender local self-government and turn over their affairs
to some national authority in exchange for a payment
of money out of the Federal Treasury. Whenever they
find that some abuse needs correction in their neighborhood, instead of applying a remedy themselves,
they seek to have a tribunal sent on from Washington
to discharge their duties for them, regardless of the
fact that in accepting such supervision they are barter-
ing away their freedom. Such actions are always taken
on the assumption that they are a public benefit.

"Somewhere, Lincoln said something to the effect
that tyrants always bestrode the necks of the people
upon the plea that it was for their good. He might
have added that the people suffered the rule of tyranny
in the hope that it would be easier than to rule themselves. We have built our institutions around the
rights of the individual. We believe he will be better if
he looks after himself. We believe that the munici-
pality, the States and the Nation will each be better
off if they look after themselves. We do not know
of any other theory that harmonizes with our conception of true manhood and true womanhood.

"We have long since realized that we have become
a Nation. But it is a Nation founded on the individual
States. Their rights ought always to be scrupulously
regarded. Unless their actions are such as to violate
the Constitution and seriously interfere with the rights
of other States, they should be left to solve their own
problem in their own way under the pressure of public

opinion, rather than have outside authority step in to attempt to solve it for them. If we are going to have local self-government, with all of its advantages, we cannot escape from some of its limitations.

"When authority is located afar off it is necessarily less well informed, less sympathetic and less responsive to public requirements. When it is close at hand it is more likely to be executed and in the public interest. Having a personal contact, it is more humane and more charitable."

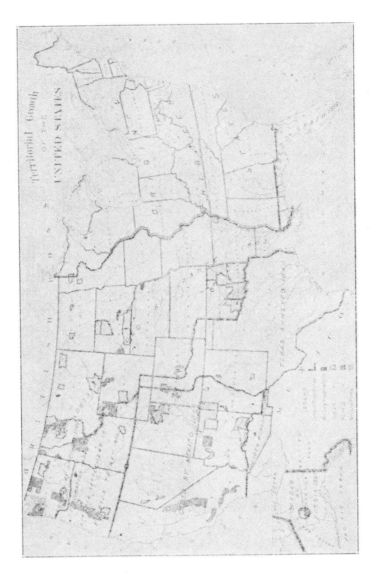

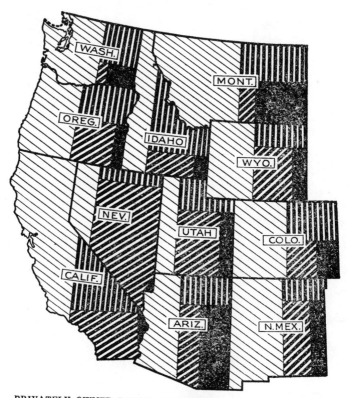

PRIVATELY OWNED LANDS   GOVERNMENT OWNED LANDS

—National Forests

—Unappropriated Public Lands

—Other Government Reservations: Indian, Oil, Mineral and Power, National Monuments, National Parks.

Map No. 1

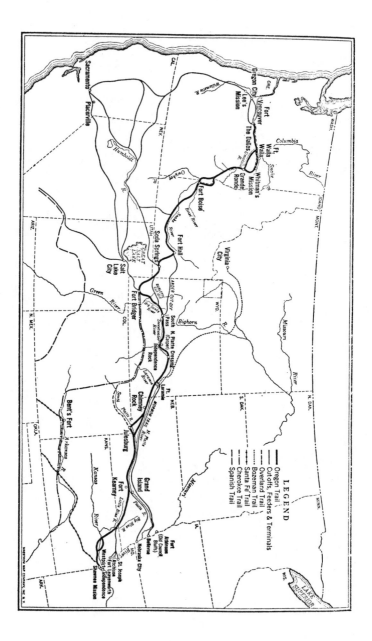

CHAPTER I.

Acquisition.

However great the temptation, it is impossible in a work of this character, which covers the disposition of our lands, to tell the romantic and fascinating story of the several great acquisitions of territory by which the Original Thirteen States and the subsequently formed nation expanded to the Mississippi, then to the Rocky Mountains and then to the Pacific. A brief outline only will be attempted.

It is to be hoped that some day a work will issue which will adequately present all of the statecraft, the diplomacy, the intrigue, the inner spirit, motives and springs of action, the exciting and dramatic incidents, the national and international relations of great moment involved in our accessions by war and purchase.

Whether it be clothed in the romantic garb of fiction or presented in the bare narrative of historical facts, which in themselves constitute national and world-wide chapters of fascinating interest, the story when fully told will grip the minds, hearts and imaginations of the American people, bring a keener realization of the meaning of American citizenship and a deeper conception of the mission of the Republic.

Original States. Treaty with England.

In that narrative you will enter the secret councils of American statesmanship, mingle with men with "empires on their brains," and vision a superb future. You will journey over the waters which Columbus sailed and in Paris follow Franklin, Jay, Adams and Laurens, the American negotiators, representing the

Confederation of the Original Thirteen States which fought and won the Revolutionary War, and thrill with them and the three million colonists for whom they spoke, when the Treaty with England was signed which ceded not only a narrow fringe of land between the Atlantic seaboard and the Alleghanies but a vast area extending westward even unto the Father of Waters; not only the historic ground from northern Maine to southern Georgia, hallowed by a hundred battles and countless sacrifices of the Revolutionary War, the ground of Plymouth Rock, Valley Forge, Bunker Hill, Saratoga and Yorktown, but that deep land of endless virgin territory in whose wilderness recesses the frontier woodsmen, patriot soldiers, fought the conflicts of Kaskaskia and Vincennes; land of the incredible achievements of George Rogers Clark and other chiefs of the border and the forest hinterland. They fought with French, Indian, Spanish, and English foes for control of that inland and its great flowing highway of navigation of which the Ohio was the main tributary to the East. Water transportation was the sine qua non of commerce and growth.

The cession went to and beyond, in the estimation of many, the utmost possibilities territorially of the new nation to be. It conveyed to America forever that entire region east of the great water artery which formed the all-important route between the Great Lakes, so near the St. Lawrence ocean outlet in the North, and the Gulf of Mexico, the sea highway of the South.

Louisiana Purchase.

Again, in 1803, you will cross the ocean and be with the American representatives, Livingston, Minister to France, and Monroe in the Court of France and fol-

low the intricate maze of diplomacy of Talleyrand and
Marbois as they prolonged negotiations through weary,
humiliating months to be suddenly cut short by the
decision of Napoleon, to the surprise of Livingston and
his compatriots and in violation of his pledge to Spain,
to sell to America not merely New Orleans, command-
ing the mouth of the Mississippi, which was vital to
American water commerce around to our own eastern
coast and for foreign export of the products of the "inland empire," but the colossal area extending from the
Mississippi to the fabled and mysterious Rocky Mountains; a second empire comprising an "unknown country" of nearly one million square miles, practically
doubling in one stroke the size of the United States.
The dream of France and England of later regaining
their lost dominion by force of arms was never realized.
Napoleon lost to Wellington at Waterloo. Pakenham
and his trained and disciplined English veterans were
defeated at New Orleans by Jackson. America's ownership was at last secure.

The Louisiana Purchase Territory was to become,
through the spirit of exploration, enterprise and heroism of the frontiersman, the abiding place of forty
millions of people, a mighty bulwark of national soli-
darity, resource, wealth and progress. Its vastness and
inexhaustible riches were but partly disclosed by the
historic expedition sent forth by Jefferson. For generations it was story-land and battle-ground in which
mingled fur-hunter, scout, Indian, soldier, buffalo,
cattle, cowboy, stage coach and pony express; the
arena of adventure, ambition, hope and realization.
The thin, steel edge of the forerunners cut gradually
through the wilderness. Behind followed the home-

builder. Tragedy, massacre, conflict, sorrow and death mingled with drama, victory, exaltation and surging triumph to final settlement and development into a civilization the marvel of which could not have been conceived by even the Napoleonic imagination.

Florida Purchase.

You next turn your faces to the southeast extremity of the nation. There lies an oblong flat, bright-hued land, not to be compared in magnitude with the imperial expanse of the purchase from the Little Corsican, yet strategically and materially vital to the security of the United States. It is the great Peninsula of Florida, Land of Flowers, extending from Fernandina on the North to Key West on the South, a half-thousand miles, containing more than 30,000 lakes in addition to Okeechobee's 1,250 square miles of shallow waters.

Here early in 1513 came Juan Ponce De Leon exploring and searching for the fabled Fountain of Youth on the Island of Bimini. This land, by the very logic of situation and integral connection as part of the mainland must be secured. Not then was it a land of fruit, grain, vegetables, cotton and fisheries. Naught but the brilliant flowers which gave it name met the eager and curious eyes of the explorers who followed De Leon: Miruelo, Narvaez, DeSoto, De Luna, Ribault, Laudonniere and Menendez.

By the Treaty of Paris, 1763, Florida was ceded to England. More than two centuries after De Leon and after the founding by Menendez of St. Augustine, oldest of American Atlantic cities, we come to the American national period; to the picturesque military exploits of the tempestuous and imperative General Jackson and of the brave feats and impressive utterances of the dignified, eloquent Indian character, Osceola, Chief of the Seminoles. In 1779 Spain declared war against Great Britain, seized the English forts in West Florida and in 1781 captured Pensacola. By the Treaty of Paris, 1783, Florida reverted to Spain. In 1810 West Florida declared itself an independent state and sought admission into the American Union. Congress annexed it to the State of Louisiana. President Madison, holding the theory that West Florida was ceded by Spain to France in 1800 as a part of Louisiana Territory and thus was included in the sale of Louisiana to America in 1803, proclaimed it under the jurisdiction of the United States. Ports on the Gulf of Mexico were necessary to America. West Florida was therefore needed as well as New Orleans. Negotiations for West Florida for this purpose in 1803 by strange chance led to and resulted in the Louisiana Purchase. The smaller object was lost in the immensely great acquisition, although the supposition remained that the lesser, West Florida, was included in the greater, Louisiana.

Again war between Great Britain and the United States was approaching, and occurred, 1812-1814. British troops in 1817 landed at Pensacola which General Jackson promptly captured and as promptly evacuated to recapture it in 1818. By the treaty of 1819 Spain formally ceded East and West Florida to the United States. This completed ownership in and possession to America of all land east of the Mississippi. Once again she looked to the West where brightly burned the Star of Empire.

Texas Annexation.

You now trek to the illimitable plains of Texas and
see and read anew the dramatic story of the Lone Star
State; how by American bravery and the unquench-
able spirit of independence its mighty area was wrested
from Mexico, after the sacrifice of Bowie and many
indomitable lives at the Alamo, through the vengeance
victory of San Jacinto; how the banner of Mexico
sank from the flag staff and the Lone Star Flag swept
up in triumph to take its place.

With absorbing interest you review its early history
in which sailed and walked and rode, as early as 1528,
the romantic figures of De Vaca and Coronado, Span-
iards, and La Salle, Frenchman. The Spanish, however, maintained their ascendancy and planted ecclesi-
astical missions, military presidios and civil pueblos.
The territory now made a province was named Tajas
(Texas) from the Indians of that name. American invasion was attempted by Philip Nolan in 1799, by
Gutierrez and Magee in 1812 who actually captured
San Antonio, were victorious over several Mexican
forces but finally succumbed, to be followed by another
abortive attempt by a former officer of the Navy,
James Long. These attempts were sacrificial forerunners of a deep need and purpose, advance eddies of the
coming current of destiny moving in the hearts and
minds of the American people; preliminary outbursts
of the ever-surging and resurging impulses to "make
way for liberty" and its necessity of room and yet more
room whereon to plant its advancing, myriad feet.

With the ratification in 1821 of the cession of Florida
by Spain, vague American claims to Texas were surrendered; but for Spain it was a hollow gain as Mexican revolution was imminent and soon followed to a

successful conclusion. Texas became a part of the Republic of Mexico. But immediately American settlement began. Austin was founded on the Brazos. The frontier people of the United States poured on Texas soil. The striking figures of Austin, Wharton, Smith, Robinson and Archer stalk into view; Johnson, Bowie and Fannin stand forth. Then came, in 1835, under dynamic General Sam Houston, the Lone Star Flag, an Independent State, the Republic of Texas.

It was American. It came unto its own in the inevitable climax. The Stars and Stripes superseded the Lone Star Flag when by joint resolution of Congress in 1845, Texas became the most gigantic state in the Union.

And so Texas came and remained and helped to fight in the war with Mexico which followed. It counts its citizens by the millions and her many great cities rise and grow and expand. Its ports give outlet over the Gulf of Mexico. Its cattle and cotton and wool and oil help to feed, clothe and transport the people of America and of the world, including those of Spain which once had claim to its immense domain.

Oregon Territory Cession.

But the great expansion was not yet at an end. The tremendous impulse of a restless, fresh, eager people was not yet exhausted. The deep-seated urge of wilderness-conquering thousands, strong and insistent, drove onward. It was yet to carry them to the Pacific in the North and in the South.

You follow up the trail of Lewis and Clark, pole-boat up the yellow-mottled Missouri, take with you as guide the most remarkable Indian woman character in all our history, Sacajawea, climb over snow-capped mountain ranges and descend to the deep valley "where rolls the Oregon."

Again, you carry the plow in ox-hauled, covered wagon over the interminable stretches of the Oregon Trail. You pass Fort Laramie, Fort Caspar, the "Firey Narrows of the North Platte," so designated by Stuart and his five companions in 1812 on their return journey from Astoria, discovering the South Pass and establishing the route which became the Oregon Trail; Independence Rock, named by De Smet "The Register of the Desert"; follow the Sweetwater River to its headwaters, swing over South Pass to Fort Bridger, travel on to Fort Hall and the Snake River. Thence you come again where sweep westward through primeval forests the blue waters of the Columbia.

Or perhaps you explore with Fremont to the summit of the sharp-ridged Wind River Mountains of the Rockies. Or hunt and trap the buffalo, bear and beaver and fight the Redmen over the mountains with the first wheeled vehicles to camp in the great basin of the Green River with Bonneville whose travels were given to the world by Washington Irving. Or you penetrate westward through picturesque Hoback Canyon to enter Jackson Hole and stand in awe before the sublimity of the granite-peaked Tetons and reluctantly pass on ever to the North and West across that wonderland, later the Yellowstone National Park, to stand entranced before Old Faithful and the dreamland of beautiful Yellowstone Canyon. Onward again till you mount the Cascades and dip down to Vancouver Bay, or portage down the magnificent Columbia to the rolling waves of the Pacific. You have reached the great objective.

Here in 1792 Captain Gray of the American Navy discovered and named the Columbia, an important factor in the Treaty consideration a half century later. You stand on the shores of the Western Sea and turning landward you behold in imagination splendid cities rearing themselves on river and hill between ocean tide and the soaring peaks of eternally snow-crowned, majestic Rainier and Hood.

Or you mingle with a group of those few thousand hardy Americans who pressed over the great trail to the Northwest between 1841 and 1843, among them heroic women, mothers of men, to stay and plant and reap and to grow. You stand with them at that critical meeting at Champoeg, in 1843, pregnant with national significance and future possibilities, that meeting since memorialized by federal ceremony and monument, that gathering "of the people" where, by the majority of two, the "settlers" carried against English, French and Canadian claims and votes a resolution declaring for the Flag and jurisdiction of the United States. They "represented" a wonderful region over which no flag of earth had ever flown in recognized right by both discovery and occupation—conquest by habitation, until the Oregon Settlement Treaty with England in 1846 surrendered it to the young, giant, puissant nation of the West. The northern boundary was fixed, regardless of our slogan "54-40 or fight," at the 49th parallel. That line of three thousand miles has ever since been one of harmony and peace with Canada.

Thus came United States authority over the Oregon Territory and in this manner was extended the jurisdiction of the new nation throughout the Northwest to the shore of the mightiest of oceans, on whose further side, five thousand miles toward the setting sun, lay the Orient with its teeming millions of olden peoples.

Mexican Cession.

With your Seventy times Seven League Boots, in which you strode in successive giant strides from the soil of the Original Thirteen States to the forested basin of the Mississippi, back southward to the everglades of Florida, westward again across the prairies to the Rockies and once again to the wooded harbors of the Pacific Northwest, you now take the final gigantic stride to the Southwest; at once, in its widely separated and contrasting regions, a land of desert and of flower; of sullen, sterile sand leagues awaiting the coming of life-giving waters and of vine-bearing gentle hills; of cold, wind-swept heights and semi-tropical lowlands; of heated valleys of death and luxuriant slopes of foliage and fruit; of barren mountain chains and rushing mountain streams; land of the ancient civilizations of the Mayan, the Aztec, the Pueblo and the Apache; land of the Missions with bells calling the Spaniard and the Mexican to worship.

After the accession of Texas in 1845 the northern end of Mexico was a barrier to the westward movement of the American people. Disputed territory lay between Texas and the Mexican line on the West. At the direction of President Polk, General Zachary Taylor crossed the Nueces and occupied the disputed ground. Clashes with Mexican armed forces occurred at Palo Alto, Resaca de la Palma and Monterey. Tampico was taken. Declaration of war followed the first bloodshed. Hostilities opened on the Rio Grande. Buena Vista saw the Americans victorious. California was occupied by American land and naval forces.

General Winfield Scott landed at Vera Cruz and marched through successive battles through Cerro Gordo, Contreras, Del Rey and ancient Chapultepec and on September 14, 1847, ran up the American Flag over the citadel of the Montezumas, Mexico City, the Capital, to remain aloft until the treaty of Guadaloupe Hidalgo, the following year, ceded the great Southwest to America.

Of this accession Webster said in the United States Senate, March, 1848, discussing the land indemnity from Mexico, that it was all a barren waste "not worth a dollar." Clay, however, looking intently westward and being asked of what he was thinking, said, "I am listening to the tramp of the oncoming millions."

Immediately after the Treaty with Mexico was signed in 1848, the discovery of gold by James W. Marshall, on January 19, 1848, became known. This discovery, on the American River, at Sutter's Mill, California, was the first of many similar discoveries and developments which were to pour into the coffers of the nation and its people hundreds of millions of dollars of mineral wealth.

And over this land of the Great Salt Lake, of the Golden Gate, of Mt. Shasta, and Mt. Whitney, of the Grand Canyon of the Colorado, of the Santa Fe Trail, of petrified trees, oldest of dead things, of redwood forests, oldest of living things in all the world, of hidden immense oil deposits, of unknown, fabulous lodes of copper and silver and gold an irresistible tide of Americans swept even to the south line of the small Gadsden Purchase of 1853. This line should have continued due west as it began in which event it would have included the mouth of that sinuous giant of waters, the Colorado River, and the north end and

harbor of the Gulf of California into which it throws its turbid flood.

Thus the flag of the Union was carried to the south-west shore and our territorial acquisitions rounded out. Through these dramatic and swift moving events we finally breasted the white surf of the Pacific nearly two thousand miles by coast line south of the 49th parallel at Vancouver.

And thus finally the United States of America came, under the purposes of Providence, to occupy and expand its power over the whole of this magnificent land from sea to sea and from the Rio Grande to Canada. The national spirit had swept our people in sixty years across the continent. It was the most rapid and the strongest folk movement over the greatest and richest area with the most far-reaching results known to history. Destiny determined that we must have entire dominion from ocean to ocean; that our physical base and material resources must be broad and wide and great and rich in order to be commensurate with, and to protect and advance, the great principles of free government which we had enunciated to the world. The United States has grown to be the mightiest nation of the earth. On the foundations of those principles our governmental structure of free and beneficent civilization is yet to be raised to still greater heights.

CHAPTER II.

Evidences of Destiny.

The territorial growth of this great nation is but incidental to a vastly greater truth affecting the destiny of our people. Intimately connected with the acquisition of the areas which now comprise the United States of America were events of tremendous significance not ordinarily associated with our acquirement of vast areas.

Someone once said "Providence takes care of fools, children, and the United States." This was originally spoken half in jest. There are some significant items of evidence tending to show the hand of destiny in the laying of the foundations of the nation preparatory to the later development, which was to make the United States of America the greatest and richest nation of earth and its citizens the most advanced and prosperous of all peoples.

The interposition of Providence seems to be apparent in numerous incidents and conditions associated with the treaties and cessions under which our magnificent domain has been acquired. There is nothing more impressive, heroic and romantic than the successive stories of our accessions. A series of historical novels based upon each of our seven different great territorial additions would picture among scenes dramatic and significant the gradual growth and development of the greatest Republic of all times. Tragedy, heroism, ambition, the elevation of great individuals and personalities, the intrigues of foreign courts, the gallantries of political ministers, influence of women, the despair and rejoicing of ambassadors and special

commissioners in war and peace, ruin and suffering, victory and triumph, are all involved and woven into the experiences and lives of men and nations in the cessions of empires of territory to the United States.

The ways of Providence in the making of this nation are apparent prior to the Revolutionary days. The United States of America began its great struggle for existence July 4, 1776, but 17 years prior on the 13th day of September, 1759, there occurred an event which had a profound bearing upon the territorial beginning of this Nation and without which it would have been exceedingly difficult, if not impossible, to develop and expand as was necessary to make the Nation, even though independence was won. On that date was fought the battle of Quebec on the St. Lawrence on the heights known as the "Plains of Abraham." It was in possession of the French. There extended from the St. Lawrence through the Great Lakes down the Mississippi to New Orleans a sphere and route of influence, power and dominion, which was foreign and contrary to the hopes and aims and the national aspirations of the American Colonists. It was French occupancy and jurisdiction, sustained by alliance with the Indians. Hence the French and Indian Wars. As a result of that battle fought by the combined forces of the Colonies and Great Britain, headed by the English General Wolfe on the one side, and the fortified French, under General Montcalm, on the other, the destiny and dominion of the North American continent was changed and determined forever. It was transformed and transferred from a Gallic to an Anglo-Saxon civilization. It became English.

Thus it was, when the Revolutionary War had been fought and the Treaty with Great Britain by each of the

thirteen separate States was made, England was in possession of and therefore able to include in the terms of the treaty not merely a narrow strip of territory along the Atlantic Coast but a vast domain of 571,000,000 acres extending to the Mississippi, covering approximately one-third of the final Continental area of the United States and retaining access to and command of that great artery of transportation and the protection of the Western border. Another unfoldment brought us that vast area compromised in the Louisiana Purchase in 1803, adding 529,000,000 acres, the second continental third. Another negotiation acquired Florida in 1819, 46,000,000 acres; annexation expanded us over Texas in 1845 with 249,000,000 acres; the mighty Northwest in 1846, 183,000,000 acres more, were secured under the terms of the Oregon Treaty. In 1848, the Mexican Treaty and cession brought into the United States the vast area of the Southwest, 338,000,000 acres, to which was added in 1853 the Gadsden Purchase of 19,000,000 acres. These together made up the final continental third. This completed the onward march of the mighty figure of the young American political giant from the Atlantic to the Pacific, making one great unified country and nation between the two great oceans. In 1867 was concluded the Purchase of Alaska with its prodigious area of 378,000,000 acres. The ceding nations were England, France, Spain, Mexico and Russia.

In 1800 Spain had ceded her rights to the area of Louisiana Territory to France. Thomas Jefferson, a strict constructionist, holding to his own and his party's tenets and principles, declared that under the Constitution there was no power in the Federal Government to purchase territory. These were his settled principles and yet in the workings of Providence, he it was who sent the Commission to France to negotiate with Talleyrand and Napoleon for the purchase of an additional area at the mouth of the Mississippi, the port of New Orleans. After long negotiation and apparently facing defeat in their quest the American Commission was amazed at the offer of Napoleon to cede not only the delta and port of that Spanish city stronghold but the entire area between Mississippi and the Rocky Mountain system, comprising again approximately one-third of our entire continental area. What moved the mind of Jefferson, against his announced principles, to make the Louisiana Purchase?

What moved the mind of Napoleon to give up this vast, rich area to the struggling young Republic? History says his express reasons were immediate financial requirements for war and defense purposes and the desire to build up on the North American Continent a nation which one day would rival and humble England, his traditional enemy. World events, not the United States, brought about these conditions. Thus again with the purchase of Florida, the political and war exigencies of Spain with France and England were the moving causes of her sale to us.

Consider the significance and effect of the discovery, or rather the deferment of the discovery of gold in America. In 1804 there began that magnificent adventure and journey of Lewis and Clark up the Missouri, down the roaring Oregon to the Pacific. In Northern Idaho and Western Montana the feet of the members of this Expedition nearly trod upon gold nuggets in the streams and gulches, later to produce hundreds of millions of dollars in placer and lode gold. The question naturally arises, why this failure to find this

enormous wealth at their very feet? The only answer
is that destiny had in its purpose but one thing, and
that was to advance and carry on the journey, the plan
of exploration and discovery, to the Pacific Ocean at
the mouth of the Columbia, thus completing the northern line of an oval circle, the other perimeter of
which was made by Captain Gray sailing from the Atlantic around Cape Horn up the west reaches of the
two vast Continents of the Western Hemisphere to the
mouth of the Oregon, which, upon discovery and pene-
tration into the channel, he named Columbia. Thus
the Louisiana Expedition formed one of the foundation stones of the American claim to the territory of the
Northwest. Had that Expedition discovered the gold
on the western side of the Rockies, in later years taken
from Alder and Last Chance gulches and other deposits in Montana and Idaho, there can be no doubt
that it would have been dissolved, disintegrated and
would never have reached its destination, upon the
successful accomplishment of which so much depended.

For two hundred years California had been occupied
by the Spaniard and Mexican, who then formed most
of its population, many of whom were the very men or
their descendants who had developed the fabulously
rich mines of old Mexico. They were miners. They
were familiar with mineral formations. They were
gold seekers. That quest had brought the first ex-
peditions from Spain. And yet, they did not discover
gold in California. The Treaty with Mexico, by which
we acquired the great area now comprising the States
of California, New Mexico, Nevada, Utah, parts of
Arizona, Colorado and Wyoming, was made and completed in 1848. Scarcely had the ink of the signatures
of that Treaty become dry when, lo and behold, there

became known the great gold discoveries of California. Had these been made at an earlier date there can be no question but what we would have had tremendous difficulty and possible failure of the inclusion of that wonderful area in the Mexican Treaty. Who can explain the failure of the Mexicans to find the gold deposits of California, Arizona, New Mexico, Nevada?

In 1842 there were rumors of gold in the region of the South Pass, Wyoming, through the Wind River range, on what was then the beginning of travel on the Oregon Trail. Whether by massacre by Indians of the early adventurous miners, or of the workings of Providence in other respect, the rumors died. From 1842 to 1846 stalwart Americans walked over the Oregon Trail and at the head of the Sweetwater River at South Pass tramped near surface gold deposits, which in 1868, 1869 and 1870 produced millions of dollars in the yellow metal. Who can explain otherwise than providentially the failure of these men and the later thousands of Forty-niner gold seekers, rushing to California, to discover that precious metal almost at their feet as they toiled through that pass in the Rockies, a thousand miles to the eastward from the golden Pacific?

The deferment of the discovery of gold at South Pass had a double significance. First, it permitted unchecked the flow of migration from Northern United States into Northern California. When the great crisis of '61, the Civil War, came on, California, by a small margin, provided undoubtedly by the northern blood and numbers which had arrived, determined to stand by the Union. Had the majority of the population in sympathies and its decision been otherwise, who may say what the result of the great war between the States would have been? Who can say whether we would be one Nation today? The other significant angle was that the 2,000 Americans traversing the Oregon Trail from '42 to '43 went as permanent settlers into the northwest region which fact afterwards determined the action of a mass meeting or convention called by the inhabitants for the purpose of declaring for themselves under which flag they chose to live. As related, by the narrow margin of two votes, that convention determined in favor of the Stars and Stripes and organized a local government. Had any considerable number of the travelers of the Oregon Trail destined for the great Northwest been deterred in their migration by the discovery of the gold over which they almost walked at South Pass, who may say what the results of this mass meeting might have been? Judging by the narrow margin it would have been a defeat for the Stars and Stripes. That meeting and its decision by vote was one of the main elements, if not the controlling factor, in the deliberations of the Commissions who finally formulated the Treaty between England and the United States, setting the boundary line in the Northwest on the 49th parallel, thus securing to this young nation a vast, wonderful and rich area, including that mighty artery and magnificent stream, the Columbia.

Had the gold and other mineral values of Alaska been known we probably would never have acquired that marvelous and immense land area, which at the time of its purchase for $7,200,000 was called "Seward's Folly."

Let us not forget the general fact that it was the discovery and production of gold, and other minerals, silver in the great Comstock Lode, in the northern half of western United States that enriched the North in population, free labor, production and resources and enabled it to win the war in 1865 and maintain the Union.

Not only was it vital to the destiny of the Republic to acquire dominion from sea to sea, but it was of even more importance to keep the area and the nation built upon it united.

In 1834 the greatest leader of one of the two great political parties, John C. Calhoun, advanced the doctrine of the right of a state to refuse to obey a national law. This was nullification. Any attempt to put it into actual application meant force in resistance and force in compelling obedience to the federal authority. This would be secession and war, and, if successful, the result—a divided nation. Calhoun was threatening this very thing in the State of South Carolina. The crisis was fast approaching. The sentiment was spreading throughout the South. While the President had indicated his dissent in his official acts the great question was, "Would General Jackson, head of his party, and President of the United States, acquiesce in and give sanction to the widespread and deep-rooted purpose of the large element of his party?"

A banquet was held in Washington. The President was the guest of honor. Many leaders had spoken. The speeches clearly followed and all but openly endorsed the Calhoun idea. All waited to hear the word from Jackson's lips. The trend of the times, the impulses of his followers, the weight of the powerful Calhoun were all toward defiance of the government in its administration of the new tariff law, at the port of Charleston, a policy of the opposition party. At last the President arose. His face was determined. Lifting his glass he proposed the sentiment: "Our Federal

Union—it must be preserved." The die was cast. The
Union was not to be dissolved.

Legend says that later Jackson stated that if Calhoun persisted in carrying out his intention of nullification he would "hang him to the highest tree in South
Carolina." His attitude has been attributed to jealousy
and hatred of Calhoun, personal difference with this
leader of Southern sentiment arising out of a number
of incidents and issues. How and why did these incidents arise? Fate, destiny, Providence, name it what
you will, it was Jackson, the Democrat, the advocate
of States and individual rights, the Southerner, who,
"crushed excessive State's rights, and established the
contrary doctrine in fact and in the political ortho-
doxy" of his party.

What was the source of Jackson's inspiration? Jackson, the impetuous, the violent partisan? Every tendency and influence surrounding him within his own
party was to take the view of the State. Nevertheless,
in the supreme moment he thundered the word—
Union!

"Surely the wrath of men shall praise Thee."
Back of all these rapid acquisitions of territory, alter-
nately in the North and South, lay the impetus of the
slavery agitation. The violent passions aroused by the
determination on the one side to uphold slavery and
upon the other to stop its spread contributed to the
urge to acquire more territory and thus more States
and thus more representation in the National government, first for the one side and then for the other. This
great evil and problem, this irrepressible conflict which
culminated in the war of the States, that mighty movement toward secession, all constituted a cause of extension by successive additions and cessions until we had

shoved our western frontiers to the shores of the
Pacific. Thus was demonstrated the truth of the
Biblical saying for in their wrath in this great conflict of interests and principles, in these violent and
war-like factions Providence attained its great object
of rapidly giving to this Nation a foundation reaching
from ocean to ocean and commensurate in area and
wealth with the great principles, purposes and ambi-
tions which underlie and impel the American Nation
today.

No people can advance in education, art and the
higher things of life unless and until they have the
proper basis of material welfare so that the struggle
for existence shall not consume all of the time and the
energies of men and women. Providence thus secured
for this Nation a vast resource of wealth which has
placed and will maintain it indefinitely at the head of
all Nations. If American principles are to spread
throughout the earth, if representative form of government and individual freedom and initiative are to come
to mankind, this Nation must in the first instance have
the wealth and the power to maintain itself and to extend its influence over the world. Topography, climate and altitude have long since been determined by
science to have its effect upon the character of the
people. In this vast domain affording seashore and
water trade and commerce, the immense agricultural
region of the Mississippi, the wonderful mountainous
areas from the Rockies to the Pacific we have a variety
which should and does breed a people who should en-
dure. When the culture of the East, its chief characteristic, is added to the strength of body and the
strength of mind of the agricultural center, its special
contribution, and these two great characteristics

are constantly imbued with the spirit of independence and love of liberty which lives in the hearts of the dwellers of the mountains, their main quality added to the national character, there is every reason to believe that we shall have a people and institutions such as will be permanent; with such wealth of resources, of such high education and intelligence, and of such vitality, of such longevity, of such devotion to freedom and hostility to centralization and tyranny as shall enable this Nation of ours to stand indefinitely; and to maintain in the future years its manifest destiny of leading the peoples and nations of earth in the principles of free government, constitutional security and individual liberty. Under these and under these alone, the faculties, the aspirations and inspirations of mankind may be unfolded into their full flowering to the fruition of an ever greater and more humane civilization.

CHAPTER III.

Early History.

The general subject of our public lands has been one of great importance and interest from the beginning of our national history. It was important because of the vastness of the area, its potential value, and the growth of the Nation westward from the original thirteen States on the Atlantic, first, to the Mississippi, then to the Pacific Northwest, and then to the Pacific Southwest. It affected our economic life. It was involved in nearly every public question and policy, including internal improvements, tariff, slavery, and the settlement and admission of new States. The lands came to us as follows:

First, by treaty with Great Britain at the close of the Revolutionary War, all the territory of the original thirteen colonies, and in addition all the territory west of them to the Mississippi, including what was later designated as the Northwest Territory; second, purchase of Louisiana from France in 1803; third, purchase of Florida from Spain in 1819; fourth, annexation of Texas in 1845; fifth, Oregon settlement with Great Britain by treaty in 1846; sixth, cession from Mexico in 1848; seventh, the Gadsden purchase from Mexico in 1853; eighth, purchase of Alaska from Russia in 1867.

The following table shows the source of our acquisitions, exclusive of our island possessions, the dates, the price, number of acres, and the price per acre:

Source—	Date	Price	Price per Acre	Number of Acres
British treaty, original States	1783	$	$	570,966,400
Louisiana Purchase from France	1803	15,000,000	.028	529,911,680
Florida Purchase from Spain	1819	5,000,000	.14	46,144,640
Texas Annexation	1845	10,000,000	.04	249,066,240
British Treaty, Oregon	1846			183,386,240
Mexican Treaty, Mexican cession	1848	15,000,000	.044	388,680,960
Gadsden Purchase, Mexico	1853	10,000,000	.52	18,988,800
Total acreage of United States proper		55,000,000	.041	1,937,144,960
Alaska Purchase from Russia	1867	7,200,000	.019	378,165,760
Total acreage, including Alaska				2,315,310,720

The Louisiana Purchase of 529,911,680 acres carried the then western boundary from the Mississippi to the Rocky Mountains. Out of that area were formed the States of Louisiana, Arkansas, Missouri, Iowa, Minnesota, Nebraska, Kansas, Oklahoma, and a large part of North Dakota, South Dakota, Colorado, Wyoming, and Montana. Florida was next acquired, with 46,144,640 acres, for $5,000,000. Next came the annexation of Texas in 1845, which added an area of 249,066,240 acres. In the first bill for the annexation of Texas there was a provision to waive her right and cede her lands to the United States but this bill failed of passage; and in the second bill, which was successful, Texas retained title to all her lands; but disputed portions of her territory became parts of the States of New Mexico, Colorado and Wyoming. We later paid Texas $10,000,000 to surrender her claim to an extensive region in the territory of New Mexico after the same was received from Mexico.

The Oregon settlement came in 1846, adding 183,-386,240 acres, and reaching the north shores of the Pacific. From this were later carved the States of Washington, Oregon, Idaho, and part of Wyoming and Montana. This additional area rounded out our possession and completed the full sweep to the Pacific Northwest.

In 1848 we acquired the Mexican cession, paying $15,000,000, comprising the great areas of California and New Mexico, aggregating 338,680,960 acres. The latter territory was later divided into the States of Arizona Nevada, Utah and parts of New Mexico, Colorado and Wyoming. This completed our onward march to the Southwest Pacific.

In 1853 the southern border was pieced out with a strip known as the Gadsden Purchase, which forms a part of the south end of Arizona and New Mexico, adding 18,988,800 acres, at a cost of $10,000,000.

Alaska was purchased in 1867 from Russia for $7,-200,000. This added 378,165,760 acres, which still remains under Territorial government.

Excluding our island possessions and Alaska, the total area of the United States is 1,937,000,000 acres. Of this amount, 262,000,000 comprised the original 13 colonies and States formed from their areas. There remained 1,675,000,000 acres to be "disposed of" by the national government under the international treaties, the Constitution, and under the policy determined in our early history.

As a note of interest attention is called to the remarkable distinction of the State of Wyoming in two important respects. That State enjoys the sole and unique position of being comprised of a part of each of the four great territorial acquisitions—the Louisiana

Purchase, Texas Annexation, Oregon Settlement and Mexican Cession. A further notable fact is that within an area of 150 miles square in its northwest corner are the source and headwaters of the three primary river systems of the United States west of the Ohio River— the Mississippi River, by its long arm of the Missouri, by its branches the Madison and Gallatin Rivers, these waters flow into the Gulf of Mexico; the Columbia River, flowing into the North Pacific, by its longest branch, the Snake River; the mighty Colorado, emptying into the Gulf of California, by its direct north and south longest arm, the Green River.

We now take up the exceedingly interesting history of the treaties, the Constitution, the ordinances, the waivers and cessions, the laws and policies touching all of the public lands and the erection of new States other than the original thirteen.

Even during the Revolutionary War the question of the territory west of the original colonies was agitated in connection with the growing idea of nationality. The treaty of peace with Great Britain was made with each free, independent, sovereign State which had fought in the Revolution. By that treaty all the territory westward to the Mississippi was added to their possessions. In 1782 the Continental Congress asserted the validity of territorial rights which New York had conveyed. At the request of Congress, Virginia ceded to the United States in 1784 all her extra territory; the other claimant States did the same; Massachusetts in 1785; Connecticut in 1786; South Carolina in 1787; North Carolina ceded Tennessee in 1790; Georgia gave up her western claims in 1802, out of which grew Alabama and Mississippi. Thus the area between the original colonies and the Mississippi

River was added to the new young Nation. Thus
came into being the Northwest Territory out of which
were carved Ohio, Indiana, Illinois, Michigan, and
Wisconsin and part of Minnesota, established by the
Ordinance of 1787, the year of the signing of the
Constitution but prior to its adoption, comprising all
the land east of the Mississippi and north of the Ohio.
The Ordinance of 1787 provided:

> That this territory must be erected into States and have
> their entrance into the Union on equal terms with the original
> States, and bear the same relation to the State government as
> all the original States. They shall be settled and formed into
> distinct Republican States which shall become members of the
> Federal Union and have the same rights of sovereignty, free-
> dom, and independence as the other States.

The treaty with France, conveying the Louisiana
Purchase in 1803, provided:

> The inhabitants of the ceded territory shall be incorporated
> into the Union of the United States and admitted as soon as
> possible, according to the principles of the Federal Constitu-
> tion, to the enjoyment of all the rights, advantages, and im-
> munities of the citizens of the United States, and in the mean-
> time they shall be maintained and protected in the free enjoy-
> ment of their liberty, property, and the religions they profess.

The treaty with Mexico, covering the Mexican Cession in 1848, contained the following provisions:

> * * * shall be formed into free, sovereign, and inde-
> pendent States and incorporated into the Union of the United
> States as soon as possible, and the citizens thereof shall be
> accorded the enjoyment of all the rights, advantages, and im-
> munities as citizens of the original States.

These treaties and provisions, ordinances, and cessions were, and are, the foundation of the principles of
Federal authority and procedure with respect to the
public lands. Fearing illegality of the Ordinance under
the Articles of Confederation in force at the time they

were adopted, regarding the Northwest Territory, they were reenacted August 7, 1889, after the adoption of the Constitution.

The Territories successively acquired were, at least until admitted as States, covered under Article IV, section 3, of the Constitution, which is as follows:

Congress shall have power to dispose of and make all needful rules and regulations respecting the Territories or other property belonging to the United States and nothing in this Constitution shall be so construed as to prejudice any claims of the United States or of any particular State.

And it further provides:

New States may be admitted by the Congress into this Union, but no new State shall be formed or erected within the jurisdiction of any other State.

There were two distinct schools of thought as to the validity, force and effect of the Ordinance for Territorial government. There was no authority in the Articles of Confederation of 1784 or in 1787 for Congress to become sovereign to hold or govern territory. The provision of the Constitution with reference to Federal jurisdiction, and the power over lands within the different States, is found in Article I, section 8, paragraph 17:

To exercise exclusive legislation in all cases whatsoever over such district (not exceeding 10 miles square) as may by cession of particular States and the acceptance of Congress become the seat of Government of the United States, and to exercise like authority over all places purchased, by the consent of the legislature of the State in which the same shall be, for the erection of forts, magazines, arsenals, dockyards, and other needful buildings. And to make all laws which shall be necessary and proper for carrying into execution the foregoing powers and all other powers vested by this Constitution in the Government of the United States or in any department or officer thereof.

Article III, section 2, provides:

The judicial power shall extend to controversies * * * between citizens of the same State claiming lands under grant of different States.

Article XI is as follows:

The judicial power of the United States shall not be construed to extend to any suit in law or equity, commenced or prosecuted against one of the United States by citizens of another State or by citizens or subjects of any foreign state.

No further powers were ever granted by the States or the people of the United States to the General Government regarding lands.

When the Louisiana Purchase was made it was done and held under the doctrine of inherent power of sovereignty and of implied powers flowing from the express provision in the Constitution for the making of treaties. Marshall laid down the doctrine that under the treaty making power the United States might acquire and hold territory by conquest or purchase. The Constitution nowhere expressly conferred upon the Federal Government the power to buy and hold territory. The strict constructionists pointed this out. Jefferson himself called attention to it, yet the nationalistic principle was growing rapidly and strongly under very necessity, and Jefferson, vowing that he could not do it, made the Louisiana Purchase. He later suggested the futile expedient of amending the Constitution afterward to grant the power he had exercised, but this was never done.

Under these documents, and indeed under the Constitution, the great purpose was the building up of the new, independent, sovereign States, which were to be admitted on equal terms with the original 13 States.

The theory was that lands should pass to private ownership as rapidly as possible, so that the new States might come into full sovereignty without delay in order that all States might be equal.

That this was the original, right, and American method of handling the new territory acquired from time to time is evidenced among many sources by the following quotation from the Encyclopedia Britannica, eleventh edition, volume 27, page 684, paragraphs 78, 79, 80, 81 and 82:

78. Congress and its committees had already begun to declare that it was impossible to carry on a government efficiently under the articles. Its expostulations were to be continued for several years before they were heard. In the meantime it did not neglect the great subject which concerned the essence of nationality—the western territory. Virginia had made a first offer to cede her claims, but it was not accepted. A comittee of Congress now made a report (1782) maintaining the validity of the rights which New York had transferred to Congress: And in the next year Virginia made an acceptable offer. Her deed was accepted (March 1, 1784); the other claimant States followed and Congress, which was not authorized by the articles to hold or govern territory, became the sovereign of a tract of some 430,000 square miles, covering all the country between the Atlantic tier of States and the Mississippi River, from the British possessions nearly to the Gulf of Mexico.

79. In this territory Congress had now on its hands the same question of colonial government in which the British Parliament had so signally failed. The manner in which Congress dealt with it has made the United States the country that it is. The leading feature of its plan was the erection, as rapidly as possible, of States, similar in powers to the original States. The power of Congress over the Territories was to be theoretically absolute, but it was to be exerted in encouraging the development of thorough self-government, and in granting it as fast as the settlers should become capable of exercising it. Copied in succeeding acts for the organization of Territories, and still controlling the spirit of such acts, the ordinance of 1787 (July 13, 1787) is the foundation of almost everything which makes the modern American system peculiar.

80. The preliminary plan of Congress was reported by a committee of which Thomas Jefferson (q. v.) was chairman, and was adopted by Congress on the 23rd of April, 1784. It

provided for the erection of 17 States, north and south of the Ohio, with some odd names, such as Sylvania, Assenisipia, Metropotamia, Polypotamia, and Pelisipia. These States were forever to be a part of the United States and to have Republican governments. The provision, "After the year 1800 there shall be neither slavery nor involuntary servitude in any of the said States, other than in the punishment of crimes whereof the party shall have been duly convicted," represented Jefferson's feeling on this subject, but was lost for want of seven States in its favor.

81. The final plan of 1787 was reported by a committee of which Nathan Dane, of Massachusetts, was Chairman. The prohibition of slavery was made perpetual, and a fugitive slave clause was added. The ordinance covered only the territory north of the Ohio, and provided for not less than three nor more than five States: Ohio, Indiana, Illinois, Michigan, and Wisconsin have been the resultant States. At first Congress was to appoint the governor, secretary, judges, and militia generals, and the governor and judges were, until the organization of a legislature, to make laws subject to the veto of Congress. When the population reached 5,000 free male inhabitants the Territory was to have an assembly of its own, to consist of the governor, a legislative council of five, selected by Congress from 10 nominations by the lower house and a lower house of representatives of one delegate for every 500 free male inhabitants. (When the total number should reach 25, the legislature itself was to have the power of regulating the number and proportion. Property qualifications were prescribed for electors, representatives, and members of the council). This assembly was to choose a delegate to sit, but not to vote, in Congress, and was to make laws not repugnant to "the principles and articles" established and declared in the ordinance. These were as follows: The new States or Territories were to maintain freedom of worship, the benefits of the writ of habeas corpus, trial by jury, proportionate representation, bail, moderate fines and punishments, and the preservation of liberty, property, and private contracts; they were to remain forever a part of the United States; and they were not to interfere with the disposal of the soil by the United States, or to tax the lands of the United States, or to tax any citizen of the United States for the use of the navigable waters leading into the Mississippi or St. Lawrence Rivers. These articles were to be unalterable unless by mutual consent of a State and the United States. The transformation of the Territory, with its limited government, into a State, with all the powers of an original State, was promised by Congress, as soon as the population should reach 60,000 free inhabitants, or under certain conditions, before that time.

82. The Constitution, which was adopted almost immediately afterwards, provided merely (Art. IV, par. 3) that "Con-

gress shall have power to dispose of, and make all needful rules and regulations respecting the territory or other property belonging to the United States," and that "new States may be admitted by the Congress into this Union." Opinions have varied as to the force of the Ordinance of 1787. The southern school of writers have been inclined to consider it ultra vires and void; and they adduce the fact that the new Congress under the Constitution thought it necessary to reenact the ordinance (August 7, 1789). The opposite school have inclined to hold the ordinance as still in force. Even as to the territorial provision of the Constitution, opinions have varied.

CHAPTER IV.

Contention in United States Senate, 1826-1834, for State Ownership.

From 1826 to 1834, there were presented on the floor of the United States Senate well-defined divergent views on the legal status of the public lands; the one asserted the complete dominion and right of the Fedderal Government, the other denied the capacity and constitutional power of the United States to own and hold the public lands, except a temporary control over its territories from their acquirement until their formation into States. Senator Kane, of Illinois, contended strongly and ably that from the moment of admission each State became and was absolutely sovereign over every foot of soil within its boundaries. The Governors and Legislatures of Illinois, Indiana, and Missouri, and their representatives took a similar view and asked the United States to cede back to the States the lands therein. This position was founded on the terms of the international treaties by which the Northwest Territory, the Louisiana Purchase, and Florida Purchase were acquired, and in the provisions of the waivers and cessions of the States ceding the Northwest Territory and other territory to the Union.

We quote now from the congressional debates, Twentieth Congress, first session, of January 28, 1829, No. 5, volume 4, part 1, being a speech on the subject of public lands by Senator Hendricks, maintaining the State view:

This Union is in theory formed of sovereign, equal people and independent States. In the older members of this confederacy the Federal Government sets up no claim to the waste and unappropriated lands, has no land offices, derives no revenue from the sales of lands. In the new States this Government is the lord of the soil, has established land offices, and collects millions from the sale of lands. A statement or historian making himself acquainted with our system would pronounce it in theory beautiful. With nothing would he be more pleased than with the republican equality of the States. But what would be his surprise when told that in seven of these States the soil itself belongs to the Government of the Union, while in 17 States the soil belonged to the States themselves. Would he not instantly inquire why are the States of this confederacy equal in theory when they are not so in fact? Why are they not equal in reality as they are in name? The answer to this last inquiry would be the reasons against the propositions now heard before the Senate. He would then hear, as we have so often heard, of the cessions, the pledge, and the compacts.

I am aware, Mr. President, that these are usually resorted to as the authority of this Government to hold the lands in the States; but these authorities taken in connection with other portions of the history of that day, instead of showing title in the Federal Government, may, in my opinion, safely be relied on to sustain a different position. It surely was the intention of the States ceding and of Congress in receiving these cessions that the territory thus ceded should be formed into states and should be received into the Union as free, sovereign and independent States, on an equal footing with the original States in all respects whatever. That they should thus be received into the Union was most certainly the intention of the framers of the Constitution.

It is said we may not cede the lands to the States because Congress stands bound to appropriate their proceeds to the payment of the public debt. The pledge, as it is called, is immediately referred to. This pledge, sir, I believe, is to be found nowhere else than in the act of cession of Virginia and in her deed of transfer to the Union.

Whatever the language of this pledge may be, the object of the contracting parties is plainly expressed. That object was that all the States should become and remain members of the Confederacy, and as a strong inducement for so doing it was stipulated that the proceeds of the ceded lands should be appropriated in favor only of those States that had subscribed the articles of Confederation.

This provision held out to the new States thereafter to be formed strong inducements to join the Confederacy, for, refusing to do so, they would be deprived of their respective proportions of the proceeds of the Territorial lands, while they would be chargeable with their proportions of the public debt. The inducement, too, in their case was much strengthened in the Ordinance of 1787, which prohibited them after they should become States from interfering with the primary disposal of their own soil until they should have joined the Confederation.

I have said, Mr. President, that this pledge has reference only to a Territorial form of government, and has no reference whatever to a period after the political condition of the country shall have been totally changed—after it shall have been formed into sovereign, free, and independent States.

Whenever it becomes necessary for this Government to divert any portion of the public lands from the object of this pledge it can forthwith be done; but when the fair claims of the new States are presented for the whole or a part of these lands, then, indeed, this pledge rises in great majesty and strength. Put this matter on what ground soever you please, these lands are long ago released. If bound for the payment of the Revolutionary debt, that debt, is, in amount, long ago paid; and if inseparable from the sovereignty of the States, they are in that way released, although the debt is not paid.

Can anyone believe that the ordinance would guarantee, one particular event, the admission of these States into the Union on an equal footing with the original States, in all respects whatever, if it had been the intention of Congress to retain the full property of the soil, while the soil of the original States belonged to those States?

Being recognized as States before they had joined the Confederacy, the Congress of 1787 thought proper to restrain them, previous to their joining the Union, from the primary disposal of the soil. * * * * It was contended for many of the advocates for the Missouri admission that she, having formed her constitution, convened her legislative body, enacted her own laws, was in very deed a State, and that her State sovereignty and equality included her right to her public domain.

We shall be told that Congress have power to dispose of and make all needful rules and regulations respecting the territory or other property belonging to the United States. * * * * If you say the ordinances were repealed by the Constitution of the United States, you lose the benefit of its prohibitions against the new States; and if you admit that the ordinance, with its guarantees in favor of the new States, is sanctioned by the Constitution, you must admit that the new States, * * * were entitled to admission into the Union on an equal footing with the original States.

The ordinance contemplated the public lands as belonging to the new States, after their admission into the Union, and, if all other authorities were wanting to prove this, the ninth article of the Confederation would be sufficient. It declares that no State shall be deprived of territory for the benefit of the United States. * * * * The meaning of the ordinance compared with this article becomes perfectly clear.

As a further inducement to the new States to join the Confederacy, the ordinance stipulated that they should be admitted

into the Union *   *   *   *   on an equal footing with the
original States in all respects whatever, and the Constitution,
in sustenance of the same policy, provides that all engagements
entered into before the adoption of the Constitution shall be
as valid against the United States, under the Constitution, as
under the Confederation. So that the articles of the Confederation, the acts of cession, the ordinance of 1787, and the Constitution itself, form a perfect and harmonious chain of policy—
the grand object of which was the union and equality of the
States. Then, Mr. President, if at all correct in this view, it
may well be asked, by what means have the new States been
deprived of their equality of the right of soil?

The Indiana Senator then took up the question of
compacts made with the new States, the waivers and
cessions by the new States, in the acts of admission
to the United States, and the pledge not to interfere
with the primary disposal of the soil. On this the
Senator said:

And are we to be told that although the sovereignty and
equality of the States, as well as the stipulations of the ordinance, would have given us, without the compacts, the soil of
our country, we are to be deprived of that first attribute of
sovereignty by the conditions imposed when we asked permis-
sion to form for ourselves a constitution and State Government?
These compacts, it is true, ought never to have been made,
and however soon we may get clear of them we shall have
suffered sufficiently by them. *   *   *   The territories, anxious
to gain a political elevation, anxious to gain the level of equality with the original States, did not rightly consider the immense sacrifices they were making for the name, while they
were not really acquiring the substances of equality and independence. *   *   *   Congress, upnder these circumstances, having
the power to admit or not, responded to this request of Ohio
with conditions. That part of the ordinance which prohibited
the new States from full property in the soil until they should
be admitted into the Union was made perpetual; and the prohibition of sale and taxation was imposed for no other consideration than a few sections of school lands; a few supposed salt
springs, and 5 per cent of the proceeds of the public lands, for
internal improvements.

Senator Hendricks then showed how Louisiana and
Indiana were next admitted under the imposition of the

same condition not to interfere with the primary disposal of the soil, and pointed out that if the United States had a right to impose these conditions then, it could impose others which could never be complied with and in this way exercise the power of refusal. He continues:

The public lands should be ceded to the States in which they lie, because their present condition is not warranted by the letter of the Constitution of this Government. * * * Its powers are carefully enumerated and specified; and so jealous were its framers that after each specification contained in it, it is expressly inhibited the exercise of any powers except those delegated to itself or prohibited to the States. We shall search in vain for any clause in the Constitution which prohibits to the States the exercise of any powers connected with the public lands. In all the original States this power has always been exercised by the State. * * * One of the principal difficulties in the formation of this Government was to designate the boundary betwixt it and the States, and it seems to have been the care of its framers to avoid as much as possible municipal legislation; the regulation of all local and domestic concerns. It seems to have been intended that the Federal Government should not engage in that which the States were competent to do. * * * The Compacts are unwarranted by the Constitution, and if so are not binding on the States.

I deny, sir, the constitutional power of this Government to hold lands within the limits of the States, except for the purposes designated by the Constitution, such as forts, magazines, arsenals, dockyards, and other needful buildings; and to enable Congress to hold lands even for these purposes; and consent of the legislatures of the States is declared to be necessary by the express language of the Constitution. In a question of such vital importance to the new States it would surely not be thought unreasonable that they should scrutinize the power which takes from them the public lands within their limits, impairs their sovereignty, and deprives them of equality with the original States. It would be at least some consolation to know that the power which prostrates them at the foot of the Union, which assigns them a level lower than that of the original States is based on the Constitution.

This power, Mr. President, of the States to make contracts is one thing and the Constitution of the United States is another. And although the States may have the power to make compacts by which a portion of their sovereignty may be alienated, yet it does not follow, of course, that they have a right to transfer such sovereign power to the Union or that the Union could receive or exercise such power. The boundary separating Federal and State powers may be considered the stability of our political system. This boundary may not be passed by either for any purpose; neither to usurp nor to transfer power; for in either way would our system be deranged and the Constitution suffer violence. A State may have the power of destroying her own constitution, though totally destitute of power to interfere with the constitution of another State or with that of the Union. Suppose a State to determine on its own dissolution: Could it transfer all its powers, legislative, executive, and judicial, to the Federal Government? And, if a State could so transfer its powers, could this Government receive such transfer or exercise such powers? Surely not. If one jot or tittle of power not given by the Constitution can be acquired or exercised in such way as this, then farewell to the guards against usurpation of power, placed by the wisest and best of men around the Constitution; farewell to the sovereignity of the States. Establish this doctrine and we may live to see a consolidation of all power in the hands of this Government. Then, indeed, would the Constitution have prescribed in vain the mode of its own amendment. Vain would be the provisions that two-thirds of Congress, or of the States should agree in calling a convention to propose amendments and that three-fourths of the States should be necessary to ratify such amendments, if the Constitution can be changed by transfers of power from individual States or by compacts with the several States.

I lay it down, sir, as a proposition not to be resisted that the rights of soil and taxation are inseparable from the sovereignty of every independent State.

John Marshall in delivering the opinion of the Court in the case of Fletcher v. Peck (6 Cranch, 128) said:

That the Legislature of Georgia, unless restrained by its own constitution, possesses the power of disposing of the unappropriated lands within its own limits in such manner as its own judgment shall dictate is a proposition not to be controverted.

Again, he said in Martin v. Hunter (1 Wheat. 325):

The sovereign powers vested in the State governments by their respective constitutions remain unaltered and unimpaired, except so far as they are granted to the Government of the United States.

Once more quoting Senator Hendricks on the correlated subject of internal improvements:

The question of internal improvements is one which the new States in the present condition of the public lands, can never yield. It is in vain to expect that while the lands belong to the Federal Government, while millions are drained from the country into the Treasury of the Union, these States will cease to ask aids for the improvement of their country in roads and canals. It is reasonable that they should so ask. The new States have recently seen New York finish her splendid canal. They see Pennsylvania in progress with one no less splendid. They see other States carrying on other public works. These States have all derived revenues, almost inexhaustable, from their public lands, and Pennsylvania, though one of the oldest States, has not yet exhausted the great source of revenue, for on a recent occasion she has pledged the revenues to be derived therefrom to the progress of the canal.

The public lands in the hands of the new States would put those States on an equal footing with the original States. They would be sources of revenue for the improvement of those States, and they would relieve their agricultural interests from the heavy burdens they at present bear to sustain their treasury. Few of the old States are reduced to the necessity of a land tax to meet their current expenditures, but in the new States, having few objects of taxation, lay heavy contributions on their agricultural interests for that purpose. Almost all the circulating medium of the new States is drained into the Treasury of the United States by the operation of the land offices, and the lands thus purchased are taxed heavily to support the State governments. So in no portion of the Union is agriculture so much burdened as in the new States. * * * * But the people of these States are devoted to the Union. You cannot drive them from the Union. They are attached to our republican institutions and proud of the trophies and achievements of the Revolution. They wish to perpetuate to future ages the liberties of their country and the Union of the States. They wish to preserve inviolate the Constitution, and ask for that justice which will place them on an equal footing with the original States, which will place in their hands the first attribute of sovereignty—the soil of their country. I trust they will not ask in vain.

In January, 1830, in the Senate occurred the famous debate between Webster and Hayne. It arose over the Foot resolution for an inquiry into the status of the public lands, and into the further question whether the public surveys proceeding on such lands might not be stopped and land offices closed. The debate, participated in by many Senators had proceeded for many days before, and continued many days after, the famous speech of Hayne, and the more famous Webster's Reply to Hayne, which extended into the momentous question of the right of a State to nullify a law of the United States in case the State believed such Federal law to be unconstitutional. A portion of the speeches of both Webster and Hayne relating to the public lands is now quoted as significant upon whether the emphasis should be placed upon that portion of the Ordinance which held that the land should be disposed of for the common benefit of all the States or that portion which provides for the admission of new States as free, independent, sovereign, and equal to the original thirteen States, and whether this last object did not include and comprehend the first.

In a Senate speech in January, 1825, Daniel Webster stated:

There could be no doubt if gentlemen looked at the money received into the Treasury from the sale of the public lands of the West, and then looked to the whole amount expended by the Government (even including the whole amount of what was laid out for the Army), the latter must be allowed to be very inconsiderable, and there must be a constant drain of money from the West to pay for the public lands. It might be said that this was no more than the refluence of capital which had previously gone over the mountains. Be it so. Still its practical effect was to produce inconvenience, if not distress, by absorbing the money of the people.

The Government has received eighteen or twenty millions of dollars from the public lands, and it is with the greatest satisfaction I advert to the change which has been introduced in the method of paying for them; yet I could never think the national domain is to be regarded as any great source of revenue. The great object of the Government in respect of these lands is not so much the money derived from their sale as it is the getting them settled. What I mean to say is I do not think we ought to hug that domain as a great treasure which is to enrich the exchequer.

Robert Y. Hayne, January 21, 1830, in the Senate said:

If in the deeds of cession it has been declared that the grants were intended for "the common benefit of all the States" it is clear from other provisions that they were not intended merely as so much property, for this expressly declared that the object of the grant is the erection of new States, and the United States in accepting this trust bind themselves to facilitate the formation of these States to be admitted into the Union with all the rights and privileges of the original States. This, sir, was the great end to which all parties looked, and it is by the fulfillment of the high trust that the common benefit of all the States is to be best promoted.

On January 19, 1830, he stated on the question of legal status and equitable consideration:

Sir, the amount of this debt has, in every one of the new States, actually constantly exceeded the ability of the people to pay, as is proved by the fact that you have been compelled from time to time in your great liberality to extend the credits, and in some instances even to remit portions of the debt, in order to protect some land debtors from bankruptcy and total ruin.

Come now to the claims set up by the West to these lands. The first is, that they have a full and perfect legal and constitutional right to all the lands within their respective limits. This claim was set up for the first time only a few years ago, and has been advocated on this floor by the gentlemen from Alabama and Indiana with great zeal and ability. Without having paid much attention to this point it has appeared to me that this claim is untenable. I shall not stop to enter into the argument further than to say that by the very terms of the grants under which the United States have acquired these lands the absolute property in the soil is vested in them, and must, it would seem, continue so until the lands shall be sold or otherwise disposed of. I can easily conceive that it may be extremely inconvenient, nay, highly injurious to a State, to have immense bodies of land within her chartered limits, locked up for sale and settlement, withdrawn from the power of taxation, and contributing in no respect to her wealth or prosperity. But though this state of things may present strong claims on the Federal Government for the adoption of a liberal policy toward the new States, it can not affect the question of legal or constitutional right.

* * * * While they shall continue to ask and gratefully to receive these petty and partial appropriations, they will be

kept forever in a state of dependence. Never will the Federal Government, or rather those who control its operations, consent to emancipate the West by adopting a wise and just policy looking to any final disposition of the public lands while the people of the West can be kept in subjection and dependence by occasional donations of those lands, and never will the Western States themselves assume their just and equal station among their sisters of the Union while they are constantly looking up to Congress for favors and gratuities.

The public debt must first be paid. For this these lands have been solemnly pledged to the public creditors. This done, which if there be no interference with the sinking fund will be effected in three or four years, the question will then be fairly open, to be disposed of as Congress and the country may think just and proper. * * * * I suggest for consideration whether it will not be sound policy and true wisdom to adopt a system of measures looking to the final relinquishment of these lands on the part of the United States to the States in which they lie, on such terms and conditions as may fully indemnify us for the cost of the original purchase and all the trouble and expense to which we may have been put on their account. Giving up the plan of using these lands forever as a fund either for revenue or distribution, ceasing to hug them as a great treasure, renouncing the idea of administering them with a view to regulate and control the industry and population of the States or of keeping them in subjection and dependence the States or the people of any portion of the Union, the task will be comparatively easy of striking out a plan for the final adjustment of the land question on just and equitable principles. Perhaps, sir, the lands ought not to be entirely relinquished to any State until she shall have made considerable advances in population and settlement. Ohio has probably already reached that condition. The relinquishment may be made by a sale to the State at a fixed price, which I will not say should be nominal, but certainly I should not be disposed to fix the amount so high as to keep the States for any length of time in debt to the United States. In short, our whole policy in relation to the public lands may perhaps be summed up in the declaration with which I set out that they should be administered chiefly with a view to the creation within reasonable periods of great and flourishing communities, to be formed into free and independent States, to be invested in due season with the control of all the lands within their respective limits.

It is impossible to say that a State is admitted on equal terms with the original States which retained and owned every foot of soil of the public lands within their borders and even public lands outside their boundaries, when approximately all the soil of that State is retained in and controlled and great portions permanently reserved by the Federal Government, all tax free. To draw four lines on the map and call it Colorado, without ownership of and sovereignty over the soil, even though it is given political representation, does not admit that State on an equality with the original States, for it lacks the other vitally important if not equally essential attribute.

Let us illustrate: The granting by the Federal Government to Montana of 500,000 acres of land, for state institutions upon its admission, out of a total of more than 94,078,080 acres in its area, does not change the legal and sovereignty propositions stated. Nor does the fact that this was augmented by school sections and other grants for colleges, and later Carey Act projects, constitute that equal sovereignty specifically provided in the Louisiana Purchase and other treaties, and clearly contemplated in the Constitution. A part is never equal to the whole. Anything less than the whole leaves unequal terms and an incomplete sovereignty.

As long as a given area of land was territory, the Constitution makes clear provision for its control by the Federal Government, in Article IV, Section 3:

But there is not a line in the Constitution which expressly authorized the Federal Government to retain ownership and control after that Territory is organized into a State. On the contrary, the equality among the States fixed by the Constitution demands that the State then have absolute ownership, which includes jurisdiction, power of disposition and taxation. And it applies to every foot of soil and everything in it to the center of the earth. Again, the international treaties provided for admittance of sovereign States, with "equal rights, advantages, and immunities to its citizens."

CHAPTER V.

Theory of Federal Trusteeship Adopted.

The great Public Land Committee of the United States Senate, in 1832, after a comprehensive survey and study of the public lands, made a formal report, in part, in the following words:

Our pledge would not be redeemed by merely dividing the surface into States and giving them names.

The public debt being now paid, the public lands are entirely released from the pledge they were under to that object, and are free to receive a new and liberal destination for the relief of the States in which they lie.

Nearly one hundred millions of acres of the land now in market are the refuse of sales and donations through a long series of years, and are of very little actual value, and only fit to be given to settlers or abandoned to the States in which they lie.

The speedy extinction of the Federal title within their limits is necessary to the independence of the new States, to their equality with the elder States, to the development of their resources, to the subjection of their soil to taxation, cultivation, and settlement, and to the proper enjoyment of their jurisdiction and sovereignty.

The ramified machinery of the Land Office Department and the ownership of so much soil extends the patronage and authority of the General Government into the heart and corners of the new States and subjects their policy to the danger of a foreign and powerful influence.

Thus it is seen that the true view and policy, the great consideration, the great purpose was and should be the development of the new area and of the new States carved therefrom.

In 1832, Henry Clay, in an address in the Senate presented the extreme nationalistic viewpoint of the public land question. His policy was, in fact, in large part carried out by legislation in 1834.

And it was at this point, in 1834, that the policy of our Government was settled and fixed on the principle that the Government was to hold the legal title and as trustee "dispose of" the public land. It was a trust for the reason that the Ordinance and international treaties made it so and the Constitution provides but one method of acquiring property for the United States in absolute ownership, that is, by purchase, Article 1, section 8, paragraph 16; heretofore quoted in Chapter III.

The manufacturing States of the North Atlantic by reason of their great population controlled a majority of the votes of Congress. They did not want their people and workingmen to migrate to and settle the West. They, therefore, not only denied the legal claim, but they also determined to defeat the movement for Congress to cede the lands to the States admitted, and to the subsequent States upon admission. The fact that they had had every foot of their soil and sold their public lands, and additional lands beyond their borders, and with the proceeds built up funds for the enrichment and development of their States, did not deter them.

Henry Clay, though a westerner, from Kentucky, was a member of the Committee on Manufactures. He was an expectant candidate for the Presidency. His course may have been influenced by the voting strength of the eastern manufacturing States in the Senate, House, and country. He threw in his lot with the East as against the then West on the public-lands question. The report of the Manufactures Committee of the Senate, presented and argued by Clay, was against ceding the lands to the States and favored the policy, which was adopted in 1834 by force of their votes without regard to legal rights or equities, of

MUIR FOREST—CALIFORNIA
Courtesy Chamber of Commerce, Sacramento

the continued Government control of the lands even after Territories were admitted as States.

But even they denominated the Government a trustee, stating that the lands were to be administered, the Revolutionary War debt being paid, for the benefit of the States in which the lands were located, and sold into private ownership as rapidly as possible. This was afterwards and is today perverted to mean under the phrase "for the benefit of all the States" to include all the people of all the States. Such is the position held today by the States east of the Rockies, notwithstanding they have all had their lands and everything in them. The four sons of Uncle Sam—North, East, South, West—were entitled to their equal inheritance. North, East, and South duly received theirs. Now, when the West comes of age and asks for its equal share, North, East, and South say, "Now, we will divide the last quarter among the four of us."

Nearly all the States of this Union except the present eleven public-land States, have gradually but finally, by transfer to private ownership, come into full possession, control, jurisdiction, taxation and development of all their lands and resources, including surface, forests, and minerals. This was under the trusteeship policy imposed by the East against the then West. Twenty-six of the States east of the Rocky Mountains, received their mineral wealth by and through grants, purchases, mineral locations, and homesteading of the people who settled those States.

This is generally true of the States east of the Rocky Mountains. Texas retained all of its lands and minerals for itself when it was annexed. Some States were granted all their minerals when admitted or by subsequent provision that exempted them from the operation of the mining laws permitting full title to be gained by homesteading, including the minerals.

But when it came the turn of the States of the Rocky Mountain region and westward to the Pacific to be developed, the letter and the spirit of the trusteeship, as explained and placed of record in the United States Senate by those who imposed it by main force and strength of votes, in lieu of ceding to the States, has been denied, violated, and perverted by interpretation of old laws and by the passage of new laws.

The West, unable to secure their lands and resources upon admission, acquiesced in the policy which was adopted in 1834 and adjusted itself to develop thereunder. Under it all its land, including forests and minerals, would, though gradually, ultimately pass to private ownership, and thus the Western States would have come eventually, though long delayed, into full sovereignty and development.

The West was and is agreeable to the general mining law of 1866 and 1872 and later amendments whereby mineral lands were made not subject to homestead entry and mineral rights reserved from agricultural patents, but were made subject to mineral location and conveyed thereunder, on compliance with the mining law, by patent to its citizens. The mineral lands were thus made available to the people and came into private ownership and taxation. This policy was acceptable, as it carried on the general plan of disposing of the public domain to the people, contributed to its development, individual opportunity, and State sovereignty.

The views of Senators Hendricks and Kane and of the Representatives of Indiana, Illinois, and Missouri were not accepted as to the absolute and exclusive

State ownership and right of disposition of the soil; but it was well recognized that the jurisdiction over the lands was in the States and that the provision of all treaties and cessions and laws merely constituted the General Government a trustee for the sale and disposition of the lands, and the remaining problem was as to whether thenceforth, the debt of the Revolution having been paid, the declared common benefit to all the States of the Union and their people had not been fulfilled in a monetary sense, and that thenceforth the common benefit was limited to and recognized to be solely in the settlement of the new country and the formation of new States.

The United States Supreme Court, in Kansas v. Colorado (206 U. S. 55) analyzes section 3 of Article 4, which in part is as follows:

The Congress shall have power to dispose of and make all needful rules and regulations respecting the property or Territory belonging to the United States.

Attention is called to the exceedingly significant conclusion of that section:

And nothing in this Constitution shall be so construed as to prejudice any claims of the United States or of any particular State.

The court says of that section that it is limited and purposely guarded by the tenth amendment, which reads:

The powers not delegated to the United States by the Constitution, nor prohibited by it to the State, are reserved to the States, respectively, or to the people."

The Constitution does not provide that a State, when admitted, should not have ownership and control of the soil within its boundaries. The natural assumption and logical conclusion would be that it was therefore a right reserved to the State, just such a right as was held and was exercised by every one of the thirteen original States, with which it was to be on equal terms. Ownership of the soil, which is ordinarily a necessary attribute of sovereignty, was not in the Constitution "prohibited by it to the States," nor was the right of the Federal Government to hold and dispose of the land of an admitted State among the "enumerated powers delegated to the United States." Lines upon a map do not constitute a State, even though the State be given political equality. Without ownership of the soil there is not complete and equal sovereignty. If one-half of the area of a State can be withheld from a State, then nine-tenths of its area can be permanently held by the General Government. Reductio ad absurdum.

The right of the United States to acquire territory by purchase or conquest and to hold and govern the same as long as it remains a Territory is clearly inherent in the express provision of the Constitution empowering it to make treaties, and in the express provision to govern Territory. On this basis there is no doubt that the Nation constitutionally acquired the areas from different nations and held and governed them as Territories. The question as to legal status arises upon the admission of the Territories as States. Attention is again called to this as a background lying deep behind our present problems. Lack of jurisdiction in our Supreme Court, any Court, because of international treaties being involved, prevents legal remedy. (Botiller v. Dominguez, 130 U. S. 238.) But the equities become stronger by reason of this situation.

CHAPTER VI.

Determination of Legal Status.

We find the legal status of our public lands and the
relations of the United States and of the several States
stated as follows in Thirty-second Cyclopedia (Cyc.)
776 and succeeding pages:

When the thirteen original States established their independence each State became the owner of the vacant and
unappropriated lands within its borders. (People v. Livingston,
8 Barb, N. Y. 253; State v. Pinckney, 22 S. C. 484).

And when new States were formed out of the territory of
such original States, and admitted into the Union, such new
States became entitled to vacant and unappropriated lands
within their borders, and the ownership of the United States
of lands within the limits of the original States is based upon
cessions from the States. (Pollard v. Hagan, 3 How.[U. S.]
212, 221, 11 Law Ed. 565; United States v. Chandler Dunbar
Water Power Co., 152 Fed. 25, 81 C. C. A. 221.)

But when foreign governments ceded territory to the United
States Government, the vacant and unappropriated land therein
passed to the United States (United States v. Berrigan, 2
Alaska 442; People v. Folsom, 4 Cal. 373; Woodworth v.
Fulton, 1 Cal. 295; Sims v. Morrison, 92 Minn. 341, 100 N. W.
88; Territory v. Lee, 2 Mont. 124.)

And the new States which have been formed out of such territory have no title to vacant and unappropriated lands within
their borders. (Stoner v. Royer, 200 Mo., 444 98, S. W. 601;
Bradshaw v. Edelen, 194 Mo. 640, 92 S. W. 691; Irvine v. Marshall 20 How. (U. S.) 558, 15 Law Ed. 994; Shannon v. U. S.,
160 Fed. 870; 88 C. C. A. 52).

So, also, a treaty by which an Indian nation relinquishes and
conveys to the United States its right, title, and interest in and
to certain territory vests the title in the United States. (Mc-
Cracken v. Todd, 1 Kan. 148; Robinson v. Caldwell, 67 Fed.
391; 14 C. C. A. 448).

The policy of the United States has been not to dispose of
its tide lands, but to retain them for the benefit of the future
States in which they may lie and to grant them to such States
upon their admission. (Mobile Transp. Co. v. Mobile, 128 Ala.
335, 30 So. 645, 86 Amer. St. Rep. 143, 64 L. R. A. 333; U. S.
v. Roth, 2 Alaska 257.

Power to Make Reservations.

A reservation of the public lands may be made by Congress
(U. S. v. Shannon, 151 Fed. 863; U. S v. Payne, 8 Fed. 883, 2
McCrary 289. See also Doll v. Meador, 16 Cal. 295) or by the
treaty-making power (Spaulding v. Chandler, 160 U. S. 394, 16
S. Ct. 360, 40 L. Ed. 469; U. S. v. Payne, 8 Fed. 883, 2 Mc-
Crary 289).

In addition to which, from an early period of the history
of the Government, it has been the practice of the President to
order from time to time, as the exigencies of the public service
required, parcels of land belonging to the United States to be
reserved from sale and set apart for public uses. (Grisar v.
McDowell, 6 Wall. (U. S. 363, 381, 18 L. Ed. 863; Russian-
American Packing Co. v. U. S., 39 Ct. Cl. 460, 483, affirmed
199 U. S. 570; 50 L. Ed. 314).

The authority of the President in this respect is recognized
in numerous acts of Congress (cases same as last above), and
decisions of the courts (Onderdonk v. San Francisco, 75 Cal.
534, 17 Pac. 678), independent of any act of Congress, expressly
authorizing him to make such reservations (Florida Town Imp.
Co. v. Bigalsky, 44 Fla. 771, 33 So. 450); but compare Jackson
v. Wilcox (2 Ill. 334-354).

And Congress has, moreover, by express enactment conferred
upon the President the power to make reservation of the public lands for certain purposes. (Spaulding v. Chandler, 100
U. S. 394; 16 S. Ct. 360, 40 Law ed. 469; U. S. Bleudeaner, 128
Fed. 910, 63 C. C. A. 636).

How Reservations Effected.

Forest reservations (U. S. v. Bleudauer, 122 Fed. 703, re-
versed on other grounds in 128 Fed. 910, 63 C. C. A. 636).
A reservation for the future disposal of the United States is a
reservation to the United States.

Hot Springs cases (92 U. S. 698, 23 Law Ed. 690) grants to
States in general:

The rule is that lands granted for a particular object are held
in trust for the fulfillment of the purpose of the grant and
can not be diverted to other purposes. (In re Canal Certificates,
19 Colo. 63; 34 Pac. 274).

Reservation to United States—Meaning of Term.

The term "reservation" as used with relation to the public
lands means a withdrawal of a specified portion of the public
domain from the administration of the Land Office and from
disposal under the land laws and the appropriation thereof for
the time being to some particular use or purpose of the General
Government. (Territory v. Burgess, 8 Mont. 57; 19 Pac. 558,
1 L. R. A. 808).

It should be realized and remembered that one great reason every State, admitted after the original thirteen States, did not insist on its claim that instantaneously on admission it came into exclusive absolute ownership and control over every acre within its boundary lines, was that there was no tribunal having jurisdiction to enforce the provisions of the international treaties. The Supreme Court of the United States declared it could not take jurisdiction, because the violation of a treaty provision was a matter between sovereign nations. In Botiller v. Dominguez (130 U. S. 238, April 1, 1889) the Supreme Court said:

The propositions under this Statute are presented by counsel in support of the decision of the Supreme Court of California. The first of these is that the Statute itself (9 St. 631 * * * * is invalid, as being in conflict with the provisions of the treaty with Mexico * * * * and also in conflict with the rights of property under the Constitution and laws of the United States * * * *

With regard to the first of these propositions it may be said that, so far as the act of Congress is in conflict with the treaty of Mexico, that is a matter in which the court is bound to follow the statutory enactments of its own Government. If the treaty was violated by this general statute, * * * * it was a matter of international concern, which the two States must determine by treaty, or by such other means as enables one State to enforce upon another the obligations of a treaty. This court, in a class of cases like the present, has no power to set itself up as the instrumentality for enforcing the provisions of a treaty with a foreign nation which the Government of the United States, as a sovereign power chooses to disregard. The Cherokee Tobacco (11 Wall. 616), Taylor v. Morton (2 Curt. 454), Ready Money cases (112 U. S. 580, 598, 5 Sup. Ct. Rep. 247), Whitney v. Robertson (124 U. S. 190, 195, 8 Sup. Ct. Rep. 456).

Many eminent legal minds have always recognized and now recognize that the right of the United States against the rights of the separate States as to the lands organized into States has not been clear; that it has been settled more by custom, precedent and long acquiescence than by consitutional and treaty principles. The right of the President to withdraw lands for various purposes was settled only by a divided opinion of the Supreme Court, and it was deemed wise to fortify it by act of Congress, afterwards enacted. (See Midwest Cases, 236 U. S.)

We may enter a world court. It would be interesting indeed, if France asked the World Court to entertain a suit looking to the enforcement of the express provision of the treaty by which we acquired the Louisiana Purchase, which required the admission of new States from that territory on an equal footing with the original States, which manifestly has not been done because the United States has exercised its national power and reserved millions of acres to national purposes, and granted many more millions to corporations and made other gifts and grants and leases which she could not restore to the States whose lands were granted. It would be rather startling if French capitalists who invested in the bonds of these States should insist on requesting the United States to submit the question to the World Court of restoring the security of all the lands and their resources which have been diverted or withheld from these States.

There was and is no forum in which the legal rights of the States under those treaties could be tested and enforced. Again, the Supreme Court, in so far as it has passed on the matter, has upheld the right of the Federal Government under the Constitution to control and dispose of the public lands in such manner as Congress may provide. It has further held that this authority includes the right of the Government to make reservations of public land for public purposes, under Article IV, section 3, giving the General Gov-

ernment the power to "dispose of" the "territory."
Also, that the Executive may withdraw lands from
entry for public purposes.

The decisions of the United States Supreme Court
on these subjects are stated as follows in "The Constitution of the United States of America"—annotated—1924, page 521:

The true constitutional equality between the States extends
to the right of each, under the Constitution, to have and enjoy
the same measure of local or self-government, and to be
admitted to an equal participation in the maintenance, administration, and conduct of the common or National Government.
(Case v. Toftus, 39 Fed. 732).

(Page 527)

The words "Dispose of" vest in Congress not only the
power to sell but also to lease the lands of the United States.
The disposal must be left to the discretion of Congress. (U. S.
v. Gratiot, 14 Pet. 538).

No appropriation of public land can be made for any pur-
pose but by authority of Congress. (U. S. v. Fitzgerald, 15
Pet. 421; California v. Desert Water Co., 243 U. S. 415; Utah
Power Co. v. U. S., 243 U. S. 389).

(Page 531)

The power of the President to withdraw public lands from
entry has been so long exercised and recognized by Congress
as to be equivalent to a grant of power. (U. S. v. Midwest Oil
Co., 236 U. S. 459).

(Page 530)

Congress has the power "to dispose of and make all needful
rules and regulations respecting the territory or other property
belonging to the United States" and pursuant to this power has
the exclusive right to control and dispose of the public and
unoccupied lands, to which the United States has acquired
title, either by deed of cessions from other States or by
treaty with a foreign country; and no State can interfere with
this right or embarrass its exercise. (Van Brocklin v. Tennessee, 117 U. S. 167).

This being the legal status concerning the public
lands, the western States are compelled to turn their
faces from the Courts to the Congress.

It is the exercise of this power by Congress that they invoke. The present laws and policies of Congress are working unjustly and inequitably against the Western States and proposals have emanated from the Departments which will accentuate and fasten upon them greater and more permanent injustice. It is the duty of Congress to give to the Western States the rights which they have not been able to present and secure in the Courts. The exclusion of a legal remedy ought to make the case all the stronger, in equity and moral right, before the Congress in fixing rights by its policies and laws.

The theory under which we have operated as to our public lands for a hundred years was stated by our Supreme Court in the following language in Pollard v. Hagan (3 How. 212), decided in 1845:

> Whenever the United States shall have fully executed these trusts the municipal sovereignty of the new States will be complete throughout their respective boundaries and they and the original States will be upon an equal footing in all respects.

Until the trust is executed fully, the new States are not upon an equal footing with the rest of the States, either the original or with those States in which the trust has been fully executed. The trust referred to is that which the United States has been exercising as to the public lands. The United States has not actual absolute ownership of any land within any State, except it received the same by compliance with Article 1, Section 8, paragraph 17, of the Constitution, which defines the manner in which, excepting the District of Columbia, originally provided for, it can acquire such right within a State, to-wit, by purchase under agreement or condemnation. The Court further analyzes in

Pollard v. Hagan the trust and duty of the United States, as follows:

Taking the legislative acts of the United States and the States of Virginia and Georgia and their deeds of cession to the United States and giving to each separately and to all jointly a fair interpretation, we must come to the conclusion that it was the intention of the parties to invest the United States with the eminent domain of the country ceded—both national and municipal—for the purpose of temporary government, and to hold it in trust for the performance of the stipulations and conditions expressed in the deeds of cession and the legislative acts connected with them. * * * * When the United States accepted the cession of the territory they took upon themselves the trust to hold the municipal eminent domain for the new States and to invest them with it to the same extent in all respects that it was held by the States ceding the territories. * * * *

All agree from our earliest history that even under the compacts with the States whereby the States waive or cede their rights to the public lands and agree that they will not interfere with the primary disposal of the soil, the United States is a trustee. The Supreme Court has held that these compacts in the enabling acts of the States can not and do not alter their constitutional rights. That trust has been fulfilled as to all the other States finally, except the present public-land States. It has been fulfilled by gradually "disposing of" the lands until every acre came into private ownership and under taxation by the States. But when it comes to the Rocky Mountain and Pacific Coast States, under a new policy to which all the rest of the States were never subject, the Federal Government, through Congress, has permanently withdrawn from the process of settlement and placed beyond the possibility of ever coming into private ownership and taxation 235,000,000 acres. This is for various purposes; Indian reservations, national parks, and monuments, power sites, reservoirs, naval reserves, forest reserves; and, in addition, all coal, oil, oil shale, phosphate, and sodium areas. Now, it is proposed that all the balance of the public domain shall be precluded from settlement and private ownership.

The views of Mr. Clay further show that neither he nor any statesman of that age ever contemplated that great areas of the new States should be reserved for game or timber or parks or any other purpose, but should be rapidly sold into private ownership, so that development might continue and the equal sovereignty of the new States with the old attained. He asked:

Are they (the public lands) here locked up from the people and, for the sake of their game or timber, excluded from sale? Are not they freely exposed in the market for all who want them at moderate price?

The General Government is a mere trustee, holding the domain in virtue of those deeds, according to the terms and conditions which they expressly describe; and it is bound to execute the trust accordingly.

Bearing in mind that Daniel Webster was the chief exponent of nationalism and the great expounder of the Constitution and of supreme national authority the following statement made by him January 20, 1830, in the Senate demonstrates conclusively that the most extreme national idea of the Constitution and treaties and deeds of cession was simply and solely the sale and disposition of the lands by the Federal government under such conditions as it might prescribe and that the modern idea of rentals and leases, fees and royalties, was so strange and abhorrent that they repudiated the very suggestion. Webster said:

The gentleman spoke of the centuries that must elapse before all the lands could be sold and the great hardships that the States must suffer while the United States reserved to itself, within their very limits, such large portions of soil not liable to taxation. * * * If these lands were leasehold property, if they were held by the United States on rent, there would be much in the idea. But they are wild lands held only until they can be sold; reserved no longer than till somebody will take them up at low price. Sir, if in any case any State can show that the policy of the United States retards her settlement or prevents her from cultivating the lands within her limits, she shall have my vote to alter that policy.

It may be interesting at this point to hear what the United States Supreme Court held as to the effect of the waivers and cessions required and contained in the acts of admission of the States. In the case of Pollard v. Hagan, in 3 Howard 212 (January term 1845) the court held:

The provision of the Constitution above referred to shows that no such power can be exercised by the United States within a State. Such a power is not only repugnant to the Constitution, but is inconsistent with the spirit and intention of the deeds of cession The arguments so much relied on by the counsel for the plaintiff that the agreement of the people inhabiting the new States, that they thereafter disclaim all right and title to the waste and unappropriated lands lying within said territory, and that the same shall be and remain at the sole and entire disposal of the United States, can not operate as a contract between the parties, but is binding as a law. Full power is given to Congress "to make all needful rules and regulations respecting the territory or other property of the United States." This authorized the passage of all laws necessary to secure the rights of the United States to the public lands, and to provide for and sell, and to protect them from taxation. * * * The proposition submitted to the people of the Alabama Territory, for their acceptance or rejection, by the act of Congress authorizing them to form a Constitution and State government for themselves, so far as they related to the public lands within the territory amounted to nothing more or less than rules and regulations respecting the sales and dispositions of the public lands. The supposed compact relied on by the counsel for the plaintiff, conferred no authority, therefore, on Congress to pass the act granting to the plaintiffs the land in controversy. * * * To Alabama belong the navigable waters and soil under them in controversy in this case, subject only to the rights surrendered by the Constitution to the United States; and no compact that might be made between her and the United States could diminish or enlarge those rights.

As to the United States having any Constitutional rights of municipal sovereignty, the Court in the same case laid down the following propositions:

> The United States now hold the public lands in the new States by force of the deeds of cession and the statutes connected with them and not by any municipal sovereignty which it may be supposed they possess or have received by compact with the new States for that particular purpose.
>
> The counsel for the plaintiffs insisted, in argument, that * * * by the compact between the United States and Alabama on her admission into the Union, it was agreed that the people of Alabama forever disclaimed all right or title to the waste or unappropriated lands lying within the State, and that the same should remain at the sole disposal of the United States. * * * That by these articles of the compact the land under the navigable waters and the public domain above high water were alike reserved to the United States and alike subject to be sold by them; and to give any other construction to these compacts would be to yield up to Alabama, and the other new States, all the public land within their limits.
>
> We think a proper examination of the subject will show that the United States never held any municipal sovereignty, jurisdiction, or right of soil in and to the territory of which Alabama or any other new States were formed, except for temporary purposes and to execute the trusts created by the Virginia and Georgia Legislatures, and the deeds of cession executed by them to the United States, and the trusts created by the treaty with the French Republic on the 30th of April, 1803, ceding Louisiana. * * *
>
> These deeds of cession stipulated that all the lands within the territory ceded and not reserved or appropriated to other purposes should be considered as a common fund for the use and benefit of all the United States, to be faithfully and bona fide disposed of for that purpose and for no other purpose whatever. And the statute passed by Virginia authorizing her delegates to execute this deed, and which is recited in it, authorizes them in behalf of the State, by a proper deed to convey to the United States for the benefit of said States, all the right, title, and claim, as well of soil as jurisdiction, upon condition that the territory so ceded shall be laid out and formed into States * * * and that the States so formed shall be republican States and admitted members of the Federal Union, having the same right of sovereignty, freedom, and independence as the other States.

Taking the legislative acts of the United States and the States of Virginia and Georgia, and their deeds of cession to the United States, and giving to each separately and to all jointly a fair interpretation, we must come to the conclusion that it was the intention of the parties to invest the United States with the eminent domain of the country ceded, both national and municipal, for the purposes of temporary government, and to hold it in trust for the performance of the stipulations and conditions expressed in the deeds of cession and the legislative acts connected with them. * * * When the United States accepted the cession of the territory, they took upon themselves the trust to hold the municipal eminent domain for the new States and to invest them with it, to the same extent in all respects that it was held by the States ceding the territories. * * *

By the sixteenth clause of the eighth section of the first article of the Constitution power is given to Congress "to exercise exclusive legislation in all cases whatsoever over such district (not exceeding 10 miles square) as may by cession of particular States and the acceptance of Congress become the seat of government of the United States, and to exercise like authority over all places purchased, by the consent of the legislatures of the State in which the same may be, for the erection of forts, magazines, arsenals, dockyards, and other needful buildings" within the District of Columbia, and the other places purchased and used for the purposes above mentioned, the national and municipal powers of government of every description are united in the Government of the Union. And these are the only cases within the United States in which all the powers of government are united in a single government, except in the cases already mentioned of the temporary Territorial governments and their local government exists. The right of Alabama and every other new State to exercise all the powers of government which belong to and may be exercised by the original States of the Union must be admitted and remain unquestioned, except so far as they are **temporarily** deprived of control over the public lands. * * *

We will now inquire into the nature and extent of the right of the United States to these lands. * * * This right originated in voluntary surrenders made by several of the old States of their waste and unappropriated lands, to the United States, under a resolution of the old Congress, of the 6th of September, 1780, recommending such surrender and cession, to aid in paying the public debt incurred by the war of the Revolution. The object of all the parties to these contracts of cession was to convert the land into money for the payment of the debt, and to erect new States over the territory thus ceded; and as soon as these purposes could be accomplished, the power of the United States over these lands, as property, was to cease.

Whenever the United States shall have fully executed these trusts the municipal sovereignty of the new States **will be** complete throughout their respective boundaries, and they and the original States **will be** upon an equal footing, in all respects whatever.

SALT CREEK OIL FIELD—WYOMING
Under Government Mineral Leasing Act

CHAPTER VII.

Disposition and Proceeds.

From the years 1831 to 1836 the sale of public lands markedly increased. President Jackson announced to Congress in 1835 that the public debt was extinguished and that something must be done with the surplus. Mr. Calhoun proposed, and it was authorized, that after 1836 any surplus in excess of $5,000,000 should be divided among the States as a loan.

The following sums, aggregating $28,000,000, were thus borrowed and received by the following named States:

Maine	$ 955,838.25
New Hampshire	669,086.79
Vermont	669,086.79
Massachusetts	1,338,173.58
Connecticut	764,670.60
Rhode Island	382,335.30
New York	4,014,520.71
Pennsylvania	2,867,514.78
New Jersey	764,670.60
Ohio	2,007,260.34
Indiana	860,254.44
Illinois	477,919.14
Michigan	286,751.49
Delaware	286,751.49
Maryland	955,838.25
Virginia	2,198,427.99
North Carolina	1,433,757.39
South Carolina	1,051,422.09
Georgia	1,051,422.09
Alabama	699,086.79
Louisiana	477,919.14
Mississippi	382,335.30
Tennessee	1,433,757,39
Kentucky	1,433,757.39
Missouri	382,335.30
Arkansas	286,751.49

That amount, with interest since 1836, is still due from those States participating and is still carried on the Treasurer's books as "Unavailable funds."

Thus in 1835 the first of the two stipulations of the cessions by the first group of States ceding the Northwest Territory (East of the Mississippi and North of the Ohio) was fulfilled and terminated, to wit, the application of the proceeds of the sale of public lands to the extinguishment of the debt of the Revolutionary War.

Henceforth there was but one purpose with reference to sale of public lands, that of creating new, independent, sovereign States, which was to be done by disposing of the domain to settlers until successive areas were sufficiently populated to seek and obtain admission as States. This was done gradually over a 75-year period until, with exception of Alaska and the Island Possessions the last areas were admitted and became the States of Arizona and New Mexico in 1912.

When the western States were admitted, they received grants of land for various State institutions of but 500,000 acres out of areas averaging over sixty million acres within their State lines. The Constitution gave them the right to fix their own boundaries. Iowa settled this question in 1846. It must be conceded that they were not in fact admitted on an equal footing with the thirteen original States, which were sovereign within their borders, not only as to jurisdiction but as to ownership of the soil to the complete exclusion of the Federal Government, except as under the Constitution the Federal Government might purchase areas within them, with the consent of their legislatures.

Two hundred and two million acres, not including grants for benefit of State railroads, wagon roads, and the Carey Act, were granted to the States upon or subsequent to their admission. In addition thereto there were granted to the States 37,000,000 acres, which in turn were granted by the States to railroads.

The amount of land in acres granted to each of the States is as follows:

Alabama	2,258.262.10
Alaska Territory	21,345,209.00
Arizona	10,489,236.00
Arkansas	9,372,993.37
California	8,424,840.32
Colorado	4,433,378.00
Connecticut	180,000.00
Delaware	90,000.00
Florida	21,968,478.42
Georgia	270,000.00
Idaho	3,631,965.30
Illinois	3,639,065.51
Indiana	4,306,253.49
Iowa	3,019,645.61
Kansas	3,606,783.20
Kentucky	352,508.65
Louisiana	10,994,352.37
Maine	210,000.00
Maryland	210,000.00
Massachusetts	360,000.00
Michigan	8,787,423.87
Minnesota	8,330,990.61
Mississippi	4,948,588.85
Missouri	5,574,485.70
Montana	5,869,618.00
Nebraska	3,458,711.00
Nevada	2,723,647.00
New Hampshire	150,000.00
New Jersey	210,000.00
New Mexico	12,406,026.86
New York	990,000.00
North Carolina	270,000.00
North Dakota	3,163,476.00
Ohio	2,492,925.93

Oklahoma	3,095,760.25
Oregon	4,352,132.66
Pennsylvania	780,000.00
Rhode Island	120,000.00
South Carolina	180,000.00
South Dakota	3,432,604.00
Tennessee	300,000.00
Texas	180,000.00
Utah	7,414,276.00
Vermont	150,000.00
Virginia	300,000.00
Washington	3,044,471.00
West Virginia	150,000.00
Wisconsin	6,219,970.33
Wyoming	4,138,569.00
Total	202,396,648.40

The grants to the original States, denominated "agricultural scrip" were for lands extraneous of their own areas, as they held all the lands within their boundaries in their own right.

The average amount of land granted to each of the present 11 public-land States for all purposes to date is 6,084,378 acres. This, on the average, is about one-twelfth of the area of each State.

The theory on which they were, and are eventually to become sovereign as to ownership and taxation, was the gradual acquirement by purchase, or acquirement by homesteading under the various homestead laws after 1862. Small direct purchases ceased with the laws so providing in 1862, when the first homestead law was enacted. The best of the lands were then taken up under the 160-acre law, under which residence and cultivation requirements took the place of cash payments. Later the commutation amendment permitted a reduction of the years of residence and provided, in lieu thereof, payment in the sum of $1.25 per acre. Omitting the commuted homesteads, 232,259,180 acres have been patented since the passage of the homestead law.

Under the Timber and Stone Act, June 3, 1878, 13,-827,515 acres have been entered.

Desert Land entries from passage of the Act March 3, 1877, to the amount of, original 32,724,292 acres, final 8,591,106 acres, have been taken.

Coal Land entries from the passage of the Act March 3, 1873, amount to 604,363 acres.

In 1909, owing to the dry character of the lands remaining, the size of the entry was increased on certain designated dry areas to 320 acres. As the limit of entries of the lands of this type was approached, it was again found necessary to enlarge the entry on other designated areas to 640 acres, and the character of these entries changed to a stock-raising or grazing homestead. This required improvements by buildings and fences and forage cultivation, still embodying the idea of settlement, new homes and development. 56,-134,312 acres have thus been entered, 21,289,661 patented.

In 1902, and thereafter, 19,034,330 acres, were withdrawn from entry under the usual homestead laws in order that they might be entered, after construction of reclamation works, as reclamation homesteads, under which the settlers are to return to the reclamation fund the entire cost of such projects. While this was and is a heavy burden on settlers, yet it is working out and the great and settled policy of the general government to gradually dispose of the public domain and transfer the same into private ownership, and make the States completely sovereign is being adhered to.

For the development of the West and the entire country and to the same great general purpose there were granted by the Federal Government as subsidies, from 1850 to June 30, 1925, the following railroad corporation grants, aggregating 93,255,338 acres, under provisions whereby they could be purchased by settlers at a low cost:

Union Pacific	11,935,121.46
Central Pacific	7,231,732.76
Central Pacific (successor by consolidation with Western Pacific)	461,191.24
Central Branch Union Pacific	223,120.50
Union Pacific (Kansas Division)	6,176,383.76
Union Pacific (successor to Denver Pacific)	821,324.15
Burlington & Missouri River in Nebr.	2,374,090.77
Sioux City & Pacific (now Missouri Valley Land Co.)	42,610.95
Northern Pacific	39,029,964.67
Oregon Branch of Central Pacific (California and Oregon)	3,188,412.83
Oregon & California	2,777,591.96
Atlantic & Pacific (now Santa Fe Pacific)	11,133,232.11
Southern Pacific (main line)	4,511,860.66
Southern Pacific (branch line)	2,218,139.85
Oregon Central	128,618.13
New Orleans Pacific	1,001,943.40
Grand Total	93,255,338.70

Thus, again, under this class of disposition of the public lands, the ultimate object intended and effected was the bringing of the land into private ownership, development and taxation.

CHAPTER VIII.

Reservations.

We come now to a radical change in the general policy and a departure from original and long-followed methods and purposes, a change which has given cause and rise to question, objection, protest, and cessation of settlement over immense areas in the remaining public land States. This was inaugurated by withdrawals for permanent reservations for various purposes.

The following table gives the total areas withdrawn, and for what purpose, temporarily or permanently, as to surface and subsurface:

	Acres.
Areas in national forests (net)	135,971,883
All minerals reserved (stock-raising homestead entries)	56,134,312
Areas patented with reservation to the United States for oil, gas, phosphate, nitrate, potash, or asphaltic minerals	1,571,743
Areas patented with reservation of coal in United States	14,522,906
All minerals reserved in patented lands other than stock-raising homesteads	77,273
Lands certified to States with coal or other mineral reserved	617,815
National parks	7,935,912
National monuments	130,599
Gold, silver, and quicksilver reserved to the United States, in patented Spanish and Mexican land grants (estimated)	2,040,881
Indian lands owned or controlled by the United States	70,993,326
Specific withdrawals:	
Coal lands	29,825,444
Oil lands	5,183,096
Oil shale (specific)	156,147
Oil shale (estimated)	4,000,000
Phosphate	2,004,765
Potash	9,411,939
Power sites	6,587,865
Public water	419,339

Reservoir sites	254,050
Helium	12,255
Reservoir sites (Arizona, New Mexico and Oregon)	1,074,550
Reclamation	19,034,330
Miscellaneous	7,668,627
Total	375,629,057

The withdrawals include some State and privately owned lands and some duplications. Of the above total, 235,000,000 acres have been permanently reserved, leaving a balance of 180,000,000 acres of vacant unreserved, unappropriated public domain.

Thus, more than one-half of the remaining public lands in 11 Western States, in which are located 97 per cent of the lands, are, under the system of reservations, forever withdrawn from settlement, private ownership precluded, power of taxation permanently denied and the full State sovereignty expressly provided for in the cessions, defeated.

If it be said that the homestead laws are still in effect in the forest reserves, the complete answer is that, by law, rule, or regulation, if a given tract is more valuable for timber, mineral, or other purposes than for agriculture then the entry is not accepted and cannot be compelled. In fact, then, the forest areas, being forest and generally in a mountainous country, are not open to entry for settlement. They constitute a permanent withdrawal from any possibility of private ownership, save the location of lode mineral claims.

If it be said that the laws provide for homesteading the surface of lands embraced in Government mineral permits and leases, the answer is that if that surface be more necessary for mining operations in order to extract the mineral, which is almost invariably the case, then the surface entry is defeated.

The result of reservations then, in the 11 Western States, is to leave the Government permanently in complete control of approximately 235,000,000 acres. An average of 30 per cent of the area of each of the 11 Western States is thus placed forever beyond private ownership and taxation, notwithstanding these States must extend government, maintain police jurisdiction, keep law and order, build roads, as needed over this entire area, excepting only the national parks. Will anybody seriously maintain that these States are free, independent, sovereign, and "on equal terms with the original States" and that their citizens have the same "rights, advantages and immunities" as those of the original States and the States of the Mississippi Valley, all of which were or became sovereign, according to the original intention, over practically all soil within their boundaries?

The Supreme Court of the United States never intended that their decision, to the effect that the power to "dispose of" in the Constitution included the power "to reserve," should be extended so excessively and so outrageously invading the rights of the States. Reservations have been made to an unconstitutional extent. There is a rule of reason in law and in constitutions.

To permanently reserve and keep from development and under Federal bureau control one-fourth of a State is unconstitutional, because it is an unreasonable exercise of the right to reserve. It violates the conditions imposed in the treaties under which they were acquired. It takes no legal argument to prove this. It is obvious to all as a matter of plain sense and justice. If it can be done constitutionally, then three-fourths or nine-tenths of a State can be reserved constitutionally. That is an absurdity and proves the contention.

For example, the State of Nevada is still more than 80 per cent under Government control. There is nothing in the Constitution to prevent, if this view is wrong, the reserving by the President and the Congress forever all of the area of that State, thereby preventing its settlement, development, and making it tax-free forever, except the 20 per cent which has been granted to that State or acquired by its people under the mining and homestead laws.

But the West says there is something in the Constitution to prevent such emasculation of a State of this Union. If that can be done constitutionally, and that is the position the opposition must take, then the words "Union of Sovereign States" are a hollow mockery. The West does not believe they are, but believes that its view is right—that the power to reserve is limited and retail, not unlimited and wholesale. It must not be exercised unreasonably.

While the Supreme Court has said that a reservation of the public land may be made by Congress (U. S. v. Shannon, 157 Fed. 863), it was not the earlier intention to deprive the new States permanently of great parts of their area. Indeed, it was the thought that in due time all of their area was to come into private ownership and under the sovereignty of the States.

This thought is clearly presented in the following statement, on page 521 of the "Constitution of the United States, Annotated, 1924":

The right of every new State to exercise all the powers of government which belong to and may be exercised by the original States of the Union must be admitted and remain unquestioned except so far as they are temporarily deprived of control of the public lands. (Pollard v. Hagan, 3 How. 223; Weber v. Harbor Commissioners, 18 Wall. 65; Escanaba Co. v. Chicago, 107 U. S. 688; Kinglett v. U. S. Land Assn., 142

U. S. 183; Illinois Central R. Co. v. Illinois, 146 U. S. 387 and 434; McCabe v. Atchison R. Co., 235 U. S. 151.)

Again, the Supreme Court in Pollard v. Hagan (3 Howard, 212, 1845) clearly stated that equal terms and full sovereignty of the States would not be complete until the national trust was fully executed, and all lands and resources disposed of to the States or the people of the States. The language is a follows:

Whenever the United States shall have fully executed these trusts the municipal sovereignty of the new States will be complete throughout their respective boundaries, and they and the original States will be upon an equal footing, in all respects whatever.

The denial of control by the States was considered **temporary.** These great reservations **permanently** deprive them of control. This is a complete change of policy, virtually denies ultimate sovereignty to the State, and defeats the purposes of the trust.

But even if constitutionally a quarter, a half, or three-fourths of a public land State could be forever reserved for a so-called public purpose, it would be utterly unjust and unwise to do so, not only for these States, but also for the Nation. And yet it has been done on an average as to more than a quarter of each of the Western States.

The compacts with the States upon their admission, the forced price of their entrance into the Union, their enabling acts and constitutions, whereby the newly admitted States agreed to not interfere with the primary disposal of the soil, which pre-supposes a right to the soil of the State in the State, under the decisions of the Supreme Court simply made the Government a trustee; and a trustee for all the people of that State; and they did not change any constitutional right held by the State, because it is impossible for a State to include anything in its constitution, that can add to or take away a right granted to it, or retained in it, by the Constitution of the United States.

The construction by the Courts of section 3, clause 1, of the Constitution which provides that "new States may be admitted by the Congress into this Union," etc., is expressed on page 518 of the "Constitution of the United States, annotated, 1924," in the following language:

This clause refers to and includes new States to be formed out of territory as yet to be acquired, as well as that already ceded to the United States. New States when admitted have equal sovereignty with the older ones, and are entitled to all the rights of jurisdiction and eminent domain which the original States possessed, whether such equality be stipulated for in the act of admission or not. * * * When also a State enters into the Union, it solemnly pledges to the other States to support the Constitution as it is, in all its provisions, until altered in the manner which the Constitution itself provides, and she can not, by a compact with the United States, enlarge or diminish her constitutional rights or liabilities. (Illinois Central R. Co. v. Illinois, 146 U. S. 387 and 434; Ward v. Race Horse, 163 U. S. 514.)

When those compacts were made, there were no great "reservations" of public land. They were not in the contemplation of the parties to the compacts. Hence the States have a right to have their trustee by said compacts "dispose of" the domain by transfer to the people as always theretofore and as it was being disposed of at the time; by purchase, homestead, mining laws, or grants for specific purposes, and not by reservation in immense areas in the trustee. The Government is not carrying out its part of the compacts, its duty as trustee. If not, then the compacts should be abrogated and the States at once reinvested with their rights and the land restored to them.

To that extent the complete sovereignty of these States, which was eventually, if not upon admission, to be brought about by transfer from the Federal Government to private or State ownership, has been utterly defeated.

Unless there be a change of policy and law by the Congress of the United States with reference to these great reservations, the States are and always will be denied complete control, which they have a right to expect as equal members of the Union. These reservations will remain a government within a government in each one of these States. This was never contemplated by the Constitution or the founders of this Nation, and is in effect prohibited by the Constitution, in its express inhibition against erecting a government within a State.

As to the reserved and withdrawn areas, excluding and excepting only the national parks, it is manifest that justice, equality, and dignity for these States require that ultimately all should be ceded to the States wherein they lie. The theory that the Western States can not intelligently and wisely administer these areas, for example, the forest reserves, is based on the delinquencies and wastefulness of the States to the eastward which had their resources and their opportunity, and in some cases, as States, misused and abused their rights. This constitutes no reason why the same right which they enjoyed should be denied to the Western States. The self respect and sovereign right of these public-domain States must demand and continue to urge that they shall not be discriminated against and excepted from the general rule, which has been applied to all States from the Atlantic coast to the Rocky

Mountains, of eventual, complete sovereignty over all of their areas.

It was never within the purview of the decision of the United States Supreme Court, when it held that the power "to dispose of" included the power "to reserve" that such reservations and withholding from the States should ever be extended to these enormous and unreasonable proportions. The area already permanently reserved goes far beyond anything that was contemplated 30 years ago by either the Courts or the Congress. It is unreasonable, excessive, and therefore unauthorized and unjust exercise of the power of the Congress to reserve.

Only 45 per cent of the area of the 11 western States has come into State and private ownership. About 10 per cent went to the State. Perhaps 35 per cent, on an average, is now in private ownership. The bulk of all of the benefit of the $600,000,000 received by the Government from the public lands has gone to the now non-public-land States. By these immense reservations the western States are barred to that extent from proceeds from sales in the future. It is even sought to stop the sale, homesteading and settling of the present vacant and unreserved lands by placing them under a federal regulation and lease system and repealing the 640-acre act, which is the only act under which, in view of their character, they could be taken up.

The western States did not share in the past because of their youth, being the last group of States admitted. Shortly after admission the policy of great reservations began, and the reservation of mineral rights from homesteads. They are not to share therefore in the future, as there will be no lands sold. Thus they have been and are practically outside of the limits of even the doctrine which has been imposed that the public lands were "for the benefit of all the States." While they are included in "all the States," the policy was stopped just at the time they would have participated in a small part of the benefits of the total. One billion acres were disposed of, and the benefits went almost entirely to the States east of the Rocky Mountains. Then disposition ceased and reservations were made of 30 per cent of the remaining area; and now it is sought to cease disposition of all the remainder, 25 per cent of the area of each State, figuring the average. They were too early and they are too late. Something should be done in the face of this unjust and anomalous policy and condition.

Let it be understood that in the national parks no development can ever take place. Let it be equally understood that agricultural and mining development, while legally and technically possible, has practically ceased and will not be resumed on the 149,596,379 acres of forest reserves in these Western States, and that the small proportion coming back to the States of the proceeds of grazing fees and annual timber sales is wholly inadequate to make up for the loss; likewise the return from royalties to the reclamation fund are not repayments to the West but loans which must be repaid.

The total area in acres of the forest reserves in the mainland, Territories, and Possessions is 184,463,819. The total area in acres on the mainland, exclusive of Alaska, is 163,066,062. The total area in acres in the non-public-land States, purchased in the main from private ownership, is 13,403,633. The total area in acres in the 11 public-land States reserved from the public domain is 149,596,379. The net area of the national forests in the United States proper, exclusive of private property within their exterior lines, is 135,-533,824 acres.

If these permanent reservations are to be forever retained by the United States, then why is it not just that those States from whose areas they are taken for all the people should have recompense for their value, or an annual return for their use, based on the value of that use, in view of the loss to those States of development and taxation?

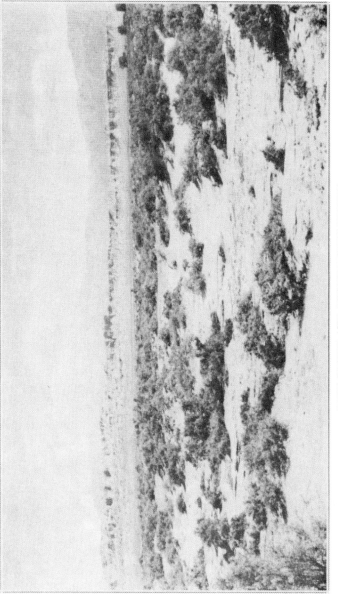

SAGE BRUSH AND DESERT—NEW MEXICO
Courtesy Chamber of Commerce, Santa Fe

CHAPTER IX.

Leasing System as to Minerals.

In 1908 there began an agitation for another change in our public land and mining laws. There had been a general settled system of acquirement of title to mineral land by location, discovery, assessment work, improvements, and patent upon the payment of $5 per acre for lode claims and $2.50 per acre for placer claims. This was all under the provisions of the general mineral law of 1866, as amended May 10, 1872, entitled "An act to promote the development of the mining resources of the United States."

Now entered the lease and royalty idea. It was proposed to withdraw all mineral land containing coal, oil, oil shale, gas, phosphate, and sodium, pending the enactment of a leasing bill. These withdrawals were made, though of doubtful validity, after hundreds of thousands of dollars of private capital had been spent to prove various structures to be oil bearing. The law was imposed upon the West by weight of numbers. The West was opposed to the leasing system, but perforce had to acquiesce and make the best leasing law possible. Strangely enough, as if in irony, this act of February 25, 1920, bears the title, "An act to promote the mining of coal, oil, oil shale, gas, phosphate, and sodium on the public domain."

Attention is called to the whole leasing system as another sweeping change in restricting and hampering, instead of encouraging, the discovery and development of mineral. It was another step in curtailing and abolishing the right of the individual to prospect, discover, and develop, and to have the fruits of his initiative and enterprise. It imposes a royalty burden of from 2 to 50 per cent. This was all done on the excuse or theory that the mining laws did not fit the location of oil placer claims. The most prominent feature of the law was the exaction of royalties for the Federal Government; a proposition that would have been indignantly opposed by the strongest nationalist in the days of Calhoun, Webster, Hayne, Clay, and Benton. The Government has collected, since February 25, 1920, royalties to the amount of $80,000,000. The injury of this new imposition upon the public-land States, for it affected them only, was attempted to be minimized by the provisions to render back out of these exactions upon the mineral industries and development of those States 37½ per cent of the royalties collected to the States of their origin, and to pay into the reclamation fund 52½ per cent of such royalties, in order that it might go back to the States in agricultural development. And yet representatives in Congress are inclined to argue that this is the money of the Nation, as though raised by taxation, and of all the States, and seem to begrudge reclamation and appropriations therefor; and this from Representatives from States such as Pennsylvania, Ohio, Indiana, Illinois, and many others which never had a foot of soil taken, reserved or withdrawn for national purposes; which received the benefits of the sale of their public lands, borrowed $28,000,000 of the proceeds of the sales of public lands, which they have never repaid, principal or interest, to the National Treasury; and which never paid a dollar of grazing fees, or of royalty from their coal and oil; and which have had all their forest wealth. The Government never received land, save by the original cessions, within the limits of the original thirteen or other

States east of the Rockies without compliance with the Constitution, which compels it to purchase the same, even for forts, magazines, arsenals, and dockyards, and then only with the consent of the legislature of the State in which that soil is located.

It is a glittering theory at best that all the public lands were to be disposed of for the common benefit of all the people of all the States. Incidentally that provision was only in the cessions of Virginia and other States ceding areas, and is not in the Constitution or the international treaties under which our Western territory was acquired. The original States have had the benefit of the proceeds of the sales of more than a billion acres of public lands; the States between them and the Mississippi have had the benefit of the sale of about a half-billion acres; the present public-land States have shared in the proceeds of probably a hundred million acres; and now after reserving for national purposes permanently 235,000,000 acres from these Western States without paying a dollar therefor, it is planned to rent out this remaining 180,000,000 acres in those States, and either make inapplicable or repeal the homestead 640-acre act, the only existing law under which it could be sold and settled; one more item to make the loss of the Western States complete, the proceeds of public-land sales would cease, and the reclamation fund, one of the methods of doing partial equity, will be the loser.

The greatest evil and injustice of the whole royalty, leasing, renting, fee system is that it is an unusual, unprecedented, unjustifiable, un-American levy upon business in those States, seriously impeding the development of the natural resources by taking a large share of the production, whether there are profits or not, discouraging capital and private enterprise and thus preventing the free development of these States. As for the individual citizen of these States, his opportunities are taken from him, he does not enjoy the "rights, privileges, immunities, and advantages" expressly guaranteed to him and expressly stipulated for him in the Constitution and by the cessions to the United States, and by the treaties under which these territories were acquired.

While our Supreme Court has reaffirmed the right and custom of Government to reserve all mineral rights in its disposition of the public lands, it was not with a view of profits in royalties on the mineral produced. It was with the intention and purpose of allowing and aiding our citizens to discover, locate, develop and own the mineral resources; and to this end, in 1866, there was enacted the general mining law which, with certain amendments, is in force today. It is from the operation of this general law that the particular minerals, to-wit, coal, oil, oil shale, gas, phosphate, and sodium were withdrawn and excepted by the mineral leasing act of February 25, 1920. Under the general mining law the prospector and miner was encouraged to locate, patent, and enjoy private ownership, which was best for him and for the State, without a royalty, without a profit to the Government. The Government is in the peculiar attitude of making a profit out of its trusteeship. A trustee is paid for service. With the Government, that means cost of administration. The object of the general mining law, stated in its title, was to promote the development of mining. Under it mining was encouraged and no tribute in the form of royalty was demanded.

The leasing act was opposed by the West until it was overwhelmed by numerical strength in the Congress. Forced to do so, it helped to make the best leasing bill it could.

If it is right to lease and exact royalties on the particular minerals named in that act, why is it not logical to broaden its terms and take in all minerals? Is that the ultimate object of the supporters of a leasing sysmet? This tendency and purpose is evident in Congress, for potash and asphalt, gilsonite, elaterite, and other like substances were brought under its terms. If it is not right as to all minerals, then, there is no excuse for maintaining it as to the minerals now embraced therein.

Let us see how it works by taking a particular example: Leases for the areas in the great Salt Creek oil field, Natrona County, Wyoming, on the east and south borders, to which no equitable claims had attached or which had been abandoned, were sold at public auction in tracts of 160 acres. The oil industry paid for those leases $1,600,000 in cash. Those who have no thought for the operators and for the States, in which the minerals and the industries are, no doubt thought that fine for the Government. But how has it worked out? Those leases exacted flat royalties of from 25 to 33 1-3 per cent. It was not long before it became evident and soon became the fact, that the owners or operators could not continue to operate the leases on these tracts at a profit. Applications are even now being made and allowed, reducing these always excessive royalties to 12½ per cent. Ultimately this same experience will be undergone by all the operating companies, even though new sands with new flush production are found at greater depth. The time will come with all when the 33 1-3, 25 or 12½ per cent cannot be paid. Then manifestly all royalties will have to be taken off or operations will cease, as the lessees can not and will not operate at a loss. The result will be, if royalties are not taken off, that production will cease with more than half of the oil still in the ground. This is the opposite of conservation.

What principle supports the plan under which the Government has absorbed one-fourth of the total production, or 12½ per cent, as the case may be, of the nearly 250,000,000 barrels of oil taken from the Salt Creek field up to this time? If Government royalties mean the ultimate cessation of drilling and production, and that is inevitable, if sometime the operations must stop and untold wealth allowed to remain in the oil sands, we will have arrived at a condition which demonstrates that the royalty system is economically unsound and of great detriment to the States in which the mineral resources lie. A great Government should function toward better and wiser ends.

Legislation is not right which must be eventually repealed to prevent the cessation of operation. It seems to be thus logically established that in every mine and every oil field affected by the Government leasing system, Government royalty should be eliminated. When we reach the point when operations are not profitable, as has occurred in some instances and will occur in all in time, with only a part of the mineral recovered, instead of promoting the mining industry it has discouraged it and then destroyed it. These large royalties have been a burden from the beginning. Mining capital must have an incentive to compensate for the hazards. Every industry must be able to build up a reserve. If such is the effect of the leasing bill in the end, was it ever justified in the beginning? The wells drilled, the mines sunk are lost capital, with but little salvage. The early profits should be high, to offset the later reduced profits and the final loss of the capital invested. The great element of risk and speculation in the mining business, particularly in oil, should be remembered. What is the net result? The Government has simply exacted as long as the traffic would stand it one-fourth of the total production. It then, in effect, says; "We have taken a large share of the rich part, let the enterprise die." The Government in its activities should be helpful. Its only purpose should be to "promote" the development of mining, as it alleges its purpose to be in the title of the leasing act. That act has laid extra heavy burdens upon the mining and oil industry.

The States have shared to some extent in the oil and other mineral royalties, 37½ per cent. If it is right to exact royalties, then the States where the mineral is produced should have it all. Let it be kept in mind that the 52½ per cent now going into the reclamation fund does not go back to the State in cash or to their citizens. It goes into the construction of reclamation works, of which the great bulk of costs are the dams and reservoirs, the title to which under the Reclamation Act remains in the Government. Nevertheless, the cost must be paid back by the settlers of the project, and eventually the fund will go back into the United States Treasury.

No one will contend that the States have not received some benefit by reason of the 37½ per cent cash return and some benefits of the loan of the money to its settlers, without interest, through the Reclamation Service. But in the long run a State would receive more benefit by itself administering the leasing system, if there must be one, taking all of the royalty. The State in fixing a royalty would at least set it at such a low or even nominal figure as will enable the State to regulate and the industry to live and develop, as well as encourage new discoveries. This whole matter of mineral resources is one distinctly for the States themselves to handle, or it should proceed under the general mining law and without a Federal mineral leasing act and royalty requirements.

CHAPTER X.

Conservation.

The immense reservations of areas, and the royalty mineral leasing act are attempted to be justified under the policy of conservation. There is no real conservation necessary or accomplished except that of the forests. The Western States know more of the facts and conditions and have a better-founded appreciation of true conservation than those who live a distance from the things to be conserved. The Western States are in direct contact with the forest areas and know better than anyone else the value of the forests in the conservation of rainfall and snowfall to regulate and restrain the floods and retain the waters for irrigation and reclamation. As to coal, oil, gas, oil shale, sodium, phosphate and potash, these things need development and use rather than to be locked up under the extreme theory of conservation. Every American farm from the Rockies to the Atlantic Ocean is in growing need of the three great elements of fertilizer, phosphate, potash, and nitrate. The imposition of royalties defers the day when these essentials can be profitably produced.

Conservation in its true sense will be upheld by the States if these lands and resources are ceded to them, and there is no justification in the policy of conservation or on any other ground for longer withholding from these States the lands and resources within them. This is true of both the reserved and unreserved areas, but attention is called to the fact that the present movement to cede the remaining public lands to the State where located refers not to the parks, the forest reserves, and other reservations which have been enumerated but to the vacant, unreserved, and unappropriated public domain.

The trouble is not to conserve, it is to develop. Immense mineral resources lie idle. Conservation means wise use, not imprisonment forever. Conservation is applicable only to the forests and to gas; even as to gas, methods have been worked out whereby the lignite coal of the West can be converted into gas. There is enough coal in one State of the 11—Wyoming—to provide the entire United States for 300 years. Other States have almost as much. It was stated by scientists and statisticians at the International Coal Co'ference, held in Washington, that there is enough coal in this country to last the United States 3,000 years. It is ridiculous to talk of conservation with respect to coal. There are yet great fields producing oil by flow or by pump. Many more fields are being and will be discovered. Deeper sands are penetrated in the known fields. When they are exhausted by flow and pump and new gas forced into the sands, we will mine the sands that are left in these fields, which will still hold 60 to 70 per cent of their original content of oil. When these are exhausted and before, there are 10,000 square miles of oil shale in Wyoming, Colorado, and Utah— the Green River formation—from 500 to 2,500 feet thick, which have been officially determined to contain 60,000,000,000 barrels of oil which will furnish new supplies. New, efficient processes are being invented to extract oil from coal. The coal deposits of the West are actually inexhaustible. Long before any of these sources of oil are exhausted, it is obvious and conceded by all that new and important sources of power, light, and heat will be discovered and applied. Coal can be pulverized and used as oil and gasoline are now used. Electricity can be generated at these tremendous coal deposits that will rival in endless quantity the hydro-electric power of our eternal rivers. It is not conservation that is needed, it is development. These great deposits of fuel minerals can not be wasted. Who will waste them, and how can they be wasted? And why, if they could be, would any State any more than the Federal Government, waste them? The State has the power of regulation and restriction. These are great manufacturing deposits rather than mining ore as with hard metals. They will produce only enough to supply the demand and no more, and that will be on a small margin of profit.

The same is true of phosphate and potash and sodium, which are also embraced in the mineral leasing act. There are in the State of Wyoming alone deposits of phosphate and potash sufficient to supply the Nation with these elements of soil enrichment for hundreds of years. Other States have vast deposits. The reports of the United States Geological Survey and of the State Geologist of Wyoming, show 200,000,000 tons of potash on the surface, in the Leucite hills of Sweetwater County, Wyoming, and with it, in the same material, are 200,000,000 tons of aluminum. It is not the saving of these things we need, it is use. Meanwhile we ship our potash from Germany and France, and import aluminum. No one as yet has ventured to suggest that the metalliferous minerals, gold, silver, copper, lead, and zinc, should be brought under a leasing bill in order to conserve them and regulate their production. They proceed under private enterprise and the Government derives only a small purchase sum per acre at the time patent is issued. So there is nothing in the argument that the Government must retain control by a leasing bill of these deposits. Let the States have them; let the States and private capital bring these resources into the channels of use; and if there be anything in the idea of regulation and royalty, let the States regulate, prevent monopoly by restricting the area which can be acquired, and have the benefit of all of such royalties as they deem necessary and wise to impose. If the Government is receiving no profit, as a former Secretary of the Interior states, and if it is not necessary that these minerals be conserved and limited in their use, what argument is there to retain the Government in this business which the States can handle with just as much, if not more, benefit to the people as a whole? Any citizen of any State or Territory can come to the western States and have the same opportunity to secure rights and seek to develop these resources. Again, the States only have the power of regulation.

All of these lands, both reserved and unreserved domain, are of great potential value, running into billions of dollars. It will, of course, require many hundreds of millions of dollars of private capital and many decades to develop their mineral resources so as to make return to the Government or to the States through fees and royalties. The Government or the States can not and should not go into Government or State ownership and operation.

Now, as to all other resources which are said to be conserved by "reservation," and "leasing" they do not need or want conservation. They need and want use and development. The range is not being destroyed and does not need to be "conserved" by a permit and fee system but, if so, the states can conserve it better than the national agencies can. There are billions of tons of coal, which, in addition to its ordinary method of use, can be converted into oil and gasoline, or ground and burned in the same manner as oil. It can be converted into gas and into electricity. A late official report estimated the amount of oil in our coal and lignites at about 140,000,000,000 barrels of motor fuel.

Again, the United States Geological Survey and the Secretary of the Interior are authority for the statement that we have in all the oil shales of this country, 92,000,000,000 barrels. In manufacturing oil from shale there will not be millions of dollars wasted in "dry holes." Every ton of shale treated will produce 10 to 45 gallons of oil.

The West wants its great deposits of potash and phosphate, aluminum and asbestos used and not kept useless by imprisonment under "conservation." So-called conservation does not justify the withholding from the States and their legitimate use of all these resources by "reservation," or leasing acts which hinder the industries with restrictions and excessive royalties. The mining law was invaded as to coal, oil, oil shale, gas, phosphate, and sodium, by the leasing act, and location and patent denied. Theoretically, the forest lands are open to homesteading and location of minerals, but in fact they are not. Entries are denied. Prospecting and discoveries have ceased. This is one of the reasons for the alarming shortage in gold production. Conservation is a great word to conjure with, especially with those who do not know and often do not care to know the facts and conditions regarding the things they insist upon "conserving." There is only one thing, upon analysis, in addition to gas, that conservation really applies to and that is the forest land. But there is no reason why the States, primarily interested, directly concerned and dependent upon the preservation of the forest, will not conserve their own forests. They will.

The Federal Government has wasted forests in the past as well as the States. The new States should not be made dependencies because of the folly of the older States which permitted the destruction of their forests.

CHAPTER XI.

The Common Benefit-State Compacts-National Parks-Reserves-Royalties-Water-Power Sites-School Sections.

It is often thought and said that the public lands and their resources are for "the common benefit of all the States." You will look in vain for any such provision in the Constitution. You will find language to that effect in the Ordinance of 1787 and in the cessions of Virginia and other States in connection with what was designated in our early history as the Northwest Territory, and other lands east of the Mississippi ceded by the original States. The idea of the common benefit at that time was the payment of the Revolutionary debt. This was accomplished in 1836. But these deeds of cession and the ordinances provided for the greater and permanent purpose of the erection of new States. If there was still to be a common benefit after the payment of that debt, it was fully recognized that it was to be received in the building of sovereign, independent, equal States, with their additional strength and wealth to the Union, in the markets they would constitute for the manufactures of the original States and in the furnishing of food products to the Nation.

In 1825 Daniel Webster said:

I could never think the national domain is to be regarded as any great source of revenue. The great object of the Government with respect to these lands is not so much the money derived from their sale as it is the getting them settled. What I mean to say is I do not think we ought to hug that domain as a great treasure which is to enrich the exchequer.

In 1830 Robert Y. Hayne stated:

If in the deeds of cession it has been declared that the grants were intended for "the common benefit of all the States," it is clear from other provisions that they were not intended merely as so much property, for they expressly declared that the objects of the grant is the erection of new States; and the United States, in accepting this trust, bind themselves to facilitate the formation of these States to be admitted into the Union with all the rights and privileges of the original States.

This, sir, was the great end to which all parties looked, and it is by the fulfillment of the high trust that the common benefit of all the States is to be best promoted.

In the same address in the Senate he concluded:

In short, our whole policy with relation to the public lands may be summed up in the declaration with which I set out, that they ought not to be kept and retained forever as a great treasure, but that they should be administered chiefly with a view to the creation within reasonable periods of great and flourishing communities, to be formed into free and independent States, to be invested in due season with the control of all the lands within their respective limits.

Such were the opinions of the statesmen of that formative period when our public land policies were settled. It is evident that the beneficiaries of the trust, after the payment of the revolutionary debt, were to be the new States and the people thereof; and in their prosperity, wealth, strength, and loyalty the further "common benefit" was to be attained; and still further in that the lands of these States could be acquired by any citizen of the United States. We have departed from that policy.

It is true the original States ceded their extra lands between their western borders and the Mississippi, an area they were surprised to receive in the treaty with Great Britain. They threw this extra territory into the common Government for the purpose of a common benefit to-wit, payment of their debts of the Revolutionary War jointly instead of severally; and immedi-

CATTLE ON RANGE
Photo by Belden

ately received the proceeds of such lands in that way. Moreover, they retained within their original and permanent lines great areas of waste and vacant land, disposed of them for their own exclusive benefit, and developed greatly by the entire proceeds therefrom. They later shared also in the proceeds of the sale of a billion acres of the after-acquired lands, which amounted to $600,000,000. The present public land States have shared little in that as a common benefit. They have received but a small fractional part of that vast sum. Each State should have had all the proceeds from the sales of lands within its borders.

State Compacts.

When the States entered into the compacts in their enabling acts, waiving and ceding to the Federal Government and pledging themselves "not to interfere with the primary disposal of the soil" within their boundaries, the policy had ever been, and was, and therefore it was with the understanding that, as the Constitution prescribed, the Government was to "dispose of" the lands; not hold them, reserve them forever and impose royalties or fees on their development and prevent settlement.

There is no bad faith on the part of the States. They do not now ask to interfere with the "disposal" of the lands. They insist upon their disposal according to the compacts into private ownership, or to the States. It is the only way in which the new States can grow to full stature and equal sovereignty. That was the object of the trust created by the treaties, Constitution, the cessions, and compacts. It is the General Government which has ceased to "dispose of" the soil by permanently reserving and forever barring from settlement 235,000,000 acres, and recommending through a former Secretary of the Interior, the permanent withholding and placing under a rental and fee system of 180,000,000 acres more; a total area twice in extent that of all of the permanent area of the original thirteen States. The trust in part created by the treaties and the waiving or ceding by the States can be fulfilled only by the disposal of the soil in the manner in which it was being disposed of at the several times the compacts were entered into.

The West wants the trust fulfilled; just as it was fulfilled as to Ohio, Indiana, Illinois, Iowa, and Nebraska. At that time, neither party to the compacts, no one, had any other idea than that "dispose of" meant to pass to private ownership through sale, grant, subsidy, homestead, or mining location, thus in time completing the full settlement and sovereignty of the States. The only possible exception to this policy would be as to the national parks. Even as to these, it should be remembered that, with the exception of one, all these western public-land States were admitted prior to the establishment of any parks therein.

Where is the justification for adopting a different policy when it came the turn of Colorado, Utah, and Nevada in the march of development to the western coast? By what right and for what reason are these Rocky Mountain and Pacific Coast States deprived of the usual orderly disposal of the soil, in the same manner as it had been disposed of for a century, without withdrawals, reservations, royalties, and fees; the manner which was in effect at the time the States were admitted; the manner contemplated and expected by all concerned when the States agreed to waive their rights to the soil that they might be admitted and so that disposition might be made under one general, federal, uniform plan.

It does not answer the requirements of justice, equity, fairness and moral right to say that the United States Supreme Court, disregarding the international treaties, has held that the word "dispose," as it appears in the Constitution, may include disposition by reservations for particular public purposes. Aside from a question of legal and constitutional right, justice and equity require at the hands of Congress, fair and equal treatment with that accorded the settled States. The western States protest against a departure from the settled policy of a hundred years; against discrimination and the imposition of burdens never placed upon the older States. They insist upon the carrying out of the compacts in their true spirit. They submit that the Federal Government by reason of immense withdrawals made, and more proposed which would forever preclude settlement of the area and complete sovereignty of the States over them, is to that extent making it impossible and is clearly failing to carry out the compacts and fulfill its trust as was the contemplation of all parties when the compacts were made.

National Parks.

The people of the West are entirely willing to let the withholding of the areas of the public-land States stand as to the national parks, although they have now increased to the number of 23, and set apart from all development or taxation nearly 8,000,000 acres. These areas are used directly for broad national purposes and are probably best administered by the Federal Government. With the adjustment of the lines of the national parks under the bills introduced in the Congress, we have reached the limit of proper park reservations and the States should vigorously oppose any further enlargements, or the creation of more parks in the public-land States.

Indian Reservations.

The whole tendency of the times' is logically in the direction of the final freeing of the Federal Government of distant, expensive, and necessarily unsatisfactory administration of the care of these local things. A Secretary of the Interior himself has recommended the transfer of the national monuments to the States where located. A representative advisory committee appointed by such Secretary to inquire into our Indian problem has adopted resolutions advising that the management of the Indians and the reservations should be placed in the respective States. This is in line with the right policy and principle, particularly since the Congress has made of the Indian a citizen with the right to vote, under State qualifications, and this carries with it the obligation of taxation. There are in Indian lands owned or controlled by the United States 70,993,326 acres.

Forest Reserves.

For the last 30 years the forest lands of the Western States have been by national laws under a conservation policy. They have been added to year by year and are still seeking enlargement, although, exclusive of Alaska, there are now 162,000,000 acres within national forest boundaries administered by the Forest Service of the Department of Agriculture. No one in this day will take a stand in opposition to the forest-conservation idea. No one would attempt to combat the principle. It should be agreed however, that conservation means not only the preservation but a proper use of the timber resources and the lands and other resources contained therein. Even the Federal view and the policy of the law theoretically is to develop and utilize to the fullest extent consistent with forest preservation. Incidentally, the States of the West might well point to the fact that whereas their forest lands are retained from them and revenues returned only in part, that the western people as taxpayers are called upon to pay money into the United States Treasury out of which the Forest Service, under the National Forest Commission, is purchasing back forest or forest areas which passed into private ownership and taxation in the Eastern States.

Proper conservation is both good and necessary. The question is propounded, however startling it may seem, why can not the States administer the forest areas within their boundaries as well as the Federal Government? Is this iconoclastic? Is it lese majeste? No; it is simply getting back to first principles. It is a habit with certain eastern citizens whose States have had and used all their resources and now want to share what is left on that peculiar principle: "What's mine is mine; what's yours is ours," and seek to inoculate the departments with the same virus, to say that the States are improvident, permit waste and sell immense valuable areas far below their value; that corrupt politics will favor certain henchmen and supporters with grants and sales and leases at less than their worth. Wise enough to retain her lands, Texas worked out a sales and a lease law and handles its own lands. Minnesota and Michigan have wisely used the mineral lands retained by them. The States have handled their school sections well. Will anyone contend that in the past the Federal Government has not been improvident; that these things have not occurred under national administrations? Where the States in the past have wasted resources on a small scale the Nation has done the same on an immense scale.

In this day and age the States and people of the West are just as anxious and determined as any of the States and their citizens anywhere to conserve all of the forests and other resources. They oppose wasting them. They, themselves, are the first beneficiaries of true conservation, and they would be the first victims of a contrary policy. The fact is that in earlier years both the Nation and the States did not know or realize the great values in their lands which the development of after years disclosed. The American people were all educated in this matter in the same way at the same time. Should the public-lands States acquire the forest lands within their confines, there is no reason to believe or say that they could not or would not administer them for the greatest good to the greatest number. The fact is that the States are now keen in looking after their land interests. In some, constitutional provisions retain certain mineral rights when land sales are made, and no doubt all State constitutions could ultimately so provide. The States should have the right to develop the untold mineral resources which undoubtedly lie in the forest areas, as well as the annual growth of timber. While mining locations are permitted in the national forests, the conditions and restrictions do not encourage but discourage the prospector and miner. They will bear witness to this fact. And if it be proper to charge the livestock industry grazing fees in the forest lands and, as is now proposed, on all the public domain, then let the States own and lease and receive directly for themselves all such returns and not a small portion of them. It may not be soon, but the day will come when, following the original plan of this Union, pursuing the American form of government, the States will come not only into bare jurisdiction as now over the forest lands for purposes of government, the preservation of law and order, the advancement of education, but, as a natural and rightful corollary with that responsibility, into full ownership and control.

Mineral Royalties.

It was never the intention of the founders of the Government or of great statesmen in the days of Webster, Clay, Calhoun, and Benton that the Federal Government should ever engage in or impose a system of rents, fees, and royalties. Webster said:

The gentleman spoke of the centuries that must elapse before all the lands could be sold and the great hardships that the States must suffer while the United States reserved to itself, within their limits, such large portions of soil not liable to taxation. * * * If these lands were leasehold property, if they were held by the United States on rent, there would be much in the idea. But they are wild lands held only until they can be sold; reserved no longer than till somebody will take them up at low price. Sir, if in any case any State can show that the policy of the United States retards her settlement or prevents her from cultivating the lands within her limits, she shall have my vote to alter that policy.

Water.

Notwithstanding the recognition by the courts of the principle of ownership and control by arid-land States of the rivers of such States as distinguished from the riparian doctrine; notwithstanding such right of these States was stated and accepted by the Congress in the constitutions of these States; in spite of the recognition of State rights in this vital matter in the reclamation law of 1902, it is undoubtedly the purpose of the Department of Justice to assert and enforce, if they can, the doctrine of Federal ownership and control of the water of the streams. The battle lines have been formed, briefs have been prepared, petitions have been drawn, and suits filed, to take from the Western States all power and authority over their streams. This must be resisted literally to the "last ditch." Every western State, separately and all together, should prepare to meet and repel this last and greatest assault of Federal encroachment.

Water-Power Sites.

Our Federal water power act, while providing regulation and a small royalty, is based on the theory of private capital and operation. These objects can be maintained as well by the States.

The States through which navigable streams run control such streams. They own their beds. Before a Federal power permit can be granted by the Federal Power Commission, the applicant must secure a permit from the State or States controlling the streams and the stream beds. By a transfer of the public lands which comprise the power sites, the adjacent lands necessarily submerged or used in the building and operation of a power enterprise, to the States wherever they are situated, authority would be concentrated in the local government, as it should be. If compacts among the States having right to a given stream, or a general water authority, are to be provided for, the States would then be in a position to proceed; and the Government would be freed from another burden, except its responsibility to preserve navigability. The States by compact, if they saw fit, would be in a position to make provision for low-cost power to their people, even though the distributing and marketing operations are carried on by private enterprise. Divided authority does not work well on water-power matters. A State obviously can block the General Government and vice versa, because the one has control of the stream bed and the other of navigation, and, in the West, of the adjacent lands. The waters also of the non-navigable streams and lakes belong to the Western States. Complete authority should be concentrated in one or the other. There is more power centered in Washington than there should be. The consolidation should be in the States. Therefore, the lands essential to water-power development, whether unreserved or reserved for this purpose in the West, should be ceded to the States, which would administer the permits and licenses which have been granted by the Federal Power Commission.

School-Section Grants.

On admission and survey each of the States was granted one, two, or four sections in each township, to be used by the States for educational purpose. If it developed these sections were known to be mineral upon survey, the State was required to select other non-mineral sections in lieu thereof.

After from 14 to 50 years in the various States, and after the States, in good faith, had sold many of the sections to innocent purchasers, who have made improvements, the Government sought to contest the right of the States and of such individual owners, and brought contests, 1,700 in number, affecting 1,700 sec-

tions, 1,088,000 acres, to eject them on the ground that
the sections were known to be mineral at the time of
the admission.   These contests were brought at the
direction of a Secretary of the Interior.   There was
no recourse to the Courts.   The Secretary renders the
final decision.   Titles were unsettled.   The States
could not sell their school lands.   Such a policy and
law was unjust and unwise.   The Government slept
on its rights in not determining and declaring the mineral character of the mineral sections many years ago.
It permitted sales and improvements without a word
of objection.   It then declared vast areas mineral which
no one formerly regarded as of mineral value.

In all justice and equity it was estopped from claiming these sections.   Twenty-six Eastern and Central
States were given all these mineral rights.   A bill to
confirm the title and issue patents to the Western
States and their grantees in all school sections granted,
received the united support of not only the West but of
the East and South as well.   Every consideration of
equity and fair dealing brought about the passage of
that legislation.

CHAPTER XII.

Unreserved and Unappropriated Domain.

To ameliorate the unprecedented and anomalous condition of the public land States it is said that out of the total of 415,000,000 acres, not in private or State ownership, which is more than one-half the area of these States, averaging 55 per cent of their entire area, 180,000,000 acres are still open to entry and will eventually be settled, and then, in that distant future day, the States will be sovereign over this area and may develop and tax, and that therefore the Government is permanently depriving these States of only 235,000,000 acres.

A magazine of national circulation, speaking of the Western States, editorially stated:

In the immense, if not heavily populated, area the sequestration of a large minority of all land from State and local control is a problem of real magnitude and a fairly constant source of irritation. * * * In the western mountain and desert States the feeling is often expressed that the tax burden would be less if only the various classes of Government-owned land were available to the assessor. * * * Speaking generally, we question the wisdom of tax exemption. The more property reached, the less the burden on any single class or group of taxables.

The governmental areas referred to above, a majority, not a "large minority," of the lands, consists of 235,000,000 acres of reserved lands, comprising forest reserves, national parks, Indian reservations, mineral withdrawals, monuments, and power sites; and nearly 180,000,000 acres of unreserved and unappropriated domain, 97 per cent of all of which are in the Western States, distributed in the States as follows:

Area of Vacant, Unappropriated, and Unreserved Public Lands.

State—	Area in acres Surveyed	Unsurveyed	Total
Arizona	8,084,880	7,096,000	15,180,880
Arkansas	190,969		190,969
California	11,294,395	5,339,093	16,623,488
Colorado	6,825,425	1,202,043	8,027,468
Florida	12,245	6,652	18,897
Minnesota	189,845		189,845
Montana	6,510,937	90,740	6,601,677
Nebraska	22,628		22,628
Nevada	30,064,688	21,389,805	51,454,493
New Mexico	14,316,481	1,347,640	15,664,121
North Dakota	146,505		146,505
Oregon	12,976,725	92,411	13,069,136
South Dakota	439,880		439,880
Utah	12,378,068	11,503,377	23,881,445
Washington	906,382	14,202	920,584
Wyoming	15,185,722	743,728	15,929,460
Grand Total	128,301,266	50,678,180	178,979,446

What is now proposed to be done with this balance of the unreserved, unappropriated public domain? Some western Senators and Representatives, apparently at the request of livestock associations of the country, are not only agreeable to, but active in, the proposal to now put this great area of remaining free-range public lands under a federal system of regulation and charge for grazing. Two departments saw this great opportunity to extend their administration and power. Bills in Congress are sought to be made law which would give the administration of all the balance of the public domain to the Secretary of Agriculture to close it forever for free range, which has been the custom from the beginning of the Government, as handed down from the free commons of England, and to issue 10-year permits under a fee system. Thus bills are pending to put the Government deeper and deeper into business operations, into absent landlordism, into Federal exactions of fees, charges, tributes, levies and Government operations. The excuse is that the cattle and sheep men war over the range, overstock it and deteriorate the range grass. This last is a theory advanced for many years. Sheepmen have gone into cattle raising and cattlemen have gone into sheep raising. There are no range wars. They use the range in harmony. The days of range wars are long since gone by. The evidence of stockmen is that of late years the range is as good or better than it had been in many years; and as against conditions of 40 or 50 years ago, the range is superior. It is reasonable to suppose this to be true in every range State. Temporary deterioration by drought does not affect the question and should not be considered.

This proposed radical departure from past policies is dangerous and detrimental to the interest of range States and to the country. It is wrong in principle. It will practically stop all settlement and development and hopes of private ownership, which has ever been the true principle and policy. Even though the bill provides these lands be still subject to settlement under homestead laws, it will be as with the forest reservations; in actual practice entry can not and will not be made, unless for nuisance and extortion purposes. If entries can be made as before, the permit is worthless to the proposed permittees. The live stock permittees will prevent and defeat the homestead entrymen if they can. One will succumb to the other. It is an impossible situation that one or many homesteaders could go into the heart of a permittee's area and each take up an entry. The conflict of the range-war days against the settler will be revived. If entries are stopped, then we will have a system of perpetual Government landlordism utterly foreign to the American idea, with all the bitter and expensive accompaniments of more Federal agents and espionage.

It is sought to take the stigma out of the proposition and make western stockmen more complacent in swallowing this radical change by provision of a very nominal charge, practically the cost of administration. The western stockmen realize that when the forest reserves were created it was first said by no less an authority than Pinchot himself that livestock would not be interfered with; that they would continue to range just as they had, without change, as the only object was to preserve the forests; that the running of livestock in the forests was a help to preservation of the forests because it removed a large part of the grass and brush which spread forest fires. They remember that notwithstanding this a small nominal charge was made; that soon that charge was increased, until it is now admitted by the Forest Service that the present charge is more than three times the cost of administering the grazing. They do not forget that now it is firmly proposed to double the present charge, so as to call for what the Forest Service denominates the "commercial value" of the grazing.

By what process of reasoning or favor of fate can they hope to escape the same history and experience if once the fee system is fastened on the unreserved public domain? They will be called upon in time, as sure as time passes, to pay the "commercial value" of the grazing on the remaining public lands, as well as in the forest reserves. "Commercial value" is equally right or wrong as to both forest reserves and non-forest domain.

But aside from the money cost the plan is unwise and vicious, because it will stop development and settlement and the great purposes of the trust reposed in the Federal Government will be abandoned and defeated. If there were any doubt as to the prevention of settlement under this plan, it is made absolutely certain by the official recommendation of a Secretary of the Interior that the 640-acre homestead act be repealed. Bills in Congress provide expressly that the domain shall not be open to such entry.

Who can calmly contemplate, whether he lives in the West, East, North, or South, a plan which is the final step to engraft a permanent system of Federal landlordism upon the public-land States involving 25 to 50 per cent of the area of those States, with all its costs, agents, regulations, restrictions, interference, and prevention of settlement? Is not the question most serious whether the passage of such a bill is not equivalent to a practical refusal of the Federal Government to continue to execute the solemn trust reposed in its power, its justice, and its good faith? The duty of the Government is to dispose of these lands, create homes for the increasing population of the country, and eventually bring about the too-long-delayed complete sovereignty of these States over that much more territory within their borders, or give over that duty to the States.

Thus it is actually proposed by a former Secretary of the Interior, and bills have been introduced in Congress, to repeal homestead laws and place the remainder of the public domain not already reserved under a Federal leasing system! "System" is the correct word. That system abides and constantly enlarges. The system, year after year and decade after decade, continues in office, building precedent on precedent, always advancing, enlarging their scope, claiming and taking more and more power, by new interpretations and by securing the passage of laws when their objects can not be gained by rule and regulation. Bureaus and Boards are made up of officials who are perfectly honest, hardworking, able Government servants; but they are imbued with the very essence of the spirit of the system. Their viewpoint is the Federal viewpoint. They work and build accordingly. When they pass their successors carry on. The heart of the system is human nature, which seeks expansion and power. A bureau perpetuates itself and its spirit. Every new precedent established is another inch gained for Federal power and, of course, incidentally, the power of the bureau and its personnel. The system grows from that upon which it feeds. The more it feeds the stronger its appetite. The stronger its appetite, the more it feeds. And always its food is the rights of the States and the individual citizens of the States. "On what meat doth this our Caesar feed that he hath grown so great?" On the substance and freedom of the citizens of the local self-governments. The people of the West believe in a strong central government, in the Union, in a nation as builded upon the Constitution; but that Constitution reserves certain rights in the States and the people. The West is for the whole Constitution, which designed a balanced Government, Federal and State. It is striving to maintain that balance.

This proposed grazing lease system on all of the balance of the public domain means perpetual Government control, it dooms those great areas to the status of a Federal pasture. It means that the remaining

SHEEP ON RANGE
Photo by Belden

lands could never be entered, acquired, and transferred to private ownership or the ownership of the States. It involves still another imposition in the form of grazing fees in addition to the long list of fees, royalties, charges, tributes which have already been exacted from the western resources. It means another profit-making reserve of 180,000,000 more acres in the 11 Western States; making a total, with the areas already reserved, of 435,000,000 acres, which amounts to 55 per cent of their total area, of which the Western States are to be forever deprived as to sovereignty, settlement, and taxation.

The Western States can never be convinced that such usurpation of more than half of these States can be constitutionally done or that it is wisdom, statesmanship, right, or justice, or in the best interests of the United States of America.

Take, for example, the State of Wyoming, if such a grazing bill passes. Wyoming would never be sovereign or be able to tax not only the 16,000,000 acres now reserved and withdrawn, but 16,000,000 acres more, the amount of its present unreserved domain; a total of 32,000,000 acres; 52 per cent of its area! And its people would be subject forever, as to that great part of her surface with all it contains, to bureau landlordism and to pay tribute for its use at the same time. And yet it must at its own expense extend over all its 62,000,000 acres police jurisdiction, preserve law and order by its courts, and provide roads and schoolhouses for what people might be scattered over all this area. The same condition would prevail in nearly every Western State.

It is an amazing proposition which is intolerable to contemplate. The highest interests of the settler, the ordinary stock grower, the average livestock companies and corporations, and of the State as a whole demand its defeat. It is the first duty of the public-land States to see to it that such additional shackle is not clamped upon them.

The pending bills providing for grazing permits or leasing systems with imposition of fees in renewable periods of 10 years will cause all settlement and home building to cease. One of the bills expressly repeals the 640-acre stock-raising homestead act. Secretary of the Interior Work recommended its repeal. Even if permitted under the terms of the bills, homesteading would not be carried on simultaneously with a permit or leasing plan. No man wants a homesteader in the middle of his leased area and no homesteader wants a home surrounded by leased lands. Conflict would be inevitable. A Secretary of the Interior twice stated in his annual reports and in letters and addresses that the character of the land now left cannot be successfully settled under the 160, the 320, or the 640-acre acts. So that it is not to be expected that a Secretary will designate any of the remaining area for homesteading, even if the proposed grazing bills should so provide. The same Secretary has recommended, if a grazing bill should not be passed, that the stock-raising homestead area be enlarged from 640 acres to 1,280 acres, having come to the conclusion that such an area is required to make a home and living on the remaining lands.

The people are still land hungry and desirous of making homes in the West. The proof of this is the large number who filed entries under the homestead acts during 1929, aggregating 1,700,950 acres. Homesteading results in the raising of more livestock than the open range. The consumer benefits thereby.

The West is opposed to the repeal of the homestead laws and the substitution therefor of Government regulation of the remaining unreserved public domain, under 10 or 20-year renewal permits, all under a fee system, as proposed in bills now pending in the Congress, and as recommended by the Department of the Interior in a previous administration.

It will prevent entry and settlement of the remaining great areas in 11 public-land States.

It will deprive the reclamation fund of the proceeds of public lands paid in under the homestead laws and direct sales.

It will establish permanent Government landlordism.

It will put the Government deeper in business in the States when it should be getting out of the public land and other business which can be conducted by the States.

It reverses the steady policy of this Government, which under the Constitution is "to dispose of" these lands to make homes, create private property, and build up the States, which must maintain organized government and order over these domains.

The immemorial right of free range should continue, leaving the land open to settlement, and until they are settled.

Fees should be decreased rather than raised.

They should be abolished rather than to create more burdens upon our industries.

The cattlemen and sheepmen together use the free range now in entire harmony, and it is not proven that the free range is being overstocked and injured.

The small livestock growers should be encouraged and protected by liberalizing the 640-acre stock homestead act, reducing the required cash expenditures and increasing the area to four sections.

Unless the homestead law is so amended, then the Federal Government should either sell the balance of public domain, the best having been taken, for 50 cents to $1 per acre or it should cede the remaining lands, with all their resources, back to the States, so each can handle them according to the best interest of each State as their own conditions require.

In any event, the Federal Government should now proceed to get out of the land business.

Preparatory to that, it should cease levying tribute to which the original States and the Central States were never subjected.

It was never contemplated under our system of Government that the Nation should continue to exercise ownership and dominion over all these lands.

It was the purpose, and should be, to encourage the settlement of the lands, for the building of homes and the development of the States. It is an anomaly and an unnatural condition that the Federal Government retain control forever of more than one-half of the area of these western States.

The proposed bill to repeal homestead laws and regulate and charge for grazing on the public domain, making one-fourth of the area of these States a Federal pasture for all time, is wrong in principle and contrary to the best interests of the West, and of the Nation.

The balance of the unreserved and unappropriated domain of 180,000,000 acres in the West, which is now planned to be placed under a leasing system, should be left open as free range until proper disposition is made of it; that disposition should not be by further Federal reservations for any purpose, or held forever under any leasing or permit system preventing acquisition by the people. The disposition which is commanded in the Constitution and the settled policy of this Nation should be made, to wit, transfer by direct sale, mineral location or enlarged homesteads to the people; or by cession to the States.

The Government has disposed by subsidy, sale, homestead, and mining location of approximately 1,100,000,000 acres, and has received into the United States Treasury from this source, in round numbers, $600,000,000. It has received in mineral royalties about $80,000,000 since February 25, 1920, under the leasing act, which is included.

If we take the average ratio of valuations of real property and improvements of exempted to taxed property in the 11 public-land States, we find according to the ofifcial report of 1922, the figure to be 38.79 as compared to the average ratio in the non-public land States of 11.45. Yet the public-land States while having the burden and obligation of jurisdiction, maintenance of law and order, spread of education and road building, do not derive one cent by way of taxation from this large, Federal-controlled portion of their total valuation.

The fact that west of the Mississippi the territory was acquired by purchase, and therefore the title went direct to the United States instead of by cession from the States as it was of the area east of the Mississippi, should not and does not change the fundamental plan and genius of the American system of erecting new States with the same powers as the original States.

There should not be two different bases and policies with respect to the relation of the States to the Federal Government and their development. The Federal Government has received back its purchase price outlay of $55,000,000 and $545,000,000 in addition.

The average price per acre paid by the United States for the 1,336,000,000 acres in the United States proper secured by purchase was 4 cents. The price per acre paid for the 378,165,760 acres constituting Alaska was 2 cents. The average price paid for all, including Alaska was 3 cents. For the approximately 1,100,000,000 acres which the United States has disposed of it has received an average of nearly 55 cents per acre.

Approximately one-half the area was disposed of by reservations, grants, gifts, or free homestead. For the actual amount "sold" or from which there were receipts, the other half, the Government has received approximately $1.25 per acre.

The Government has long since been repaid many times over the purchase price paid for it for the territory west of the Mississippi. It can well afford to cede these lands to the States without repayment by them of the cost of the land purchases.

CHAPTER XIII.

Future Policies and Legislation.

A crisis is near in regard to our public lands and the destiny of the public-land States. It has been steadily approaching with every diversion of great areas of land from State and individual to Federal purposes. It will affect the entire Nation for good or ill.

A final policy must soon be determined by Congress as to the vital and tremendous question of the ultimate disposition of all the lands not now privately owned, unreserved and reserved, comprising vast bodies of land within 11 States of this Union. The matter goes into the framework of our political structure. It penetrates to the very heart of our system of government. It should challenge the earnest attention of every member of Congress; indeed, of every student of State and governmental relations, looking to the future of our country.

In this discussion on the public-land States and the Federal Government it is not the purpose to speak of the administration of the public land and mining laws. Naturally, the States in which public lands lie, and the individual citizens of such States, desire and contend for the most liberal interpretation and administration of mining and land laws for the benefit of such States and their people, but we are not at this time dealing with that subject.

These States are deeply interested in principles, policies, and legislation. What is presented is with a view to future legislation determining and fixing permanent policies in the interests of the public-land States. In the long view they profoundly believe that what is best

for these States, as to the public lands and their resources, is best for the Nation, because their development and equity make for the good of the Union.
Their lack of development and inequity create conditions that harm the whole country infinitely more than
is offset by any money gain to the Treasury of the
United States or the exercise of national power.

They are today concerned with this 235,000,000 acres
forever reserved under the present policies and laws,
and with the remaining 180,000,000 acres of the unappropriated and unreserved public lands. We again
refer to and emphasize the fact that there is a well-
defined movement, crystallized into bills now pending
before Congress, to place the remaining unreserved
area on a lease or rental, or grazing-fee system abolishing the free range, and to repeal or make inapplicable the 640-acre stock-raising homestead law. The
West is therefore face to face with the question
whether not only the areas heretofore reserved, but a
total of 415,000,000 acres of the area of the present 11
public-land States, is never to be settled, never to pass
to private ownership or made taxable, but is to forever
remain under the Federal Government as a perpetual
landlord.

The West is utterly and forever opposed to this condition and this idea. The people of the public land
States are unalterably determined against such a destiny. The acreage thus proposed to be always withheld from the States and private ownership comprises
an average of over 55 per cent of the whole area of each
of the States of Montana, Idaho, Wyoming, Colorado,
New Mexico, Arizona, Nevada, Utah, California, Oregon and Washington.

They maintain that such a condition can not be permanently endured. These States can not live and develop half State and half national as to their land areas. These States desire to live and develop and to obtain sovereignty over their soil. A perpetual condition of half-local and half-federal sovereignty simply can not be contemplated as to any State or States in this Republic. Imagine the consternation of Eastern or Central States were it even suggested that the Government should own and control more than half their areas. No one contemplated such a condition when the conservation policy was initiated. Such a status is foreign and antagonistic to our basic principles and to our organic law. It is subversive of the American system provided by the Constitution.

Under our structure of Government, every one of these States is entitled to now have and certainly to eventually come into absolute and full sovereignty over every foot of soil within its borders; excepting only the national parks. The 11 public-land States have not been on an equal footing such as was expressly provided. They are not now on equal terms with the original States or any of the other States, and if Federal control is to continue indefinitely and increase instead of diminish, they never can or will be upon parity or equality. This is a clear violation of the intent, express purposes, provisions, and stipulations of treaties, ordinances, the Constitution, and the compacts with the States and of the policy of this country in force for a hundred years.

All of the States, except the present public-domain States, have come into complete sovereignty, not only politically but as to their soil, to the same full degree as the original States by the "disposition" by the Fed-

eral Government of all their lands by sale and purchase, homestead, and mining location. The present
public-land States never can under the present laws
and policies, attain such sovereignty. They are now
definitely and permanently, unless Congress changes
its laws and policies, deprived of that possibility.

The Government, through Congress, by the afore-
mentioned withdrawals which have actually been
made and are in force, has not only withheld them
from the States and the people of the States, who are
the rightful beneficiaries of that trust, but it has been
exacting rent from the forest reserves initiated in 1900,
and since 1920 a royalty from the minerals enumerated
in the mineral leasing act, and has retained the bulk
of these revenues. It has repaid to the said States
only 25 per cent of the forest grazing fees, plus 10 per
cent for roads, and but 37½ per cent of the royalties.

The rights of the States of production to have any
return, save a paltry 5 per cent from the proceeds for
school purposes from the sales of public lands, was
belatedly and partially recognized when the reclamation fund was established in 1902. But even as to this
fund, great and important and beneficial as reclamation, it is not a return of the money to the State. The
52½ per cent of the proceeds of public lands and royalties which constitute the reclamation fund is a loan
and not a refund. The settlers must repay. It aids in
development and settlement and affords opportunity
to create taxable wealth in the land and improvements.
These values are, however, produced by the capital and
the labor of the settlers. Let it be realized that money
of the reclamation fund expended in the construction
of reclamation works, is a loan and not a repayment; a
loan without interest, it is true, but nevertheless a loan

from the proceeds of royalties and the sale of public lands and not a return of the money to the State. Incidentally, lest we forget another phase of this matter, the 26 States existing in the year 1836 divided up the then proceeds of the sales of public lands amounting to $28,000,000, calling it a loan. Nevertheless, while some Representatives of these same Eastern States oppose reclamation and criticise the settlers on the reclamation projects for not paying up promptly in full each year the amount stipulated under their contracts, and that in an era of agricultural depression, the Eastern States receiving those loans in 1836 have never repaid a dollar, either of principal or interest. It stands on the books of the Secretary of the Treasury as "unavailable funds." The amount today, if bearing the usual interest, is over $2,000,000,000.

For the present let us limit the discussion and confine this presentation to the status and disposition of the unreserved and unappropriated public domain, amounting to 180,000,000 acres, 97 per cent of which is in the 11 Western States, and which constitutes approximately 25 per cent of their total area. They are now open, as they have been since 1862, to homesteading. Again, let it be recalled that a serious effort is being made under the recommendation of a former Secretary of the Interior, representing only the national and Federal viewpoint, to repeal the homestead law under which they are being taken and settled, to-wit: The 640-acre grazing homestead act.

In lieu of this it is sought to substitute a perpetual Government landlordism in the form of a regulation and fee permit or lease system. If successful, this would clearly defeat and make impossible forever the execution of the government's solemn trust to the people of these later States and abandon a century-long policy of this Government. It would destroy the possibility of settlement, development, and taxation and complete State sovereignty of 25 per cent more of their area in addition to the 30 per cent now permanently reserved. This would perpetuate for all time the Federal Government in control of the greater part of the area and value of property and resources in each of these States.

It is incredible that such a proposition should receive serious consideration. It is contrary to the genius of our American system of Government. It is a violation of the purpose of our forefathers and of the Constitution.

The unreserved public lands should be disposed of by the Federal Government to private ownership as to the surface by again enlarging the homestead area from 640 acres to 1280 acres, or by direct sales of surface rights in limited amounts not exceeding 2560; or cession to the States wherein the lands are located of the surface and mineral rights. The drift of opinion and sentiment favors, this last plan. We now wish to present herewith the manner and effect of ownership and administration of these public-land areas by the States. There has been already disposed of the suggestion that, because some of the older States are alleged to have wasted their mineral, forest, and swamp lands, therefore, the Western States should not have the same right as enjoyed by all of the States east of the Rocky Mountain Range.

Texas retained and administered all of her public lands and resources and eventually worked out a system which has resulted in great beneficial permanent funds for her universities and schools.

Michigan, Wisconsin, Minnesota, Missouri, and Oklahoma have made good use of the mineral rights and resources that they were permitted to retain, or their citizens to acquire patent for without mineral reservations, and built up endowment funds for State Institutions. It is an unwarranted reflection upon the Western States that they can not or will not conserve and wisely use their own resources. No one can now question the intelligence, integrity and wisdom of the people of the Western States. Federal control has not been infallible.

It has been said that this course would stop the Federal reclamation policy, and therefore and thereby harm the development of the arid West, because the fund would be deprived of the receipts from royalties coming to the Federal Government through the mineral leasing act, 52½ per cent of which goes under the law, to the reclamation fund. In answer, first, the 19,000,000 acres withdrawn for ultimate reclamation development by virtue of that withdrawal is not a part of the unreserved and unappropriated public domain and would not, therefore, be ceded to the States if cession were made; second, while it is true that future payments into the fund from the sale of public lands and royalties under the leasing act would cease and the States would receive such receipts under their own laws and provisions, there is a permanent reclamation revolving fund of $240,000,000 which will remain.

The great projects such as the Boulder Dam and the Columbia River Basin are not to be financed and never can be from the reclamation fund. This **fund** will continue to revolve and be replenished by repayments by the settlers upon the projects under the contracts. For 1930 they repaid over $5,000,000. These payments will be increased under their contracts. With the settlement of vacant areas and the completion and settlement of present authorized projects, these repayments will approximate eight to ten million dollars annually. With these annual repayments, the Federal reclamation policy can proceed.

It has been said that if the Federal Government parts with the remaining public lands and they come thus into the possession and control of the States, this would stop the homestead policy, and thus interfere with the settlement of these States. Passing over the inconsistency of this argument made by those who would expressly repeal the 640 acre grazing homestead act, on the contrary, these separate States will each be able to create and maintain a homestead policy of their own which will be better suited to their separate needs, and bring greater benefits to all concerned than the present Federal homestead act. Some States desire to have the area of the grazing homestead remain at 640 acres; some desire to increase it to 1280; some have adopted resolutions by their legislatures, in view of the character of the remaining lands, the best having been taken, asking Congress to increase the area to four sections, or 2560 acres. The representatives of some States desire to administer the public domain under a regulation and fee permit or lease plan. The present Federal homestead law is rigid and applies alike to every State, regardless of its special conditions. If owned by the States, each State could adopt the policy best suited to its lands and needs. The greater number of the Western States, will, inaugurate and maintain, if these lands are ceded to the States, a better homestead system than now prevails or can prevail under a uniform or any Federal law.

The States, once the ownership of the public lands is granted to them, can take the following courses:

First, they can preserve all the present free range, which has been threatened with extinction.

Second, they can create, maintain and administer a better homestead law than the one now in force.

Third, they can sell such areas in such limited amounts for such reasonable prices as will best subserve the State and the livestock industry.

Fourth, they can lease for nominal or low rates until sales are made.

Fifth, they can retain title to certain minerals in all these lands and lease for mineral purposes under a royalty system. The rate of royalty would be governed by the best interests of the State and the mining industry, keeping in mind the encouragement of prospecting and development. Inasmuch as the State now receives back from the Federal Government only $37\frac{1}{2}$ per cent of the royalties collected, the State could fix a lower royalty and encourage the mining industry and make possible mineral development, which otherwise could not take place, by reducing the royalty materially below the amount now required by the Federal Government and still receive for the State treasury a far greater amount than under the present system, because they would receive 100 per cent of such royalty, reduced only by the cost of administration.

The added proceeds from these sources of public land sales and leases of grazing and mineral rights would provide a fund whereby, if it was desired, the State could build reclamation projects and thus hasten the general development.

It has been suggested that cession to the States of the public lands would change the policy from the benefit of "all the people" to the people of these particular States wherein the lands are located. It has heretofore been shown that the people of the States of each area were and are the rightful beneficiaries of the lands and resources within their borders; that it is not just that the States east of the Rocky Mountains should come into possession of all of their lands or resources, either to the State or to private ownership, and that the same privileges or rights should be withheld, as is now done and further proposed, as to the States from the Rocky Mountains to the Pacific.

The following paragraphs are presented as some concrete suggestions for the policies and laws Congress should adopt:

Enlarge Homesteads.

1. Following the policy heretofore applied since 1862 of enlarging the area of homestead entries, as the lands become poorer and greater areas are required for successful home building, provide for a stock-raising homestead of four sections, in noncontiguous tracts where necessary, under liberal terms, low cash outlay requirements, with additional rights to that limit of acreage and a 90-day preference to all present homesteaders.

The only reason the 640-acre stockraising homestead act has apparently reached the limit of its usefulness is that the character of the land left requires more than that area to successfully apply it. We advanced for similar reasons from 160 acres to 320 acres and from 320 acres to 640 acres. The time has come for another and greater advance. This should be 2560 acres, four sections, to insure the great object, which is that of creating a home and affording a living. In the long run this area may be the most practical-sized unit for

POWER PLANT, BAKER CITY—WASHINGTON
Courtesy Chamber of Commerce. Seattle

all stockraising. More and better stock may be raised under this plan eventually than under the old large-herd, free-range system, which is inevitably giving way to the new order. If otherwise, then the lands by economic laws and business evolution will reach the natural highest and most efficient use.

Again, parts of these sized areas will develop by intensive study and effort, scientific application, and new, hardy, forage crops into cultivation and crop growing, permitting the fattening of livestock for market and the better livelihood of the homesteader. It will require great labor, but will eventually be worth while. No man can say that this will not develop. There was a time when all Nebraska was called a part of the great American desert, and experienced men declared it would never make farm land. By the time our western lands without irrigation attain productive capacity other than livestock, the American people will need all the foodstuff these lands can be made to produce. What higher or greater purpose can be sought or desired for these lands? It will make citizens, create and maintain homes, bring private ownership, taxable values, and bring enrichment and strength to State and Nation. Is this not their logical and rightful destiny? It was the original purpose. This policy, which has been the true theory and practice under homestead laws for 65 years, should be maintained.

Direct Sales.

2. If homesteading is to cease, except on reclamation projects, then let the Congress provide for the outright sale of surface rights of the remaining domain at a price of from 50 cents to $1 per acre, as was the policy of this country from the beginning

until the homestead laws were passed. This should be done with a limitation of the area which could be acquired by any person, company, or association, thus giving the largest number possible the opportunity of becoming land owners and home builders. Congress should fix this at 2560 acres maximum. All sales should be under restrictive and equitable rules and regulations. The receipts of the Government from this source would provide a reclamation fund sufficient to build all possible reclamation projects and all reclaimable areas would be excepted from the sales act.

Cede to the States.

3. In lieu of all these methods, all remaining public lands with all their resources should be ceded to the States wherein they are situated.

It is fully realized that there are some difficulties and some disadvantages in a transfer to and administration by the several public-land States of the lands within their borders, but there are no insuperable obstacles, and none really serious.

As to the equity of such a transfer to the States, it becomes apparent when we consider that only a small fraction of western land is susceptible of irrigation and agriculture. In the State of Wyoming, again for example, there are but 2,500,000 acres of irrigated farms, including both private and Federal irrigated areas. Twice this amount, or 5,000,000 acres is the utmost limit for which water can be found and applied. This is 8 per cent of the state's area. Dry-farm areas are likewise limited. Yet Wyoming must maintain government over 62,000,000 acres. The value of Federal property in that State not taxable is greater than the value of all the private taxable property.

As to minerals, 26 States of this Union, or their citizens, received all their minerals—the original 13, their 4 offspring, and Missouri, with her lead and zinc; Wisconsin, Michigan, with her immense copper deposits; Minnesota, with her inexhaustible iron; Alabama with her coal and iron; Florida, Kansas, Texas, and Oklahoma, with their incalculable oil resources.

The interior Department reports that, on the whole, it is administering the public lands at a loss. Why continue so to do?' Secretary Work, speaking of the total receipts and expenditures in 1926, states: "The net deficit or loss to the Federal Government in administering the public lands, was therefore, $1,305,657." The deficit for 1929-1930 was $1,300,000 according to the annual report.

The Secretary, in a report on a bill, estimates that the total royalty and sale value of public lands and resources is $13,697,500,000 and $1,550,000 annual return from water power. This sounds immense, but what becomes of it on analysis? First deduct the value estimated for the national forests, $1,000,000,000; next deduct for the present the estimated value of Alaska, $1,002,500,000. These are not in the unreserved and unappropriated public lands within the States, now proposed to be ceded to the States. It will take 10 years and several hundred millions of capital and labor to bring even a small part of this royalty. At the present admitted rate of Government administration expense the figures in that time will show over $13,000,000 more paid out than received. The States, under local administration, can do infinitely better for themselves and for the Nation.

In view of this history, of these facts and figures, equity to the public land States demands that directly or indirectly all the proceeds from their land and resources be repaid to the States of origin, except the cost of administration.

One of the following courses then should be taken as to the remaining public lands, which are the poorest, as they are the last, and a small area compared to what has been disposed of:

1. Enlarge the area to be taken under the stock-raising homestead law to four sections; or

2. Sell and dispose of these lands by direct sale at a nominal cost of 50 cents to $1 per acre, or

3. Cede these remaining lands back to the States in which they are situated, with full right to all their resources, and let the States dispose of them.

It is the spirit and the purpose of the present mining law to give patent to individuals, companies, or corporations having valid discoveries and claims; and under the leasing act the royalties go to the States, either by direct payment or to the reclamation fund. The 10 per cent retained by the Government is used in the administration of these lands so that under its own figures the Government is not only losing nothing by ceding these resources to the States, but will save over a million dollars annually, and will be relieved of complicated, vexatious, and burdensome administration.

The Government, after 140 years, should now close out the land business, as to the remaining unreserved and unappropriated and non-irrigable public domain, in the quickest manner for the benefit of the people of the States in which the lands are located.

The President and many public men, regardless of party, have repeatedly warned against too much centralization and in favor of leaving those things to the

States which the States can perform. It is conceded that the tendency at this time should be away from bureaucracy and arbitrary authority and toward the States and local self-government in order to preserve the true equilibrium which is the peculiar genius of our system of government. Principles of nationality, the principles laid down by Washington, Hamilton, Adams, Marshall, Webster, Clay and Lincoln call just as much for the preservation of the rights of the States as of the Federal Government, in accordance with the Constitution.

The time has come for the withdrawal of the Government from the land business within the States. A century and a half is long enough for the controlling hand of Federal power. It is time now that the sovereignty of the States over their lands, so long delayed, shall be, in some manner, made absolute, full, and complete, to the end that the American system of equal benefit and identical status and power among the States shall at last prevail and a "more perfect Union" be secured.

Aside from questions of legality and equities the people of the West propound the inquiry as to why any State or group of States, original thirteen or otherwise, should now in this day and age have an interest in land or the proceeds from lands or a voice in the control or disposition of lands within another State or group of States? The original price paid for the Territories was nominal. The National Treasury has been repaid more than tenfold. The genius of our institutions and the American system and spirit call for the fulfillment of the plan of the Union. Let every State be in fact as in theory, free, independent and sovereign. Let it be equal in standing and dignity. Let us have not only a sovereign Nation but a "sovereign Nation made up of sovereign States."

Our Supreme Court, in a famous antitrust case, announced a "rule of reason." A course of conduct within reason is not a violation of the law, and a legal right can be used so unreasonably as to become illegal because it is an invasion of rights of another. The permanent reservation of one-half or one-fourth of a State of this Union by the Federal Government is an absolutely unreasonable exercise of national power against such State under the right to control the disposition of the public lands. Such an exercise of right constitutes invasion of the just rights of the States, depriving them of their soil, of the power to tax, of the right to develop, and is a denial of that equality and sovereignty retained by the States under the Constitution.

That is what the Federal Government has done to the Western States as to one-fourth of their area and what is now proposed to be done as to more than one-half their areas. The doling out of a part or even all of the income of the Government from these areas and their resources back to the States does not right the wrong or make that constitutional which is unconstitutional.

Either they are States of this Union and entitled to all the rights of a State, or they are mere dependencies. They are not dependencies. If they are, there is no Union of sovereign States. Why should the other States of this Union or any group of them controlling a majority of the Congress, through their representatives desire and seek to impress or maintain such a status upon 11 sister States of this Union? How can the States of the East, in the full enjoyment of their soil and sovereignty, deny to the public land States of the West what they have demanded and received for themselves as their constitutional right?

Notwithstanding the payment back to the States from which the proceeds of lands and resources are derived of a portion of such proceeds, amounting to 25 per cent of receipts from the forest reserves, with an added 10 per cent devoted to roads, and 37½ per cent of the royalties coming to the Government under the mineral leasing act, there is universal dissatisfaction in the Western States because of the inadequacy of this return from their resources and because of the American spirit of independence which demands, regardless of material return, full recognition of these States with complete independence and sovereignty on an equality with the original States, as provided in the international treaties, the ordinances of 1787 reenacted by Congress after the adoption of the Constitution, 1789, and the Constitution.

CHAPTER XIV.

General Observations.

The public-land States must take their stand upon this underlying fundamental principle—that it is the purpose of the treaties, the Constitution, it has been and should continue to be the policy of this Government to transfer as rapidly as possible to the people, in limited acreage for business, living, home, settlement, development, State taxation and sovereignty purposes, every acre of public domain that is now left.

The trust in the Government was not created to go on forever. It is time it was finally executed and terminated. In no other way than in transferring to the people of each State or to the States the lands left in such States can the Federal trust be executed. Any other course is a breach of that national trust, a violation of a sacred obligation to the States—the States wherein the lands lie, for they and their people are the true and lawful beneficiaries of that trust and not those who have already had their inheritance either by retaining it originally or by having the later imposed trust fully executed and receiving the complete rights to which they are entitled. The West is now entitled to its lands.

As to the fourth of the area of the Western States which is now reserved in parks, forests, Indian reservations, power sites, monuments, mineral withdrawals, and oil reserves, these reservations are utterly unreasonable areas to be withheld forever from the States. With the exception of the national parks, which the West is willing to concede as a possible legitimate exercise of the power of reservation as long

as the areas are reasonable or as a distinctly national
resource which they agree shall be enjoyed by all
the people under Federal management, ultimately all
the reservations should be turned over to the States.
If they are not so returned, then all of the people for
whom they are taken should pay to the part of the
people from whom they are taken their reasonable
value. The General Government should make recompense by payment of their value or pay annually an
amount equivalent to what would be collected in taxation from them on a valuation based upon their developed resources. Each Western State is entitled to
its own,—no more no less—just as the States or the
people of the States east of the Rockies have received
their own.

One of these two courses, either cession to the States
or compensation for these great reservations, must be
adopted if justice is to be done. The Western States
take their stand on that declaration without doubt,
hesitation, equivocation, or "shadow of turning." That
position is founded on the rock of right—and it can
never be overthrown. It is just, logical, imperative,
and inevitable. Right must prevail.

The Supreme Court has held in a strict legal sense
that these States have been admitted on an equal basis
and are fully sovereign when they are granted, as they
have been, full political equality and representation
in the Congress and the Government; and that the
phrase "admitted on equal terms with the original
thirteen States" means political equality and does not
apply to the soil and land; but from the standpoint
of equity it is obvious that States which do not have
ownership control and the power of taxation over more
than one-half of their areas and the resources con-

tained therein, are not on an equal footing with other States which have come into such full jurisdiction and dominion.

The power lies in Congress and in Congress only. There is no possibility of recourse to the Courts. The theory strongly debated and presented in the Senate of the United States from 1826 to 1836, and never successfully answered, that, under the international treaties, the Ordinance of 1787, the cessions by the original States, and the Constitution, every State upon admission came into full ownership, possession, dominion, and jurisdiction, for all purposes, can not be advanced in the Courts for want of jurisdiction because the provisions of an international treaty are concerned. Therefore, the only way in which justice and equity can be done is for Congress to change its laws and policies and now finally terminate the trusteeship which it has now been administering for more than a century, and make these States, at least to the extent of the remainder of the public domain, in truth and in fact sovereign and equal to the other States of the Union.

The Western States are not looking for a great gift. The cession of these lands and their minerals would not mean sudden available wealth. They want and would have, if lands and resources were ceded to them, the opportunity to work out, by the capital and brain and skill and brawn of the investor, the capitalist, the employer, the farmer and laborer, their industrial and agricultural development.

The claims and basic equities of the States have been recognized partially in numerous acts of Congress: In the reclamation act, the federal water power act, in the forest reserve act, in the mineral leasing act. This is but a part. They are entitled to the whole.

They have been forced by virtue of this anomalous condition of vast areas owned and controlled by the Federal Government within their borders to go to Congress with many requests for aid. They have been humiliated by this necessity and often unjustly denied. Give them their lands and resources, as the other States have had theirs, and they will cease to importune Congress for financial and other aid to develop The relation, as it were, of guardian and ward and the consequent doling out of appropriations for various purposes for which they must beg is not compatible with the dignity of the rights of sovereign States in this Union. They are not, and ought not to be, in a class of provinces or dependencies. They ought not to be compelled to remain in the attitude of suppliants asking for annual support or gratuities, allowances doles, or gifts. They claim the status of sovereign States and the right to develop. Return their lands and resources and they would disdain to seek from the hands of Congress one dollar of Federal aid for any purpose which does not apply equally to all the States. They will be gratified and delighted when that day comes, as it must come, when, standing on an equality with all the rest of the States of the Union, they shall take part in and ask only to be participants and beneficiaries of those things which come to all of the States of the Union by reason of the general national policy of internal improvements.

Higher and greater and vastly more important than lands and resources, income, taxation, development, and material prosperity is the principle that under the Constitution they have the right to stand, and must become and remain equal and sovereign in a nation of sovereign States.

The Government should plan to cease functioning in a matter which can now be managed by the several States.

The fundamental principle which should govern the whole question of the unreserved public domain remaining is the transfer to private ownership in limited areas. That is the primary proposition. How this is accomplished, while very important, is secondary. It can be done; first, through direct sales in restricted amounts as to the surface by the Government to the people for a nominal price of 50 cents to $1 per acre according to classification, with several years in which to pay; the proceeds to be returned to the States of origin in cash or through reclamation projects. Secondly, through the enlargement of the area of stock-raising homesteads to 1280 or 2560 acres, with less cash requirements for improvements and less burdensome rules as to residence and cultivation; permitting those who have homesteaded to take additional areas to make up the total enlarged area.

In either of these two ways the ultimate best use of the land will be effected to the greatest good to the greatest number. Once privately owned, these lands will inevitably find their greatest use and best economic level. In case either of these methods is used it would be for surface rights only. The mineral rights now included in the mineral leasing law, and all minerals should be made over to the States to handle as their legislatures may determine.

Third, most simple and comprehensive, the lands with all their resources should be ceded to the States, so that the States could make the disposition to private owners as to the surface and evolve such plan of handling the mineral resources as they see fit, looking to the best interests of agriculture, of livestock, and the mining interests, and of the State as a whole for all its people, in accordance with the conditions in each State.

Eastern representatives and people frequently complain of and oppose Federal aid in reclamation, roads, colleges, schools, land grants for certain objects, and other purposes, forgetting the fact that the Federal Government holds these great public reservations and vast areas of public domain, which are non-taxable. Why should not the Government give even greater aid then it has when it holds the greater part of these States without taxation and prevents settlement?

Turn the balance of the public domain with all its resources over to the States and they will cease calling upon the Government for special benefits on account of this unusual condition. They will gladly attend to their own needs and welcome release from the necessity of making these requests. They will then ask for no more than the rest of the States of the Union, with whom they have the right to proportional benefits of any general plan of internal improvements under the national policies.

Thus, by one of these three methods, will the States come into that full sovereignty and equality with the other States to which they are entitled as a matter of equity and right, equality and dignity, as sister States of the American Union and receive the material return, not in part as a dole from Washington, but in full, in their own right, from the resources with which they have been endowed. That endowment no man, no party, no administration, no group of States however powerful and numerically strong in Congress, no just nation and trustee should withhold.

Government titles of a century should not be overthrown. The Western States have been compelled to acquiesce in the railroad grants, the national parks, the forest and Indian reservations. In an indirect way these States have been and are benefited. The Government, as trustee, may impose the actual cost of administering the trust upon these great areas and national resources of these States. But that is enough— beyond that these States should not have one dollar exacted from them; and if it is exacted, then in all justice and equity every such dollar so exacted should be returned to those States of origin or devoted to reclamation funds, road funds, educational funds, agricultural funds, as equitably theirs, and in addition share with the other States in a fair proportion of national moneys for internal improvements. Thus and thus only can equity be done, in view of and in lieu of the deprivations of those States of the full, complete and absolute ownership and control of all lands and resources within their borders, as was contemplated, and of that equal sovereignty expressly stipulated in the deeds of cession.

The eastern States had the benefit of the profits in private ownership and taxation of all their forest lands acquired at a nominal price or as an incident of homesteading. When forests became valuable in the West they were withdrawn entirely and the eastern States share in the proceeds of the sale of the annual crop of timber; but 25 per cent is returned to the States of origin. When forest reserves were created in the East, the western States in taxes contributed to the money necessary to buy the great bulk of these reserves from private owners.

We here recapitulate some of the discriminations and equalities as we see them in the national legislation and policies as between three great groups or divisions of States. Generally speaking, all States east of the Missouri obtained the full title to all coal contained in their homestead entries, or by coal-land purchase from the Government at a nominal cost of from $10 to $20 per acre. When the time came when it was possible to develop the great areas of the present public land States, all coal areas were withdrawn and then restored under a price classification which ran from $50 to $500 per acre.

All the other States and their citizens either through homesteading or for a nominal cash price secured title to their lands including all minerals. The present public-land States and citizens settling them, under conditions of greater hardship and poorer land, paying the same amount or more, secure only the surface, all minerals being reserved.

The States east of the Rockies never paid any fees, charges or royalties. The Rocky Mountain States are required to pay grazing fees and royalties which are a burden on the livestock and mining industries, even though the proceeds are in part, since 1920, returned to them in cash or by way of the reclamation fund.

The eastern States never have had land withdrawn or reserved for resources, for parks, and forests, and other purposes. The Western States have 235,000,000 acres forever reserved from settlement and State sovereignty.

The determination of the control of all these lands having been against the claim of the States, and in

MOUNTAIN (MILLS) LAKE—COLORADO
Courtesy Colorado Association. Photo by Eddy

favor of the General Government, the matter of express provisions of the international treaties of acquisition being ignored by reason of non-jurisdiction in our Supreme Court over matters of treaties between sovereign nations, there remains, however, equity; and the undeniable fact of the trusteeship of the Federal Government. As trustee it is inconceivable that the Government should administer its trust for profit, but only in the interest of the beneficiaries. Equity demands that the beneficiaries shall be the people who settle the lands and the States wherein such settlement is made.

The Nation decided on retaining control and administering the trust. After the payment of the debt of the Revolutionary War the rightful beneficiary of that trust was the people settling the areas and the States they brought into, and which were incorporated into, the Union. In the last 25 years only has the equity been recognized substantially in the application of the funds from the proceeds of sales of the public lands in those States back to those States by a reclamation fund under the reclamation law, and in the last ten years further in the return of royalties collected under the national leasing act of February 25, 1920, partly in cash and partly through the reclamation fund. It is not equity to return only 25 per cent of the grazing fees collected from their livestock industry. It is not equity to begrudge and refuse or complain of appropriations for highways in these Western States. First, they are entitled to them as States as a part of a great national improvement. Second, as long as the Government claims to own and control, for example, 16,000,000 acres of public land in the State of Wyoming, numbering two and one-fourth persons to the square mile, it is impossible that it should build highways over that enormous area, to be used principally by non-resident travelers going through the State.

These States have a right to settlement and development and the creation of taxable property values; and the lands should be settled, "disposed of," in the language of the Constitution, into private ownership. In other words, full equality, not only politically in representation and voice in the Union, but physically and materially in land and soil which in fact if not in law is inseparable from full sovereignty.

Are they to be States or Provinces? They hold these truths to be self-evident—that all States are created equal; that they are endowed by the organic law with certain inalienable rights; that among these are, "life," which implies and requires equal sovereignty over their soil and all the riches therein, as the means of existence; "liberty," which means freedom from discrimination and ultra-Federal control not imposed on most of the States, and freedom in local self-government to the same extent granted to any of the States; and the "pursuit of happiness," which means development under the same conditions for the new and later States as were enjoyed by the original and other States, with equal rights and advantages for their citizens in their lands and resources, which are essential to the well-being of their people.

A State can not develop as it should unless its soil and resources come eventually, if not upon admission, into private ownership or State ownership, and thus to private control and development. The international treaties under which these purchased areas were acquired contained the same express provisions regarding the building of new sovereign States upon an equality with the original States and like "rights, advantages and immunities" of their citizens, as were provided in the Ordinance of 1787 and the cessions from the States of the area east of the Mississippi. Again, the original States retained great areas of public land within and without their final boundaries which they sold and applied the proceeds to State development.

The theory laid down all through our history was that eventually all these lands would be disposed of so as to come into private ownership and thus finally the sovereignty of the State would at last be full and complete and equal to that of the original States. What of 35,000,000 acres of Indian reservations? What about 150,000,000 acres permanently held as forest reserves? They can never come under State sovereignty and private ownership, development and taxation. Are they legally the property of the United States? They are claimed to be, under our national laws, but as trustee for the benefit of those who were to settle these areas. Can it withhold any part of the trust and alienate great areas in view of the express provision of the treaties and cessions? And can it do it constitutionally in view of the fact that the Constitution makes treaties equally the Supreme law of the land?

It is realized that if these lands and the resources are ever ceded to the Western States it must be done by the votes in the Congress of the United States, coming from the States east of the Rocky Mountains. The arid States of the mountainous West have less than 35 Representatives in the House out of a total of 435. They can not demand and force their claims. They feel that if this great object is ever attained it will be by virtue of knowledge, information, education, argument and persuasion. They know of no stronger force or method than an appeal to intelligence, fairness, justice, and equity. They are certain that when eastern representatives have the time and the opportunity to give to this question their full and fair consideration they will come to the conclusion the Western States are right in their position. No group of States in this Union, however large and powerful, will, when once convinced of the justice of these claims, refuse them.

President Coolidge, in his notable address at Williamsburg, Va., May 15, 1925, on the rights of the States, said:

* * * No method of procedure has ever been devised by which liberty could be divorced from local self-government. No plan of centralization has ever been adopted which did not result in bureaucracy, tyranny, inflexibility, reaction, and decline. Of all forms of government those administered by bureaus are about the least satisfactory to any enlightened and progressive people. Being irresponsible, they become autocratic, and being autocratic they resist all development. Unless bureaucracy is constantly resisted it breaks down representative government and overwhelms democracy. It is the one element in our institutions that sets up the pretense of having authority over everybody and being responsible to nobody.

* * * While we ought to glory in the Union and remember that it is the source from which the States derive their chief title to fame, we must also recognize that the national administration is not and can not be adjusted to the needs of local government. It is too far away to be informed of local needs, too inaccessible to be responsive to local conditions. The States should not be induced by coercion or by favor to surrender the management of their own affairs. The Federal Government ought to resist the tendency to be loaded up with duties which the States should perform. It does not follow that because something ought to be done the National Government ought to do it. * * *

These principles of independence, of the integrity of the Union, and of local self-government have not diminished in their importance since they were so clearly recognized and faithfully declared in the Virginia convention of 150 years ago. * * *

Let us complete the American system of local government over local things, stop centralization in Washington, eliminate bureau government, relieve the people generally of costly national machinery, perfect the sovereignty of the public-land States, so that indeed and in truth the Western States will be on equal terms with the original and all the other States. They ask no more than the Eastern States have had. They ask the status of States of a Union. They ask equality and full sovereignty. They plead that the plan of the American Union be completed; that the process of building "independent, sovereign, republican States" be perfected; that thereby their citizens have "equal rights, immunities, and advantages with the citizens of the other States," and a "more perfect Union" be secured.

CHAPTER XV.

Outline of the New Public Land Policy
by
Secretary of the Interior Ray Lyman Wilbur.

On the 15th day of July, 1929, at Boise, Idaho, in an address to western representatives and officials of several states, Ray Lyman Wilbur, Secretary of the Interior, suggested a new public land policy which would transfer to the states the control of the surface rights of the unreserved and unappropriated public lands, which means all public domain not included in National Parks, National Monuments, Naval Reserves, Indian Reservations and Forest Reserves. The full text of his address is here given:

We now have scattered settlements all over the western part of the United States based on better farming, better selected seeds, and irrigation. Those who depend upon the regular rains of the summer have no conception of irrigation and its peculiar responsibilities.

Great civilizations have matured and some of them have died in the arid regions of the old world and some are now on the way in the new. It demands communal living and thinking and peaceful conditions, for people to join in together to finance and maintain large water distributing systems.

States Better Equipped.

Even the control of the flow of water from a single ditch demands rigid cooperation and fair play. It is to this that I ascribe the responsiveness of the people of such states as are here represented to forward-looking, progressive measures for the common good, if they are properly tempered to the high initiative and sense of personal responsibility characteristic of our citizens.

It is important for us to face the present situation squarely. The safety and survival of the human race depends upon its control of chlorophyl—the green coloring matter of plants. This substance, in the presence of water and sunlight and with the materials derived from the soil, manufactures starch and other food substances for the growth of plants. From these plants we derive foods, cotton, wool, wood and rubber and by feeding animals with them we get more food, hides, and a large amount of animal service. In fact, without the milk manufactured from plants by cows and goats, we would be unable to raise our own human babies.

With our new methods of transportation the food supply of the world is coming more and more to be held in common to be drawn on by all, and the tropical sunshine beating down on a cocoanut palm 365 days in the year is competing with a reindeer feeding on the mosses of the subarctic summer in the making of fat. We now have more than sufficient food available for all.

And, while it is probable that we will breed up to the bread line, countries like our own think of the bread line in other terms than those of merely filling the stomach. They demand an economic status that would have been luxury to a king of a hundred years ago.

There is, though, a set physiological limit to the amount of food an individual consumes. We have produced too much of some kinds, and with the industrialization and urbanization of a growing percentage of our people, there has also been a shift in the type of foods eaten.

Arid Areas Increased.

This, together with the greater productiveness of favored areas with the help of better seed, better methods and more machinery, has increased the amount of so-called marginal lands where the farmer's life is a struggle against heavy odds. I know of no more painful act than to place a man, and particularly his wife, on a piece of land where they are foreordained to a prolonged agonizing failure. The economics of a new farm project must be essentially sound or a social crime is in prospect.

These facts must be held before us in considering that great part of the western United States which is still in the possession of the federal government. There has been a good deal of talk of conservation. The real conservation problem of the West is the conservation of water.

Plant life demands water. We must have plants suitable for our own uses or we can have no civilization.

From Nebraska west water, and water alone, is the key to our future. We need the mountains and the hills and a great protected back country or we cannot have sufficient water for our valleys. We must replace homestead thinking with watershed thinking, since watersheds are primary to Western homes.

We can no longer afford to think only in terms of immediate uses and selfish interests. There must be a great Western strategy for the protection of our watersheds and the plant life on them, however undesirable and unimportant some of it may seem to be.

A cactus or a sagebrush which has fought its way to maturity against drought, plays its part in furthering rainfall and in stopping soil erosion, that curse of all cultivated countries. Overgrazing by sharp-nosed animals cuts down the plant life, increases erosion, buries water holes, increases flood damage and is harmful to water conservation. Plants hold the snow and the rain, prevent rapid run-off and soil erosion and build a balanced set of natural conditions which can only be broken at the peril of those bringing it about.

Conservation Necessary.

The public-domain has been abused, overgrazed and not respected in many sections of the country, and yet, unless we cherish and care for the lands now in possession of the United States, in forests and public domain, we in the West will repeat the fall of ancient Ninevah and Tyre, which was due to the abuse of plant life and water failure, or the degradation of Korea, and parts of China with man-made barrenness, floods, erosion and decay.

We must stop thinking in terms of immediate production in viewing much of the public land of today. The forests must be protected or harvested constructively, overgrazing must be stopped and experts in plant life and water conservation must be our guides. It is difficult to understand and properly control such problems from Washington.

It seems to me that it is time for a new public land policy which will include transferring to those states willing to accept the responsibility the control of the surface rights of all public lands not included in national parks or monuments or in the national forests. With sound state policies based on factual thinking it may eventually develop that it is wiser for the states to control even the present national forests.

Such a policy will need to be worked out so as to hold the oil, coal and mineral rights of public lands subject to some form of proper federal prospecting law with development on a royalty basis of discoveries, and with due consideration to conservation for the future. The policy of transferring federal lands for school purposes is well established and could be further initiated wherever state laws and state policy warrant the transfer.

The States of the West are water conscious and they can more readily build up those wise water conservation measures upon which their very life depends than can the distant Washington Government. It would be fair too for the citizens of Western States to have the privileges already in the possession of those of the East.

Responsibility makes for real statehood just as it makes for manhood. The Western States are man grown and capable of showing it.

The National Government can still be helpful in building dams, in protecting navigable streams and in assisting with State compacts, but it should withdraw from the details of management of community enterprises properly subject to State laws.

You men representative of the Western States could well prepare your State government by proper park, grazing, lumbering and water conservation laws for the reception of the public domain. I feel that in the long run you can be more safely trusted to administer that heritage wisely than it can be done from offices in the National capital.

It will require trained vision and forward thinking if the semi-arid West is to conserve its own future.

CHAPTER XVI.

Discussion of the Proposals.

An important element in the great general plan of development of the West, intimately connected with the problem of flood control and navigation is that of that form of conservation which saves the moisture-absorbing capacity of the tremendous areas comprising the watersheds of the West. It is of course not to be controverted that over-stocking of these watersheds to the extent of denuding and hardening them causes a running and rushing off of the waters and an erosion of the fertile grass-producing top soil, which is then carried in the flood waters to fill the lowlands and river channels. It also fills the reservoirs with silt where there are dams, overflows all restraints and levees, ruins crops and property and destroys life, both animal and human. After the "run-off" comes lack of water for needed uses and reduction of navigation because of shallow channels during the dry season.

There is a decided difference of opinion as to what extent this process has been going on and what the situation is today in this regard in the eleven western States. Conditions vary in the several States. However this issue need not be fought out inasmuch as the Administration as well as the West are agreed, first, that an evil of that kind should not be permitted and should be prevented by regulation legislation of some kind, and, second, that the people of these western States through their State governments are more competent to secure and maintain such conservation than is the Federal government. Therefore cession to and control by the States will aid the great object of conservation and the general welfare. If the conditions are as bad as claimed by Federal experts under the free range then the problem is clearly best solved by State ownership and control. Self interest will move these States to wise and efficient remedies.

Passing by then the question of whether or not the public domain has been and is now being abused, over-grazed and in consequence eroded in many sections of the country (and if they have been the States had no control or responsibility in that regard, because they had no power in the premises), all can agree that whether under Federal or State control, those things should not be permitted. The State can readily agree not to permit, and if necessary, pass laws to prevent any such harmful practices. They have every interest and motive not to do otherwise. Therefore, they meet the condition imposed by the Secretary.

As to the regulations of grazing on the forest reserves which are now administered by the Department of Agriculture through the Forest Service, they will continue as long as the forests are under federal control. If in some future day, eventually, as the Secretary suggests, it may develop that it is wiser for the states to control even the present national forests there is no reason to suppose that the State will overcrowd the forest grazing. With respect to the cutting of timber on the forest reserves, it is the same as with grazing: The States should and could and would regulate that to an annual crop, the cutting of which is not only not harmful, but beneficial to the forests.

In the case of the mineral in the forests, if ceded to the States, there would be no occasion to reserve the minerals. The mineral wealth should be included. The minerals in the leasing bill, fuel and fertilizer, and many others do not occur in the forests, for the simple reason that the forests are on the mountains and geologically these minerals cannot be there. As to the hard metalliferous minerals and the precious minerals, which, with the exception possibly of iron, do occur in the forests and the mountains, because nature formed them there, they are not under a lease and royalty system. They are taken under the general mining law, under which they do not pay Federal or State royalties. So that there is no reason to hesitate, when ceding the forests to the States, to include the mineral. It does not involve any minerals to which to apply conservation, except in the most general sense of the word against waste. In its own interest, keeping in mind the welfare of the mining industry, the State could impose a small royalty and lease system on specific minerals but it would not, probably, as to all other metalliferous minerals. But that is for the State to decide in the future and the Federal Government is not interested in these minerals now subject to location under the general mining laws, and should make no conditions relative thereto in a grant.

Coming now to the minerals lying in the unreserved public domain now proposed to be ceded to the States, they exist if at all in unknown deposits, whose values are uncertain. If minerals were included as well as the surface, our Eastern brethren might hold the idea that billions of wealth were all at once to be given the States. They forget, and we must not forget, that it will require millions of dollars of private capital to begin to realize on such values, if any, in the way of annual dividends and royalties; it will require decades of time. It simply permits the West a gradual development under its own laws.

From the Federal financial viewpoint, the Government is getting but 10 per cent of all the royalties and receipts from public lands as administration expense, and each year there is a deficit in administering the lands; in one fiscal year, 1929, according to a 1930 official statement of the Secretary of the Interior, there was a deficit of $1,300,000. That was assuming that the millions which went into the reclamation fund and were expended in the West, were not to be returned to the Government; the fact is they must be repaid.

According to that official statement the government will be better off financially, by $1,300,000 annually by ceding the reserved and unreserved areas to the States with all resources included.

The present interest of the Government in the permits and leases under the leasing bill could be made over to the States and the lessees proceed without interruption. There would simply be a change in the lessor. As to conservation of oil, gas, etc., in private ownership, it has been recently recalled that all such measures are in the jurisdiction of the State, not of the Federal Government. The State has power, the Federal Government does not have.

The Secretary has well mentioned the granting of the school sections to the States, as an example of beneficial legislation and in public interest, and states that that policy "could be further initiated wherever State laws and State policy warrant the transfer;" that is, where the States will pass laws so as to retain mineral rights as to certain minerals, such as fuel, and not alienate them, and pay due regard to the principles of conservation. That would warrant the transfer.

In this connection it is very pertinent to note that four years ago legislation in Congress was passed confirming title in the States to the school sections—**including the minerals.**

On the same basis and for the same reasons the mineral should be included in the cession of the remaining unreserved lands. There is the same justification, fundamentally; also let us not forget that the rest of the States, or their citizens, got their minerals with their lands, and some States, in the enabling act creating them, were given their minerals outright, as States.

So there is only one point of difference after all between the Secretary and the Western States, and that is as to the inclusion of the minerals in the cession to the States, of the unreserved domain; his reference to the school sections is distinctly encouraging as to that. True, as to the forests, he uses the word "eventually" —but on analysis there is no real reason why the forest areas should not be included now.

The States cannot pass laws as to their administration until they have them, and so with reference to the administration of minerals on the unreserved lands they cannot pass a permit and leasing system until they have them. They have such system as to lands under prior grants. The main safeguard against alienation by the States of the fuel and fertilizer minerals could be incorporated in the grant from the Federal Government, but it is unnecessary. So there is no reason for postponement. They are ready to receive all the lands and forests and minerals in both.

The present laws of the western States cover the basic matter of mineral reservation in case of lands now belonging to the State. A State Homestead Law cannot well be passed until cession of the lands has been made. The present State lands scarcely justify a State homestead law. Again, it cannot be done while we still have a Federal homestead law.

In the matter of sale or lease of surface rights to the land if ceded to the States, due regard should be shown by the Legislatures of the States to the livestock industry, which is now using the free ranges, so far as the Constitution of the States will allow.

As to the matters of water and reclamation—the Secretary's statement is most reassuring in that he states "The States can more readily build up those wise water conservation measures upon which their very life depends than can the distant Washington Government." He truly suggests that the Government would better contribute to reclamation dams, letting the States build and manage the distribution systems, and confine itself to its right of navigation, regulation, and help, and its advice and the consent of Congress in bringing about State compacts of equitable distribution and control of water.

The West could not ask for a broader recognition of the rights of the arid states as to their streams and waters and thus settle forever the dangerous claim of certain federalists that the United States, and not the States, own the non-navigable streams and waters. The ceding of the lands contiguous to the waters, in fact and law, includes the basis of the federal claim to the waters, and would put the States in the position to benefit by the United States claim, if it has merit, and close the controversy.

The western States should feel that they are in the hands and the House of Friends when the Secretary says: "I feel that in the long run you (meaning the Western States) can be more safely trusted to administer that heritage (meaning our lands and re-

COLUMBIA RIVER, CRATER LAKE—OREGON
Courtesy Chamber of Commerce, Portland.   Photo by Cross & Dimmitt

sources and waters) wisely than it can be done from offices in the National Capital."

This statement of the Secretary, taken all in all, although not yet conceding the specific matter of our minerals to the full extent we would like, is a declaration of equity and equality for the States which is a tremendous gain and is bound to eventuate in full recognition, jurisdiction and sovereignty as becomes equal States of the Union. As to the justice, the equity, the equality of complete ownership in the States they are fully recognized by the Secretary in these words: "It would be fair too, for the citizens of the Western States to have the privileges already a possession of those of the East."

The East must be convinced—it cannot be forced. It has overwhelming representation in Congress, in the House, 402 out of 435 members. When convinced with a sympathetic administration it will grant the things the western States are asking.

The New York Times met the proposal of Secretary Wilbur to cede the surface rights of the remaining unreserved and unappropriated public lands with an editorial of opposition, setting forth the following propositions:

Serious Blunder.

Complete reversal of a century old policy.

Western States have for years resented federal supervision of the public domain.

They have not only attempted to gain control, but have opposed the creation of national forests.

(On the grounds that this runs counter to the original intention of Congress that the Federal Government should ultimately "dispose of" the public domain.)

Secretary's theory is O. K. Much to be said for the Secretary's reasoning that States more immediately concerned than Washington Government.

But—when he specified—over-grazing, destruction of trees

and plant life, control of floods, can be better handled by the States.

He ventures into realm **theory**, and **practical politics** are in conflict.

History of the West replete with illustrations—persistence of older ·pion_er attitude toward matters of conservation.

They have fought the sensible efforts of the forestry bureau to restrict grazing so as to preserve the ranges.

They have sought to deprive the Indians of their lands.

They have welcomed the exploitations of forests, mines and waters, all without a thought of the distant results.

Categorical denial of these allegations is made. The proof of what western States will do with lands and resources is what they have done with school sections granted. What eastern States did with their forest lands and swamp lands has no bearing on the case, except to note here the fact that in 1850 the Government ceded to the then States and Territories 64,433,-870 acres of swamp land. None of the present public lands States except California and Oregon shared in that cession. What the eastern States did with these resources simply proves their early delinquency. Further, this is a different day and age. The value of forests and vegetation and water, and the need for their proper use and preservation has gradually become known and realized by all the public simultaneously in the last 30 years. But it is not within reason that the East can know and does know, as do the people of the West, the supreme need of these things to the West.

Can an Easterner who knows nothing of irrigation, who has never seen a reclamation project, who has never attempted to subdue a raw piece of land and make a cultivated, crop-producing farm out of dry grass and sagebrush areas know as much as the Westerner about the need of water on that land? Or know as much about the source of that water being in the great packed falls and drifts of snow of the mountains, and the absolute necessity of timber on those mountains to retain the snow banks and the moisture to deliver it gradually through the spring and summer months, as the Westerner who has applied that water to the land for a livelihood?

Flood control? Who, as much as the Westerner, appreciates the two-fold nature, the double purpose of, first, building Dams and Reservoirs to catch the flood waters so as to prevent the floods and regulate the flow of the streams, and second, applying those flood storage and regulated waters to cover more dry lands for beneficial production, which thus themselves become underground, flow-regulating reservoirs?

Why would a State, if it owned and controlled the forest lands as well as the remaining unreserved areas, permit excessive cutting or denudation? It would not. From a purely economic basis, the people of the Western States know that nothing carries the burden of taxes more than a developed, irrigated agriculture, which once attained, lasts forever. Are they going to destroy their own resources, wealth and prosperity? On the contrary, no one in Washington or the East can possibly have the direct interest and care that the people of these States have where these things are. The people of the East cut down their forests. They are said to have mishandled their swamp lands. The West knows better than to do as they did.

But there are other resources in the forest areas and on the remaining unreserved public domain. The forest areas are on the mountains, and the minerals, except coal, oil, oil shale, gas, phosphate, potash, gypsum, sodium, etc., the hard metals, the precious metals are in the mountains where nature formed them.

The States would adopt a system of mining laws

which would encourage the finding and development of these resources. They would pass Acts to actually "promote" the discovery and opening up of these great resources needed by the whole people.

The general mining law was intended for this purpose—its title read: "To promote—" and it functioned well until two things occurred: First, the creation of forest reserves with their restrictions of the miners and prospectors, and, second, the mineral leasing bill affecting coal, oil, oil shale, gas, sodium and phosphate, and then potash and gilsonite which were added; which not only took these minerals out of the general mining law, making it impossible to locate and acquire these minerals, by discovery, development and patent, but which can be abrogated and suspended indefinitely by the Secretary of the Interior, "in his discretion"; thus making them obtainable by neither location and patent, nor permit and lease.

The fact is that under the federal laws now in force, and in part suspended, prospecting, locating, patenting private ownership, permit and lease, all discovery and all development on all minerals, with very few exceptions, have ceased. They have been throttled. Technically the federal laws still permit both homesteading and mineral locations in the forest reserves but we know that practically there is now no more homesteading or mineral location on these areas. The homesteader, the prospector and miner verify the statement—those who have tried under present federal laws to homestead and locate mineral claims in the forest reserves. It is not being done. There may be rare exceptions. Is not this the explanation of the very serious fact of non-discovery and low production of gold in the United States?

The States would cure that situation to their own and their citizens' advantage and the benefit of all the people of the United States. As to the minerals subject to the leasing act, the State would make them obtainable by permit and lease under a State royalty system which could cut down by 50 per cent the royalties now demanded and taken from the lessees, and still receive into the State Treasury more money than they are now receiving back from the Federal Government. Reclamation should be excluded from consideration in this connection as long as the Reclamation Fund is advanced as a loan and must be repaid.

These western States have an equity right to the ownership and control of all of these areas Secretary Wilbur has partially recognized that right and the wis dom of conceding that right with reference to the surface of lands. It should extend to all the minerals in the land as well as the surface, under proper safeguards in the grant, which the States may be entirely willing shall me made—such as that the State shall never alienate its title to the fuel and fertilizer minerals in the land.

As for over-grazing, destruction of the ranges and erosion, so far as they exist, which is problematical, first, the stockmen are intelligent business men who do not want to and will not annihilate their own business by ruining their range; and secondly, as to the statement that our people should cease being "homestead minded" and become "watershed minded" they are, and will be both. The intimation of the Secretary is that homesteading should cease and the range preserved so as to hold the vegetation and water and reduce erosion. The denial of a homestead law would be a blow. Both objects can be continued and attained.

It has been estimated that a 640-acre tract, grass or sagebrush, fenced, with buildings for stock, cultivated in part, will hold up more water, absorb more moisture, raise more fodder and produce for man and beast ten times over that which it will do as range grazing.

The State can harmonize the interests of range stockmen and the homesteader. Let the settler under a favorable State homestead law, more liberal than the Federal homestead law, thus develop eight million acres for example, of Wyoming's comparatively level grass and sage brush area. It will still leave eight million acres of rough land for the free range stock growers; and in addition the stockmen would have all the mountain forest growing areas, the forest reserves, approximately nine million acres. There is no irreconcilable conflict between homesteader and stockman. If the West had had 10,000 homesteaders raising grain and various kinds of fodder in 1928 in all parts of these States its stockmen would not have had to pay such enormous prices to ship in feed the following winter. Let everything be developed according to its best use.

As to National Parks, contrary to the New York Times' statement, the West has been very liberal in its acquiescence in the creation of Parks. Again, for example, two million acres in Yellowstone Park, with another 100,000 acres in the newly-created Grand Teton National Park comprise a goodly portion of Wyoming. Westerners appreciate and value and use our parks as much and more than do their eastern brethren.

Further, in this day and age neither the western States or their people are seeking to deprive the Indians of their lands and they do not desire their resources "exploited without thought of the future."

As to a "Complete Reversal of a Century Old Policy"—alleged by the Times, in case even the surface of unreserved lands, as suggested by Secretary Wilbur, should be ceded to the States—the writer of the Times editorial should read up on the history of the public lands. He is in error.

The change of a hundred-year policy was made thirty years ago and since, against the West, by immense reservations never dreamed of by the Congress or the Courts when Conservation began in 1898, by eliminating minerals from homestead patents, by increasing restrictions, by amending the general mining law, by leasing acts, by royalties, by grazing fees, administrative cost, increased charges for all entries, cessation of development and stopping the establishment of taxable homes and mines and industries in and by reason of the 149,000,000 acres of forest reserves in the West.

The Constitution says that Congress shall have power to "dispose of" the public lands; (to the people) manifestly to provide homes, to make new industries, to permit new Sovereign States to be formed and permit those States to grow. The makers of the Constitution certainly had in mind nothing about reservations of 25 per cent of a State's area and leases and rents and royalties. Neither had the statesmen of 1832 when the permanent policy of trusteeship and disposition to the people was adopted. Nor had the Congress in 1898-1902, or Roosevelt when he began "Conservation." The Federal Government has ceased "to dispose" as was the policy of this Government for a hundred years. This is not saying that "to reserve" is not "to dispose," legally; the Supreme Court has settled that. The discussion is about equity and what Congress should do.

The States east of the Missouri River have come into sovereignty over all the lands within their borders. These states receive taxes from every part of their lands and resources. That was the "Century Long Policy."

But the Eastern States through their representatives, by force of numbers, decreed "a change of policy" after getting everything within their borders. They have put the Western States under Federal Laws which now hold one-quarter of our area forever Federal and untaxable, and during the last administration threatened to make the balance of their area, 30 per cent more, a total of 55 per cent, forever Federal and impossible of private ownership, development or taxation, by Federal regulation and repeal of the homestead law. The West stands today, 55 per cent Federal controlled—untaxable! And they of the East, those who share the views of the New York Times because of misinformation, wish to keep it in that status permanently. "To dispose of" has come to mean "to appropriate."

It is high time that a conference of the West, was held, a policy determined upon and action urged at the next Session of Congress. At such conference the Secretary's suggestion of surface rights should not be rejected off-hand. It should be given every consideration, looking to further investigations and other proposals which may lead to the ultimate goal.

CHAPTER XVII.

The Letter of President Hoover Before the Conference of Western Governors
Salt Lake City, Utah, August 26, 1929.

At the above Conference, called to consider matters of importance to the Western States, a letter from President Hoover was presented by Assistant Secretary of the Interior Joseph M. Dixon.

This was one of the most important communications ever addressed to a body of Governors in the history of the country. It will go down in history as epoch-making. By a coincidence the day, lacking five, the month and year were just a decade from the time when a general Governors' Conference was held in the same place. Out of that General Conference came a memorial, signed by twenty-two Governors, addressed to the Congress of the United States, respectfully urging that all the unreserved lands of the nation be ceded to the States where located. A copy of said memorial and others of the same character will be found in the closing pages of this volume.

For the first time in our history the Chief Executive of the United States proposed a change of policy with reference to our Lands and resources, a great movement to transfer rights over an enormous area, 235,-000,000 acres, and recognizing the superior capacity of the western States to administer their own resources. Moreover it was a declaration that with greater control in the States the cause of conservation would be advanced and secured. It stirred the country. It was an emancipation proclamation for the West!

The following is the full text of President Hoover's Letter:

My Dear Secretary Dixon:

I have for some years given thought to the necessity and desirability for a further step in development of the relations between the federal and state governments in respect to the public lands and the reclamation service. The meeting of the Governors of the public-land states at Salt Lake City which you are attending offers an opportunity for consideration of some phases of these questions, and I should appreciate it if you would present them to the Governors.

It may be stated at once that our western states have long since passed from their swaddling clothes and are today more competent to manage much of these affairs than is the federal government. Moreover, we must seek every opportunity to retard the expansion of federal bureaucracy and to place our communities in control of their own destinies. The problems are in large degree administrative in character, both as they affect the federal government and the government of the states.

It seems to me that the time has come when we should determine the facts in the present situation, should consider the policies now being pursued and the changes which I might recommend to congress.

Proposes to Appoint Commission.

That these matters may be gone into exhaustively and that I may be advised intelligently, I propose to appoint a commission of nine or ten members, at least five of whom should be chosen from leading citizens of the public-land states, and I should like to secure the cooperation of the governors by submission from them of names for such a commission. This commission would naturally cooperate with the department of the interior.

As an indication of the far-reaching character of the subjects which could come before such a commission, I may recount certain tentative suggestions for its consideration. No doubt other subjects and other proposals would arise.

The most vital question in respect to the remaining free public lands for both the individual states and the nation is the preservation of their most important value—that is grazing. The remaining free lands of the public domain (that is, not including lands reserved for parks, forests, Indians, minerals, power sites and other minor reserves) are valuable in the main only for that purpose.

Transfer Surface Rights to States.

The first of the tentative suggestions, therefore, is that the surface rights of the remaining unappropriated, unreserved public lands should, subject to certain details for protection of homesteaders and the smaller stockmen, be transferred to the state governments for public school purposes and thus be placed under state administration.

At the present time these unappropriated lands aggregate in the neighborhood of 190,000,000 acres, and, in addition, some 10,000,000 acres have been withdrawn for purposes of stock watering places and stock drives which might be transferred as a part of a program of range preservation. In addition, some 35,000,000 acres have been withdrawn for coal and shale reserves, the surface rights of which, with proper reservations, might be added to this program of range development in the hands of the states.

Reports which I have received indicate that, due to lack of constructive regulation, the grazing value of these lands is steadily decreasing due to over-grazing, and their deterioration, aside from their decreased value in the production of herds, is likely to have a marked effect upon the destruction of the soil and ultimately upon the water supply. They bring no revenue to the federal government. The federal government is incapable of the adequate administration of matters which require so large a matter of local understanding. Practically none of these lands can be commercially afforested, but in any event the forest reserves could be rounded out from them where this is desirable. Therefore, for the best interest of the people as a whole, and people of the western states and the small farmers and stockmen by whom they are primarily used, they should be managed and the policies for their use determined by the state governments.

But Little Added Burden Would Be Imposed.

The capacity which the individual states have shown in handling school lands already ceded out of every township, which are of the same character, is in itself proof of this and most of the individual states already maintain administrative organizations for this purpose, so that but little added burden would thus be imposed. They could, to the advantage of the animal industry be made to ultimately yield some proper return to the states for school purposes and the fundamental values could be safeguarded in a fashion not possible by the federal government. They would also increase the tax base of the state governments.

A question might arise upon the allotment of the federal road fund as a result of a shift of the public land ownership. It would only be just if this allotment could be undisturbed for at least 10 years while the states were organizing their range conservation measures.

It is not proposed to transfer forest, park, Indian and other existing reservations which have a distinctly national, as well as local, importance. Inasmuch as the royalties from mineral rights revert to the western states either direct or through the reclamation fund, their reservation to the federal control is not of the nature of a deprival.

Reclamation Service Needs Reorientation.

It seems to me that the vital questions here are to reorient the direction of the reclamation service primarily to the storage of water and to simplify its administration.

The reclamation fund and the reclamation service were created in 1902 and the situation has since changed materially. The present plan, as you are aware, is that receipts from sale of public lands, mineral royalties and repayments by the beneficiaries for expenditure upon projects all accrue to this fund. The reclamation service undertakes special projects upon the authorization of congress, which are financed from the fund on the basis of return by the land owners or purchasers of the cost of the project, but without interest for a term of years. A total of approximately $182,000,000 has been expended from the fund.

The present reclamation act is based fundamentally on the reclamation of government-owned lands. Possible areas available for reclamation have now passed almost wholly into private ownership and the use of the reclamation fund for further projects may be legally criticized owing to the fact that the land is no longer part of the public domain and circumlocution by voluntary agreements may not always be possible.

Moreover, the application of the fund under the present organization results in very large federal administrative activities within the states of a character which was never originally contemplated and which could be much better administered by the local state governments themselves. In many ways it duplicates the state water administrations.

There are several tentative suggestions for more effective handling of the fund. For instance, the reclamation service for all new projects might well be confined to the construction of permanent works; that is, dams and such construction as results in water storage, and at the completion of such construction the entire works be handed over to the states with no obligation for repayment to the reclamation fund except such revenues as might arise from electrical power and possibly in some cases from the sale of water until the outlay has been repaid, or, in any event, for not longer than, say, fifty years.

Again there are certain instances of insufficiently capitalized, community-owned irrigation projects which are at the point of failure for which the reclamation fund might be made a proper vehicle to rescue homes that are now in jeopardy.

A further activity which might be considered for incorporation in the reclamation service would be the authorization to join with the states and local communities or private individuals for the creation of water storage for irrigation purposes.

The primary purpose of these suggestions is thus to devote the federal government activities to the creation of water storage and a reduction of other activities within the states.

Under such arrangements the states would have the entire management of all new reclamation projects and would themselves deal with the irrigation land questions and land settlements. It is only through the powers of the states that reclamation districts can legally be organized which would incorporate the liability of privately owned lands for irrigation expenditure and by such organization it ought to be possible to finance the subsidiary works.

Secure Large Increase in Irrigable Area.

By direction of the reclamation service in some such manner the large provision of water storage would ultimately secure a very large increase in the irrigable area of the various states. It is evident to every engineer that water storage is not always directly connected with an irrigation project, but vital to expansion of irrigation. This emphasis and this direction of federal activities to water storage rather than land development has also an incidental importance to flood control and navigation.

It is not suggested that the states should take over the administration of the established project, but that the system should be set up for future undertakings. If it were instituted it would, of course, be necessary to set up some safeguards to cover interstate projects. No doubt each new project as at present should be specifically authorized by congress.

It must be understood that these suggestions are only tentative; that they have no application to dealing with power questions except that which is incidental to storage of water for irrigation or its further incidental use in navigation and flood control. Moreover, the question of the advisability or inadvisability of opening new areas of land for cultivation in the face of present obvious surplus of farm products does not arise because the activities outlined herein will only affect farm production ten or twenty years hence, by which time we shall probably need more agricultural land.

Mineral Resources Offer Many Problems.

The policies to be pursued in development and conservation of mineral resources of the public domain present many problems. They are problems of a national as well as a local character. I know that the western as well as the eastern states agree that abuse of permits for mineral development or unnecessary production and waste in our national resources of minerals is a matter of deepest concern and must be vigorously prevented.

Because of such abuse and waste I recently instituted measures to suspend further issue of oil prospecting permits on public lands and to clean up the misuse of outstanding permits and thereby clear the way for constructive conservation. It may interest the governors to know that when this decision was taken on the 12th of March there were prospecting permits in force covering over 40,000,000 acres of the public domain. We have now determined that over 40 per cent of these holders had not complied with the requirements of the law; that the large portion of these licenses were being used for the purpose of preventing others from engaging in honest development and some even as a basis of "blue sky" promotions. After yielding to the claimants, the widest latitude to show any genuine effort at development under the outstanding prospecting permits, the total will probably be reduced to about 10,000,000 acres upon which genuine development is now in progress. The public domain is, therefore, being rapidly cleared of this abuse. The position is already restored to a point where measures can be discussed which will further effectually conserve the national resources and at the same time take account of any necessity for local supplies.

These suggestions are, of course, tentative pending investigation of the full facts, but generally I may state that it is my desire to work out more constructive policies for conservation in our grazing lands, our water storage and our mineral resources, at the same time check the growth of federal bureaucracy, reduce federal interference in affairs of essentially local interest and thereby increase the opportunity of the states to govern themselves and in all obtain better government.

Yours faithfully,
HERBERT HOOVER.

CHAPTER XVIII.

Address of Assistant Secretary of the Interior, Joseph M. Dixon.

In presenting and analyzing the letter of the President, Assistant Secretary of the Interior Joseph M. Dixon said:

Lists Public Domain Remaining.

On June 30, 1929, there remained of the public domain, in the 11 major public-land states, exclusive of a much smaller acreage in North and South Dakota, Alabama, Arkansas and Minnesota, and exclusive of national forests, Indian reservations, national parks, stock driveways, water holes, etc., as follows: Arizona, 16,911,367 acres; California, 20,209,421 acres; Colorado, 8,218,875 acres; Idaho, 10,734,420 acres; Montana, 6,-900,114 acres; Nevada, 53,410,938 acres; New Mexico, 16,282,-582 acres; Oregon, 13,227,141 acres; Utah, 25,147,867 acres; Washington, 951,903 acres; Wyoming, 17,035,537 acres.

From the federal school land grants alone, the states of the west have built up their present public school funds, which, year by year, are steadily growing in magnitude and from which is annually distributed millions of income to the school children of our respective states.

Taking my own state as a yardstick, in order to visualize the actual result of the surrender value of the remaining public lands within her borders and we find that the total area of school sections granted under her enabling act to have been, in round numbers, 5,000,000 acres. The present proposal gives Montana, in round numbers, 7,000,000 acres additional.

Not Equivalent of School Lands in Original Grant.

Naturally, the remaining 7,000,000 acres are not the equivalent, acre for acre, of the school lands embraced within the original grant and still my judgment is that the granting of the remaining 7,000,000 acres will almost double the income of the permanent school fund of Montana, and to that extent lift the burden of local school taxation from the homes and farms and business interests of our state.

My judgment is that we have not, as yet, half developed the future and potential water supply on these vast areas of grazing lands.

The sinking of wells a few hundred feet, at almost any place in the two states just named will develop abundant water for stock raising and domestic use, if the proper rewards were offered through honestly administered, long-term leases by the states.

At the present time, these millions of acres of the public domain bring to the federal government, from the surface rights, not one dollar of revenue.

The federal government has never attempted to coin revenue from the disposal of the public lands, except from the royalties imposed upon oil and coal, which are immediately turned back into the reclamation fund for the development of the arid lands in the west.

Proposals for Leasing Remaining Lands.

From time to time, there have been proposals for the leasing of the remaining grazing lands by the federal government, but I have never yet seen one that was not most cumbersome in its proposed operation, and worst of all, inevitably lodges bureau control at Washington, in the administration of the lands here in the west.

That is what the President now proposes to abolish, by giving to the states themselves the ownership and right of control. The individual states have the machinery already set up for doing this very work, through their efficient state land boards already functioning in the administration of the present state-owned school lands.

There is another and even bigger matter involved in the President's proposal: Any man who is intimately acquainted with the present physical condition of our federal-owned grazing lands, well knows that they have been pastured down to the grass roots. We know that they are not now producing one-fifth of the natural forage that they would produce if intelligent use were applied.

The old days of the luxuriant bunch grass has disappeared under the present ruinous practice of indiscriminate grazing, without any restriction whatever.

Intelligent Use Easily Trebles Carrying Power.

Intelligent use of our western grazing land would easily treble their carrying power, in the matter of production of cattle, sheep and wool.

There is another matter involved, that to the far-seeing man may even assume bigger proportions than the immediate one of the increased carrying capacity of our ranges, and that is the very serious impairment of our watersheds from overgrazing, which has already resulted in a much lower carrying capacity for the annual snow and rainfall, with the resultant quick run-off in the spring and disastrous floods that inevitably follow.

SOURCE OF WATERS, MOUNT RAINIER—WASHINGTON

Reclamation Committee House of Representatives. Courtesy Chamber of Commerce, Seattle

The people of the east can make no better future investment than that of granting to the people of the West the remaining public lands, if we can assure them, in turn, that our administration of the trust involved will result in better protection of the watersheds, through a better use and rehabilitation of the natural soil covering and through a continually expanding program of impounding at the head of our rivers, by dams and reservoirs, constructed primarily for irrigation, the flood waters that now pour down each spring in disastrous floods to the lower reaches of our great rivers.

Proposes to Make Reclamation Act More Flexible.

In his letter, the President calls to your attention his proposal to make the present reclamation act more flexible and of far greater consequential value to the west.

As a whole, the federal reclamation projects, providing for long-term repayments without interest, have been far more successful than those constructed with private capital, involving the heavy interest charges on the bonds.

It is common knowledge to us from the irrigation states, that many of these privately constructed projects are now in a bad way and that many meritorious projects of this type are threatened with disaster because of their inability to refinance themselves.

In the President's proposal, he points out that in these meritorious cases, the reclamation act might well be given more flexibility, so as to take care of this type of privately constructed project, where the settler is already upon the land, by long-time loans advanced from the reclamation fund, with a low interest rate. To me, there is no more practical way of extending intelligent help to agriculture at this time.

Advance Money Necessary for Dams and Reservoirs.

He also proposes, if the individual states will take over the job of administering the work of reclamation, that the federal government, in its future commitments from the reclamation fund, advance the money necessary for the construction of the dams and reservoirs, without repayment from the states; the individual states in turn to have supervisory control of the digging of the main canals and laterals.

This plan would very materially reduce the acre cost of future reclamation to the point where successful land settlement would be assured.

I judge that the President, in recommending this joint plan, believes that the nation itself is fully justified in making this contribution of the dams and reservoirs, both for irrigation and an offset against the lessened danger from floods and as a more comprehensive plan of national flood control.

The individual states would reap no actual benefit by a surrender of mineral rights to the states. The individual public land states are now receiving, through the reclamation act, every dollar of revenue that comes from mineral royalties, except 10 per cent of the receipts which the Federal Government retains for its supervisory control and administration of the underground mineral wealth.

Only recently, I heard the comment that turning over the surface title to the public lands, without the accompanying mineral title, was like presenting the egg shell without the meat. Certainly no man from the west, who has a comprehensive knowledge of the facts involved, will give patient ear to such loose and foolish conversation.

Plan Involves Favorable Congressional Action.

There is also another side to that question that we might as well face first as last. All this proposed plan for turning over the public lands and making more flexible the present reclamation act involves favorable congressional action.

I believe that under the kindly and intelligent leadership of the President, these two things are possible; and that the congress will follow his leadership in bringing it to a successful conclusion.

But a proposal to congress to turn over the coal, oil, potash, phosphates, and metalliferous ores to the several states, with our minimum of representation in the house and senate, would be hopelessly impossible from its inception.

The same is true of the national forests. In the administration of the national forests, the federal government is spending each year far more than it receives from the sale of timber and the grazing receipts.

In our enthusiastic support of a program that we ourselves favor, we are sometimes prone to overlook an inventory of the cold facts.

The public domain was acquired by gifts from some of the older states, by purchase from foreign governments and as indemnity from Mexico as a result of the war of 1845-47. No public land state has ever added one single acre to our flag.

The mineral wealth underlying our public lands does not belong to the public land states and never did.

Neither should we forget that the constitution reposes in the congress the exclusive authority to dispose of the public lands and to adopt the rules and regulations regarding their disposal.

President Can Only Recommend Action to Congress.

The President can only recommend to congress such action as he deems wise and beneficial to the nation as a whole, of which we of the west are an integral part.

Our only hope for bringing about the desired change in present conditions, that we believe is fraught with such big possibilities for the development of the West, is through orderly procedure and the presentation of our case in a way that will appeal to the far-seeing congressmen and senators from the eastern states.

In order to bring this about the President now proposes to name a commission of nine or ten men, five of whom shall be from the public land states of the West, to study this matter and then to make report to him of the result of their findings. Backed up by a favorable recommendation of this kind, he is of the opinion that the congress will favorably respond by the enactment of legislation that will bring to early fruition the program outlined in his letter to you.

We can accomplish nothing without mutual cooperation and leadership. I have faith to believe that out of this conference will come great good and bigger things for the future development of the great republic to which we all hold allegiance and especially to that portion which we affectionately call "the west," with its great mountain ranges, valleys and plains, irrigated lands, undeveloped water powers and mineral wealth.

In his letter to you the president has outlined his plan for turning over to you a great heritage. He has also pointed the way whereby the irrigation states of the west can develop their now arid lands under their own control to full fruition.

Propose Method of Cutting Gordian Knot.

He has proposed a method of now cutting the Gordian knot that will free you from bureaucratic control at Washington, of which we have complained in the past.

May not we of the west, under the leadership here assembled, now confront an opportunity that if taken at its flood tide will surely lead on to bigger and better things in the years just ahead of us?

CHAPTER XIX.

Argument of Charles E. Winter Opening Debate.

Extract from Report of Conference of Governors and Representatives of the Public Land States.

THE CHAIRMAN: We have next on our program a Discussion of the Public Domain, Reclamation and Public Land Policies, by the Hon. Charles E. Winter of Wyoming. (Applause.)

Governor Balzar, other governors present and all representatives at this conference; I believe the presiding governor this morning expressed the desire that the discussions in this conference should be full and free and frank. After listening to the preceding speaker's address I think you will all agree with me that it is full and free and frank. (Applause.)

A member appearing upon this program with a prepared paper, and unlimited as to time, manifestly has a decided advantage over any one called in for a limited period of time to discuss the subject matters covered. It is manifestly impossible for any one to discuss this tremendous subject in fifteen minutes. Therefore I can only indicate a few of the high spots which, in my judgment, stand out and should be emphasized.

With much that Governor Dern has enunciated here I am in hearty sympathy and accord. I do not agree with him in all of his statements, nor in all of his conclusions. Those who have been acquainted with me for the last six years, during which time my labors were in the Congress of the United States, where I had the high honor of representing the State of Wyoming, as Representative at Large, perhaps know that

I have given some little study and consideration to this question of the public lands and resources.

I have taken a very "full, free and frank" attitude upon this question for several years. In my interest in that subject, some years ago I searched clear back to the beginning of this entire question, and back of the formation of the Union, into the time of the first Ordinance of 1787, and then into the international treaties under which all these great areas were acquired, a large part of which are now the subject of discussion. I found, to my satisfaction,—it is perhaps a theoretical or abstract proposition, upon which I should not take any time, but I simply want to mention the fact,—that in an early period of this government the proposition was laid down in the Senate of the United States and there argued by great senators and great lawyers who knew the express stipulations of the international treaties,—that not only the lands east of the Mississippi, which were ceded to the United States by the States, and did not come to the States from the United States, but west of the Mississippi as well,—that the States, the moment they became States and ceased to be Territories, became the legal owners of every foot of land and of all the resources contained within their boundaries.

The only reason, in my judgment, that in all these years that proposition has not been tested out from a legal standpoint, is that an international treaty is a matter of concern between sovereign nations. Therefore there was nobody, no forum, no Court in the United States, or elsewhere, capable of taking jurisdiction of that question and determining it. In other words, the United States Supreme Court said, in effect: "An international treaty, or a provision of an international treaty is involved, therefore we have no jurisdiction. We refuse to take consideration of the case. We have no power. If a treaty stipulation has been violated by the United States that is a matter to be settled by the usual methods between nations." So that I see no legal remedy, and for some years have held the conclusion that the only remedy for what I have conceived to be the rights of the Western States is relief by a change of laws and policies by the Congress of the United States; and that is the situation today.

I do not need to assure any of you, and particularly those who have known of my attitude on this question for several years, that I have not changed in any respect from what I have heretofore advocated; and what I have heretofore advocated is the absolute, full jurisdiction, sovereignty, ownership and power of taxation over every foot of soil within the States, with the exception of the National Parks. I take that attitude today. Therefore it is manifest that the proposal which is laid before us today does not go as far as I would like to see it go. It falls very much short of reaching the point that I would like to see it attain.

But here is the situation, and here is probably where there will be difference of opinion as to what conclusion this conference should arrive at, and what, if any conclusions, it should express in the way of resolutions.

I do not agree with my able friend upon the utter lack of value of the surface of the remaining public lands. I believe that they have a large present value, and certainly it is a considerable area with which we are now dealing and what we are now considering— one hundred ninety millions of acres—one-fourth of the entire area of the eleven western public land states. So that at least as to area it is something tremendous. It involves the ownership and jurisdiction over one-fourth of the area of our States.

All States would profit substantially if they owned the surface rights, by an annual income from leases. In some States this might amount to a half million dollars. The day of the free range is over. We have fought federal regulation which would repeal the homestead law and impose a charge upon the stockmen for permits or leases. But regulation of the range by that method is coming very soon, either by the United States or the States. Federal charges will increase just as they did on the forest reserves to a basis of so-called "commercial value." It is not a question whether the stock interests prefer the free range to a charge system. The question is whether the sheep and cattle men prefer to pay the Federal Government or their own State Government. The States in fixing charges for grazing leases should be and no doubt would be considerate of the livestock industry in the transition from the free range to State regulation by permit or lease.

Further, I believe that much of this area of one hundred ninety million acres will prove of great value. It is of great potential value now, and I believe it is only a matter of comparatively small number of years when this potential value will be disclosed and realized.

I believe that there is a great deal to the proposition of the possibility that, underlying these areas, or large portions of these areas, there are subsurface waters; of raising water from underlying or flowing water levels. That possibility alone would seem to indicate that it would be the part of wisdom for the

States, when they have an opportunity to acquire these tremendous areas, to do so. I could go further upon that particular line, with something very interesting regarding new water-lifting inventions and devices, but simply cannot extend upon that point.

We recognize that with various States the character of the land remaining is widely different. In my own State, for example, it is largely a sagebrush and short-grass covered area. Much of it is poor. Much of it does require the area suggested to furnish feed for a single sheep for a certain period of time. But that does not describe the area as a whole or on the average.

I do not know how it may be with other States, but in our State (approximately) I would say that out of sixteen million acres of land, eight million acres of it would always remain of this broken, rough, sparse grazing nature; but I am firmly of the opinion that practically every acre in our state which bears sagebrush and grass will some day be raising grain and fodder of much value, even if there is not disclosed water underneath the surface that can be raised.

Coming on the train the other day I noticed particularly, as we came to elevation after elevation on the Union Pacific, approaching Cheyenne, fields of alfalfa, as well as of corn and of grain. Gradually approaching the city, which has an altitude of six thousand feet, I saw within a few hours ride of that city, at that altitude, fields of corn, if you please, apparently fairly good stands of corn. Immense amounts of grain and of fodder which will carry livestock through the winter season, will be raised on these lands. We had a severe lesson on the need of that last winter.

Good crops will yet be raised upon from eight to

nine million acres in the State of Wyoming by homesteaders; and, incidentally, let us all ever bear in
mind that there is no reason in the world why, if the
surface areas are turned over to the States, the States
can not, if they desire, enact a better homestead law,
suitable to each State, than the rigid Federal Homestead Act.

I look forward, in the state of Wyoming at least,
to the time when we will have a better state homestead law, and we will settle up with homesteaders
approximately one-half of the present public land area
of sixteen million acres.

We have contended for, and we are still contending
for the complete ownership in the State, and for an
amendment of our laws by Congress, that we shall be
deeded or ceded all of the land except the National
Parks. All of the waters should be clearly understood
to belong to the States. We are now subject to suits
to the contrary, on the theory that they are the property of the Federal government. We contend that there
should be finally ceded all the forest land, and ultimately that all the minerals shall come to the States as well
as the surface rights. These are the four great elements—the land, the forests, the minerals and the
water.

And too, it seems to me that there is a direct connection with reference to the ownership of the surface
of the lands, and the claims of the Federal Government as to the ownership of the water. I cannot take
any time on the subject but you all know that suits
are pending, that there has been a dangerous contention, on the part of the Department of Justice, and
of the legal division of the Reclamation Service, that,
contrary to the provisions in the Enabling Acts, the

Constitutions and in the Desert Land Act, the Reclamation Act, and the Federal Water Power Act, and in a number of the other acts, that the States do not own their water. We are in the presence of an imminent danger. Suits have actually been filed in Federal Courts and are ready to be pressed, contending that the Federal Government is the owner of the waters as well as of the lands.

That theory, really, is based on the proposition that when you take all of the language of all of the present acts, indicating control and ownership in the States, taking them altogether, you do not find in them the language of an express grant; and without an express grant the Government has not parted with its title. And since we start from the proposition that originally, when the Government paid out money for these western land acquisitions, and was ceded all of these lands from foreign governments, it became the owner of the land and of the waters. We have to meet that.

We contend that the Federal Government, if its legal title did not pass to the States upon their admission along with the land, has released its claim to the waters—it has waived its right to the waters. The Department of Justice says it has not waived it, and that the United States is still the owner of the waters. So that this proposed ownership by the States of the surface of the public lands remaining, which are contiguous to those waters and comprise portions of reservoirs or areas which are possible for future dams and reservoirs, it seems to me, will help to put our Western States in a position to successfully combat this claim of Federal ownership of the waters. In other words, we are planting our feet in the government's footprints, from which standpoint it was claiming the right to the waters of the States. We should give very serious consideration to this question.

Now, I do not agree with some of the conclusions of the preceding speaker. He seems to see no hope. I do. I am equally dissatisfied, with the exception of the items which I have mentioned, with the limited proposal which is now being made to the Western States. I would like to see it go further at this time, and I want to say right now and here that I have no doubt whatever—not the shadow of a doubt—but that it is only a question of time when we will own all of the minerals and all of the forests, and have complete jurisdiction and full sovereignty over every foot of our soil except the National Parks. (Applause).

It is only a question of time until that will be accomplished. Nothing in the proposition which has been presented to us precludes another step in the future.

I had based some of my ideas on the statement of the Secretary of the Interior, made at Boise, Idaho. I have called attention to the fact that in that statement—and I still think it has much significance—the Secretary of Interior himself, presumably with the knowledge of the President of the United States, said in so many words that "It may eventually develop that it is wiser for the States to control even the national forests." Note the significance of that. Moreover, he expressed approval of the legislation which had turned over to the States the school sections. I am sure that he did not forget, when he made that statement, the act which has been referred to, of two years ago, which confirmed and settled in the State, not only the school sections, which were supposed to be non-mineral, but all the school sections, including the mineral. Therefore I find in that statement with reference to the school sections something hopeful for the future as to the cession of the minerals as well as the surface rights. In other words, that this proposition now before us is not one which would, if accepted, close the door to the development of the West and be a final decision and determination for all time to come.

I see nothing objectionable in the proposals of the President, or of the Secretary, or of our good friend, Assistant Secretary Dixon. There is nothing to prevent us from ultimately acquiring everything that we believe these States should have. Before I leave that let me çall your attention to this opening sentence in the statement of the President, which was read today.

I am simply giving my own impressions, as an individual, I do not have the present honor of bearing a title of any kind, I am not an official of any State or of the Government. I am a private citizen, interested in the West, and intensely interested in this particular subject. I am speaking from that standpoint, but I have a right to draw my deductions from the language of the proposal.

The President says:

"I have for some years given thought to the necessity and desirability for" What? "a further step in the development of the relations of the Federal and State governments in respect to the public lands and the reclamation service."

Why is it not possible and is it not certain that there may come a time within a reasonable period, when there may be another step taken? What are the successive steps which will bring us into full sovereignty and jurisdiction?

First, the surface areas,

Second, the mineral resources,

Third, the forests,

Fourth, the waters.

All of these things are coming as sure as we are assembled.

We are to determine, as a matter of policy and expediency, at this time, what our position shall be with reference to these successive steps; whether they shall be successive steps, or whether we shall demand two of them at this time, or three of them, or all four of them,

I believe that the present administration does not hold as drastic views with reference to the Federal claim for water as the previous administration held. There is language in the President's statement here, and in the Secretary's statement, to the effect that the States are water conscious, and in a better position to administer these local affairs, with reference to the division and use of water, than the federal government. So that while these suits are pending, and it is a dangerous claim on the part of the Government, I think the water proposition is in a fair way to be settled right in this administration. We are not facing the acute danger that we were facing prior to last March 4th. Still, everything must be taken into consideration; all of these four great elements that we are ultimately desirous of acquiring which are the foundations of the prosperity of the State. All may be possible some day in the good judgment of the President. We do not know what further may be in his mind. I am not saying that he has in mind these future steps; I haven't time to go into it; but all through this document, time and again, you have heard that we are better competent to administer all these things than the Federal government. That is the ultimate thing and the proposition that will determine this matter in the end. We can see it coming, therefore I say this is but one of the several great necessary steps to bring this whole thing about, which we have wanted and desired for the last thirty years. So we should be very, very careful, and we should give these proposals our most profound consideration.

Let us first ascertain the full value, the full possibilities over a term of years, of the ownership of the surface areas alone. I have indicated some of them. The water possibilities alone would make it worth while.

I have followed this matter up for six years. I have discussed it with numerous members of the House of Representatives, and it is a fact that we have a considerable number of converts to this idea, some of them having independently and disinterestedly expressed their views, in the closing days of the session last winter, before the House Public Lands Committee. The record shows three senators in one day to have risen on the floor of the Senate, and in so many words stated they were in favor of ceding the public lands to the states, and they made no reservations.

Yet in spite of these indications of a growing appreciation of this thing, we must all realize that the East is utterly ignorant of the conditions that we know and which are the basis of our contentions. It is a matter of education and it takes a long while. I want to say that this splendid representation of the Western States is one which I "long have sought, and mourned, because I found it not." I regard this conference as one of tremendous importance. In fact, we should have met and discussed some of these questions before this. I wonder why we did not do it? Partly because of little differences of opinion, or a little jealousy between the States, or a little difference in the character of the lands, or the matter of the over-grazing of flocks from one State into another. A lot of little things have kept us apart; but let us realize the fact that all of these things we have the intelligence and the honesty to solve when it comes to be a matter between the States. Let us not allow them to close our eyes and put a cloud before us, preventing our seeing the great main objectives that are just ahead.

We are now dealing with a nation and with a House of Representatives, as has been said, of four hundred thirty-five members, of which we have but thirty-three; but we have at least, after all these years of claiming the rights of the West, come to a period when we have a powerful administration at least willing to go with us to this extent. If we have the hope, as I claim we have, and have a right to deduct from everything that has been said, this is but one step, and the only reason that the other step is not being taken at this time is that it is impossible to convey to the East—and secure the support of the Representatives of the East—our ideas and convince them as to these other propositions which may therefore have to come along at a later date.

So the question before us is: Are we now going as far as we can when we have the opportunity? We might go further than the first proposals; at least we then will be in a position, a much firmer position; our feet will be planted upon the soil that will be our own and we surely can take the other step when the

ARROWROCK DAM—IDAHO—GOVERNMENT RECLAMATION PROJECT
Courtesy Chamber of Commerce, Boise. Photo by Grove

time has arrived, when the East can be convinced of the justice of the further step, just as the time has now arrived when they can be convinced, with the strong argument and the strong arm of the President of the United States, that the surface rights should be ceded to the states. (Applause)

I have only hit a few of the high spots. My conclusion is, first, that after full consideration, this conference will not reject the proposal that has been made. Second, I have no objection to—as my own record will prove, indeed I am in favor of, at all times—claiming all that we think we have a right to. My position is well known on that. Standing on that position I say it is well for this conference to make clear what it believes we should have; but in some way combine a statement of that kind with a proposition of support of the President, as far as he has gone. Do you imagine for one moment that this thing is to be put through by only a wave of the hand, because the suggestion has come from the President? Oh, no. It will take much labor. It will yet take much argument. Some of you possibly saw an editorial in the New York Times, immediately following on the heels of the statement of the Secretary of the Interior, made at Boise, Idaho. I have it here. The writer of that editorial is utterly opposed to the suggestion made by the Secretary. He is opposed to the ceding of even the surface rights.

ASSISTANT SECRETARY DIXON (Interposing): I am glad you have that.

HON. CHAS. E. WINTER (continuing): I refer to this just to show you what we are up against, what the President and all of us will have to overcome in order to bring about this first step.

I for one propose to defend the Secretary of the Interior, our Assistant Secretary, Mr. Dixon, and the President of the United States against that kind of opposition; and I think we can all do that. Let us do that, and let us finally in this Conference express ourselves in such a way that we will not mortgage or foreclose our future; make it clear as to what we consider our full rights to be; but then say we thank the President and that we can and will support the proposal which is now before us, to appoint a commission on which we shall have representatives, to consider a change of public land policy. I thank you. (Applause.)

CHAPTER XX.

Resolution of the Governors' Conference
on the
Message From the President.

WHEREAS, The President of the United States has tentatively proposed that the national government cede to the several states, for the benefit of the public schools, the surface of the unappropriated and unreserved public lands within their borders; and

WHEREAS, The President of the United States has also tentatively proposed certain changes in federal reclamation policies; and

WHEREAS, The President of the United States furthermore definitely offers to appoint a commission of nine or ten members, at least five of whom shall be chosen from leading citizens of public land states, to investigate and analyze the effects of those proposals and report to him on their desirability and feasibility;

THEREFORE, BE IT RESOLVED, That we, the Governors and other representatives of the eleven western states of this Conference, express our hearty appreciation of the message from the President of the United States, and our deep interest in the proposals contained therein, and we hereby endorse the offer of the President to appoint a commission to study the western land and reclamation problems and pledge our cooperation in the work of such commission.

BE IT FURTHER RESOLVED, That this conference recommends that the Governor of each State here represented submit to the President of the United States the names of three qualified citizens for consideration by the President for appointment on such Commission.

Committee on Conservation and Administration of the Public Domain.

The Committee on Conservation and Administration of the Public Domain, authorized by Congress, with a membership of twenty-two, as finally appointed by President Hoover is:

Ex officio members:
> Ray Lyman Wilbur, Secretary of the Interior, Washington, D. C.
> Arthur M. Hyde, Secretary of Agriculture, Washington, D. C.

Chairman:
> James R. Garfield, Attorney; Secretary of the Interior during Roosevelt administration, Cleveland, Ohio.

Members:
> I. A. Brandjord, commissioner of State lands and investments, Helena, Mont.
> H. O. Bursum, former United States Senator, Socorro, N. Mex.
> Gardner Cowles, publisher, The Register and Tribune, Des Moines, Iowa.
> James P. Goodrich, attorney; former Governor of Indiana, Winchester, Ind.
> W. B. Greeley, secretary-manager, West Coast Lumbermen's Association; former Chief of the United States Forest Service, Seattle, Wash.
> Perry W. Jenkins, vice-president for Wyoming of the Great Lakes-St. Lawrence Tidewater Association, Big Piney, Wyo.
> Rudolph Kuchler, president, State Taxpayer's Association of Arizona, Phoenix, Ariz.
> George H. Lorimer, editor, Saturday Evening Post; vice-president, Curtis Publishing Co., Philadelphia, Pa.
> Geo. W. Malone, State engineer of Nevada, Carson City, Nev.
> Elwood Mead, Commissioner, Bureau of Reclamation (representing California), Washington, D. C.
> Charles J. Moynihan, attorney, Montrose, Colo.
> I. H. Nash, State land commissioner, Boise, Idaho.
> William Peterson, director of experiment station and extension division, Utah State Agricultural College, Logan, Utah.

Mary Roberts Rinehart, author, Washington, D. C.
Huntley N. Spaulding, treasurer, Spaulding Fibre Co.;
former Governor of New Hampshire, Rochester, N. H.
Ross K. Tiffany, hydraulic engineer, former State super-
visor of hydraulics, Olympia, Wash.
Wallace Townsend, attorney; member of the Arkansas
River Association, Little Rock, Ark.
E. C. Van Patten, president, Van Patten Lumber Co.,
Ontario, Ore.
Francis C. Wilson, attorney; interstate river commission-
er for New Mexico, Santa Fe, N. Mex.

On their assembling at Washington, D. C., they
were addressed and instructed by President Hoover
as reported by the Associated Press in an authorized
statement as follows:

The purpose of the commission, the President said, is to
study the whole question of the public domain, particularly
the unreserved lands. We have within it three outstanding
problems:

First, there has been overgrazing throughout these lands,
the value of the ranges having diminished as much as 80 to 90
per cent in some localities. The major disaster, however, is
that destruction of the natural cover of the land imperils the
water supply. The problem therefore in this sense is really a
problem of water conservation.

Second, the question as to what is the best method of applying a reclamation service to the West in order to gain real
and enlarged conservation of water resources.

Third, the commission is free to consider the question of
conservation of oil, coal and other problems that arise in connection with the domain.

I have recently put forward some tentative proposals for
consideration at the governors' conference in Salt Lake City
and a survey of public officials show that, while three states
seem generally opposed to the idea of the states taking the
responsibility for conservation of grazing values, by transfer
to them of the surface rights, seven states are in favor of this
idea, with some secondary modifications.

Public opinion in those States generally seems to support
the tentative suggestions for reorganization of the reclamation service. The suggestions, however, were entirely tentative, and the whole subject is open to the commission.

CHAPTER XXI.

Report of Public Land Committee.

On January 16, 1931, President Hoover's Committee on the Conservation and Administration of the Public Domain made its Report formulated after many months of investigation, hearings and conferences, as follows:

To the President of the United States:

The committee appointed by you, in accordance with the act of Congress approved April 10, 1930, to make a study of and report on the conservation and administration of the public domain, respectfully submits the following report:

You have submitted to the committee problems for consideration which we summarize under five major topics:

1. The future disposition of the remaining vacant, unreserved, unappropriated public lands and the adoption of a definite program of conservation of grazing resources either through ownership or control by the States or by Federal administration.

2. The use and conservation of water resources including reclamation and flood control.

3. The conservation of subsurface mineral resources with respect particularly to the position which the States should occupy in any program.

4. The conservation of timber resources with special consideration of national forest areas, their usefulness within present limits, and the matter of additions to or eliminations from those limits.

5. Changes in administration which might produce greater efficiency in the conservation and use of the natural resources of the Nation.

Consideration of the questions submitted has led the committee to the following general conclusions and specific recommendations.

General Policies.

It is the conclusion of the committee:

1. That all portions of the unreserved and unappropriated public domain should be placed under responsible administration or regulation for the conservation and beneficial use of its resources.

2. That additional areas important for national defense, reclamation purposes, reservoir sites, national forests, national

parks, national monuments, and migratory-bird refuges should be reserved by the Federal Government for these purposes.

3. That the remaining areas, which are valuable chiefly for the production of forage and can be effectively conserved and administered by the States containing them, should be granted to the States which will accept them.

4. That in States not accepting such a grant of the public domain responsible administration or regulation should be provided.

5. We recognize that the Nation is committed to a policy of conservation of certain mineral resources. We believe the States are conscious of the importance of such conservation, but that there is a diversity of opinion regarding any program which has for its purpose the wise use of those resources. Such a program must of necessity be based upon such uniformity of Federal and State legislation and administration as will safeguard the accepted principles of conservation and the reclamation fund. When such a program is developed and accepted by any State or States concerned, those resources should be transferred to the State. This is not intended to modify or be in conflict with the accepted policy of the Federal Government relating to the reservation stated in conclusion No. 2 above.

Special Recommendations.

1. That Congress pass an act granting to the respective public-land States all the unreserved, unappropriated public domain within their respective boundaries, conditioned, however, that in order to make the grant effective, the States desirous of accepting it shall so signify by act of legislation. A copy of the accepting act signed by the governor and attested by the great seal of the accepting State, when transmitted to the President of the United States, shall operate as an application for the clear listing of the lands granted, and the proceedings thereon shall follow under the direction of the Secretary of the Interior, as in the case of selections heretofore made by public-land States under State land grants.

2. That for States not accepting the grant Congress shall include in the act a provision that upon the application of the State land commission, or State land commissioner, as the case may be, authorized thereto by the State legislature, the President should by Executive order designate the unreserved, unappropriated public domain in such State as a national range.

Existing laws and appropriations pertaining to the national forests should be extended to national ranges in so far as applicable, including grazing research and range improvements, and disposition of receipts, homestead provisions, and the prospecting for and utilization of minerals.

National ranges should include public lands withdrawn for mineral or other purposes when the use of the land for grazing is not inconsistent with the purpose of the withdrawal.

3. In the same act of Congress it should be provided that in the absence of legislation by any State within 10 years thereafter dealing with the control and administration of the unreserved, unappropriated public domain, the President, by Executive order, may establish, when authorized by Congress, a national range in such State, comprised of all such public domain, including lands withdrawn for mineral or other purposes whose use for grazing is not inconsistent with the purpose of the withdrawal.

4. Areas of unreserved and unappropriated public domain granted to the States shall be clearly listed by the Department of Interior in accordance with established procedure as to mineral or nonmineral character. In the case of lands classified as nonmineral in character, those passed to the States should be in fee simple, and pending the transfer of lands to the States the Federal Government should recognize in so far as possible any method inaugurated by the States to regulate the movement of livestock on such lands to prevent overgrazing that is not discriminatory between the States.

In the case of lands classified as mineral in character, title to the State should be in fee simple, except for the reservation in the United States of specified mineral or minerals found by the Interior Department to be present in the land at the time of clear listing, and with reservation in the United States, its permittees, lessees, or grantees, of the right to enter upon the lands, to prospect for, mine, and remove such minerals.

5. There should be temporarily excepted from the grant the areas shown on map No. 1, submitted to this committee by the Forest Service, entitled "Areas proposed by Forest Service as additions to existing national forests or for establishment as new national forests." In order to determine what, if any, areas should be taken from or added to the national forests, a board should be created for each State composed of five members, one designated by the President of the United States, one by the Secretary of the Interior, one by the Secretary of Agriculture, and two by the State. The power and duty of such boards shall be: (1) To decide what, if any, lands within such proposed areas shall be added to the national forests; (2) to decide what, if any, areas within existing national forests shall be restored to the public domain; (3) additions to national forests should be limited to areas chiefly valuable for forest purposes, except upon request of the State involved; (4) the board shall endeavor to correct and round out the boundaries of national forests by the consolidation of areas wherever practicable; (5) the board shall report its findings from time to time to the Secretary of the Interior and complete its findings within one year from appointment of the board.

The committee recommends the use of map No. 1 merely as a basis for consideration of the board, not as an expression of opinion or suggestion that those areas be added to the national forests.

The committee believes that this method of procedure will expedite clear listing of the remaining lands.

Whatever areas are not included within a national forest as a result of the decision of the board shall then pass to any accepting State to be clear listed in the same manner as the general grant.

The Board herein created shall be organized upon the passage of the act and any State may elect to defer acceptance of the grant in paragraph 1 until the determination of the board has been made.

6. The Board shall also be authorized to select additional reservations important for national defense, for reclamation purposes and reservoir sites, for national parks and monuments, and for migratory-bird refuges, and to recommend that they be set aside for the purposes indicated and be excluded from lands granted to any accepting State, and such recommendation when received by the Secretary of the Interior shall have the effect of excluding such areas from the grant; provided, however, that the recommendations shall be filed with the Secretary of the Interior prior to the clear listing to the State of any of the land which might be so reserved.

If a majority of the board, or in the case of national defense, and/or for reservoir sites on interstate streams, two members thereof request that a definite area for the purposes stated in the preceding paragraph be excluded from the clear listing of any tract for further study to be given the subject, then the Secretary of the Interior shall exclude such definite areas from the clear-listed lands.

This board shall also have the power and it shall be its duty to make recommendations to the Secretary of the Interior for the elimination of lands from existing reservations, withdrawals, and classifications when such action is deemed proper by the board.

7. Areas restored to the unreserved and unappropriated public domain through the cancellation of any rights or claims or release of withdrawals should be subject to adjudication and clear listing or reservation, as herein provided.

8. The Secretary of the department having jurisdiction over any of the lands classified and disposed of as herein provided and remaining in public ownership should be authorized to exchange any of such lands with States or private owners for other lands of equal value with a view to consolidating ownership for more effective utilization and administration. In the making of such exchanges long-standing priority of use of grazing areas should be given due consideration and no exchanges completed until after full hearing has been accorded. Similar authority should be extended by an enabling act to

the States as to any public lands granted thereby, and also as to any lands granted to the State by previous enabling or other acts.

9. In order to bring about the consolidation of existing State holdings within the States not accepting the general grant, so that administration and control may be more efficiently exercised, the State should be authorized, in the discretion of the Secretary of the department having jurisdiction thereover, to select any isolated area not in excess of four sections of the unreserved, unappropriated public domain, such as consolidated with near-by areas of State-owned lands, would effect the purpose mentioned; and upon clear listing of such selections, title should then pass to the State as in the case of other State land grants.

10. The Secretary of the Interior should be authorized to clear list areas previously withdrawn for the protection of stock-watering places and areas withdrawn for stock driveways upon a showing by the State that they are no longer required.

11. As to all grants provided for in the act, the land should pass to the States impressed with a trust for administration and rehabilitation of the public domain and for public institutions and with such restrictions as Congress might deem appropriate.

The following general restrictions are deemed desirable:

(a) The lands passing to the several States under the provisions of this proposal shall be subject to lease, sale, or other disposition as the State legislature may determine; provided, however, that all sales of such lands shall be made only at public auction after previous advertising and with reservation of subsurface minerals.

(b) None of such lands, nor any estate or interest therein, shall ever be sold or leased except in pursuance of general laws providing for such disposition.

(c) All proceeds arising from the sale or other permanent disposition of the lands and every part thereof shall be placed in a permanent fund to be safely invested and to be guaranteed by the State against diversion or loss.

12. The present conservative policy of reclamation development should be continued. Under it, construction expenditures each year are restricted to the payments from settlers and the income from other sources provided for in the law. If payments are not made, works will not be built. This makes of reclamation a sound business policy and is a strong influence toward maintaining the integrity of the contracts.

Where projects require a larger investment than can be met from the reclamation fund, they should be dealt with by Congress in special acts similar in character to the Boulder Canyon project act.

We recommend that, in the undertaking of any project, there should be no interference with the laws of the State relating to the appropriation, control, or distribution of the water or with vested rights secured thereunder.

Past experience, coupled with the urgent need of additional funds for accelerating and continuing construction work on irrigation projects, points conclusively to the desirability of adopting a definite policy relative to hydroelectric development, under which the power receipts should be used; first, to repay the cost of the power plant and appurtenant works; second, the cost of the reservoir and dam which regulates the delivery of water to the plant; and after that, all net revenues should be credited to the reclamation revolving fund.

The policy should be continued of having a central organization to design and build works, but to transfer these works to the control and management of the water users as soon as the projects are settled and developed.

13. We approve and adopt from the Report of Committee of the Irrigation Division of the American Society of Civil Engineers made October 4, 1928, the following:

"The conservation of the water in the rivers and lakes of the country should be under public control and in order to lay a proper foundation for the making of comprehensive plans the Federal and State Governments should gather data, compile statistics, and conduct studies necessary to determine the feasibility of projects.

"The regulation of the flow of streams for the prevention of floods and for the best possible utilization of the waters should be undertaken by the States, or jointly by the United States and the States under such suitable forms of cooperation as may be appropriate under the constitutional authority now delegated to each. They should prepare and adopt comprehensive plans for such regulation and should bear an equitable portion of the cost of water storage and flood-control work when the economic aspects after full investigations are found to be favorable, and the remainder of the cost should be allocated to flood-control, irrigation, power-development, municipal water-supply, and other purposes.

"Where protection against flood waters results from the regulation of stream flow by means of reservoirs or otherwise, the proportion of the cost of the flood-control work not assumed by the Federal or State Government should be assessed against the lands and other properties which receive benefit therefrom."

14. Whatever be the method adopted for the use and disposition of the public domain, any final administrative act must be based upon a survey of the areas involved. It is therefore recommended that the Congress be asked to provide appropriations sufficient to enable the General Land Office to proceed immediately with the survey of the remaining unsurveyed areas.

15. In the administration of the public domain as a national range it is recommended that consideration be given to those

methods which will perpetuate the best interests of the live-stock industry, including long-time permits for grazing, and developing watering holes to permit the complete use of the range. The program should include consideration of a year-round permit system allocated so as to make the best use of the entire grazing areas of the State.

Careful consideration should be given to those areas vital for both grazing and watershed protection to the end that both interests receive constructive administration.

16. That the present ratio of participation by the Federal Government in the construction of Federal-aid highways be continued for a period of 10 years.

17. The location and protection of stock driveways should be given immediate consideration. Pending the determination of the extent to which they should be transferred to the States accepting the grant, cooperative action between the Federal Government, the States, and the stock-raisers' associations as to use, location, and policing should be entered into where possible. Interstate driveways should be retained in the Federal Government and held subject to use determined by inter-state agreements.

18. We adhere to the principle that in all matters clearly involving the interest of two or more States, but not that of the other States of the Union, all questions arising there-from should be settled by agreement and compact so far as possible and not by Federal intervention, save an appeal to the courts where necessary. This principle has proved very effective recently and should be more frequently resorted to in the future.

19. It is the conclusion of the committee that as to agricul-tural and grazing lands, private ownership, except as to such areas as may be advisable or necessary for public use, should be the objective in the final use and disposition of the public domain.

20. In order to provide for a more effective administration of the public domain and the various reservations and areas now under the control of the Federal Government and to promote the conservation of natural resources, it is recommend-ed that the Congress be asked to authorize the President to consolidate and coordinate the executive and administrative bureaus, agencies, and offices created for or concerned with the administration of the laws relating to the use and dis-position of the public domain, the administration of the nation-al reservations, and the conservation of natural resources.

It is fair to assume that President Hoover's recom-mendation to Congress will be practically to the same effect as the Report of the Commission.

Apparently the plan is a compromise between those

who favored the initial administration proposal to transfer to the States surface rights only, over the unreserved and unappropriated domain, and those who, on behalf of the States, advocated the cession of subsurface rights as well, that is, including the mineral resources—a complete grant of the unreserved areas, and also the reserved areas, excepting national parks.

The essentials of the compromise seem to be that the reserved areas shall be held by the Government, and the grant of the unreserved areas shall be in full with fee simple title; where the areas are known to be mineral the grant will also be in fee simple but with reservations of specific minerals to the United States. After the Government and the States agree upon a conservation program on specific minerals and Reclamation has been provided for, then these minerals also are to be made over to the States.

Thus the main question which will be considered by Congress and on which the greatest difference of opinion exists is whether Federal mineral reservations of specific minerals on known mineral areas should be made in the grant.

The people of the Western States will not be satisfied with this partial restoration, cession of the unreserved and unappropriated area only, even though it be a fee simple title, because of the mineral reservations. Great values of the public lands are in their mineral content, although there is some considerable value in surface rights and a greater potential value in the possibility of sub-surface water development which would undoubtedly go with and be attached to surface rights.

If the fertilizer minerals, potash, phosphate, and nitrate, are included in the minerals, as well as the fuel minerals, coal, oil, gas, and oil shale, (not to mention all other minerals), a tremendous area in many states would come under the mineral reservations. The minerals mentioned are in the Federal Leasing Act.

It is a matter of uncertainty whether in time the advocates of more Federal power and centralization will not urge and secure the inclusion of all minerals, including gold, silver, copper, lead, zinc, etc., in the Mineral Leasing Act, thus practically doing away with the general mining law which provides for location and patenting of mineral claims into private ownership upon payment of sales price to the government of $2.50 to $5.00 per acre. There is evidence of this intention on the part of extreme federalists.

The States could and would preserve general mining law principles, as to all minerals except possibly those now under the Mineral Leasing Law, by which is meant location and patent, private ownership and fee simple title. For that matter this object could be insured by making it a condition of the grant.

A lease from the government, which is the method of the Departments of handling the minerals reserved to the government, means the imposition of a royalty to be paid into the National Treasury. The burden of a royalty often causes the development to fail, in that lease-holding companies can not continue to operate profitably under such burden, and that capital will not undertake operations, even under a low royalty, of such deposits as gypsum, asbestos, aluminum, potash, phosphate, and nitrate, because such mining can not pay any royalty and build up new industries in these deposits, particularly when they are unprotected by any tariff duties and are shipped in in enormous quantities from abroad by low-cost water transportation, and coming as they do from cheap labor countries. Even coal companies are having a difficult time to maintain themselves where they are operating under government lease and the consequent royalty burden.

If it be said that a leasing act can provide for constantly reducing amounts of royalty and ultimately to the vanishing point, to adjust itself to the necessities of the business of the lessees, then it becomes apparent that the entire theory of governmental royalty leasing system is wrong.

The report naturally and logically provides for time and continued federal administration during the transition, as it will doubtless require several years after passage of a grant by Congress, before the surveys and classification can be completed and negotiations with the Western States concluded, including the acceptance of the grant by the legislatures of the several States affected.

It recognizes the right of the government in flood control and navigation. This was necessary under the Constitution, and it emphasizes the Federal function under which marvelous development may go forward, for example, in a tributary storage policy, with its tremendous power and irrigation possibilities. as well as cheap water transporation.

It is encouraging that the Committee unites in recommending and recognizing the basic rights of the States of ultimate administration, policing, range control, compensation or partial return of proceeds from water power sites, inter-state agreements as to water control and ownership of all water within their boundaries, with elimination forever of theories of Federal ownership and control of waters of the States, and general recognition of State Sovereignty in dealing

IRRIGATED FIELDS—IDAHO
Courtesy Chamber of Commerce, Boise

with control, development and utilization of resources. The assistance of the United States is accepted where more than one State is involved and a compact is necessary. States desiring it can accept Federal regulation.

Agreement is voiced in the Report with President Hoover's original suggestion that in any event, there should be a continuance of the governmental appropriations in the highway program on a more equitable basis for the States of small propulations and great public areas. This is as it should be.

With respect to the vital matter of water power storage construction, proceeds and division, control and administration, the Committee's tentative plan is supplemented by a definite recognition and recommendation by Secretary of the Interior Wilbur of the province and jurisdiction of the States. On November 28, 1930, the Associated Press dispatches from Washington, D. C., stated that:

Control of water power developments primarily by the states was urged Thursday by Secretary Wilbur to end confusing duplication of authority with the federal power commission.

In his role of chairman of the power commission the Interior Secretary said state and federal agencies should find a basis whereby they may supplement each other or elements of conflict might impede desirable developments.

He advocated such co-ordination as the administrative policy of the commission in its annual report, which cited complaints from the states that the government was encroaching upon their rights with resultant snarls in jurisdictional questions.

The recommendation that there should be a definite policy as to hydro-electric power from the power plants erected by the government in connection with Reclamation Projects and that the proceeds of such power should be applied first to repayment of the cost of the power plant, then to repayment of cost of the reservoir and dam, is satisfactory to this point. But the further recommendation that all proceeds thereafter be credited to the Reclamation Fund ignores the right of the State which owns the water, and the beds of streams. The States where such works are located should receive one-half of the proceeds from the power, after plants and dams have been paid for. Indeed, it would do equity to provide for a percentage of the proceeds to be paid the State annually from the beginning of the sale of power rather than compel the State to wait for its participation until the total cost of all construction has been repaid.

The Commission rightfully holds that as to agricultural and grazing lands private ownership should be the objective. It will be observed that the proposals of the Committee are limited to the unreserved and unappropriated public domain. This means that their recommendation retains under government ownership and control the 235,000,000 acres which are now reserved as National Parks and Monuments, Naval Reserves, Indian Reservations, Water Power Sites and Forest Reserves.

Full recognition of the rights of the States and the principle of the sovereign jurisdiction of the State in our Constitutional structure can never obtain until the reserved as well as the unreserved lands and resources are ceded to the States. Voluntary exceptions should be made as to National Parks, but as to all other reservation they should ultimately be transferred. It is recalled that Secretary Wilbur suggested that eventually it may prove wise to have the States administer the Forest Reserves. These constitute three-fourths of the area of all the reservations of the West. But it may be that consideration of the reserved areas may have to wait another day.

It is the part of wisdom perhaps at this time not to create an issue as to the reserved areas, but confine the present effort to a complete cession of the unreserved areas. Nothing less than a complete transfer of all, however, will answer the demands of equity and justice to the Western States. This will not be obtained unless the representatives of the West unite in a determined campaign to convince Congress. There is little doubt but that there will be strenuous opposition from the East to the ceding of even the surface rights, and more decided hostility to the transfer of fee simple title to even the non-mineral areas. Congress will witness a determined conflict before the Western States succeed in the fight to obtain both surface and mineral rights of all the unreserved public domain. There are those in the East who do not yet realize the truth of the statement of President Hoover, that the Western States are no longer in "swaddling clothes," but are full grown and are in fact not only as capable but even more fitted than the Federal departments to administer their lands and resources.

The progress made in the last few years, as indicated by the report of the Commission is most remarkable. Not over three years ago the idea was characterized "Impossible" even by Senators representing the West. Some of these national representatives of the Western people have changed their minds and are now advocating the cession if it include the mineral as well as the surface. The proposal as it has been advocated always included the minerals. Surface rights only were unthought of. Great credit is due those advocates of the West who, in season and out of season, in office or in private life, have waged and advanced the cause of the public land States. The whole western people can well take heart and renewed encouragement. They are now fortified by a distinct advantage, a great forward step, in the recommendations of the President's Committee, made up, as it is, of eastern members to the extent of practically one-half of its membership. Congress may go farther than the Committee has indicated. A united effort may convince a majority of its members that the grant should be, as to the unreserved lands, full, free, and without reservations or conditions. If successful the Western States will receive incalculable benefits, and the nation as a whole will benefit thereby. The balanced structure, between Nation and States, as contemplated and provided in the constitution, will be restored. Equilibrium and harmony will make for better progress.

CHAPTER XXII.

Secretary Hubert Work States the Case for Continued Federal Control.

Hon. Robert N. Stanfield, Chairman,
Public Lands Committee, U. S. Senate,
Washington, D. C.
My dear Senator Stanfield:

I have your request for report on Senate Bill No. 4605, entitled "A bill to cede unreserved public lands to the several States."

The bill is similar to Senate Bill No. 906, 68th Congress, and Senate Bill No. 3901, 69th Congress, upon which reports were submitted under dates of March 27, 1924; April 3, 1924, and April 19, 1926, respectively, recommending that the bills be not enacted.

Senate Bill No. 564, now pending in the House of Representatives, proposes concessions to the States in aid or for the support of public schools, and I am now preparing a substitute bill, which will secure to the States mineral as well as non-mineral numbered school sections, the former having been heretofore generally excepted by the terms of the granting acts. This will be of distinct advantage to the western States particularly, in the way of enlarging and enriching the grants to those States for the support of common or public schools.

The present bill, as indicated by its title, however, proposes to cede the entire unreserved public lands to the several states in which located, and it is deemed important to again briefly review the extent and estimated value of the grant proposed by Senate Bill No. 4605, and its effect, if made.

The remaining public domain, outside of Alaska, includes an approximate area of 200,000,000 acres of unreserved public lands. One of my predecessors a few years ago made an estimate of the value of the national asset in the remaining public-land areas, substantially as follows:

Sale value of the surface of public lands outside national forests ....$	310,000,000
Value of national forests and resources...............	1,000,000,000
Royalty value of coal in public ownership; bituminous, 10,000,000,000 tons at 10c; subbituminous, 30,000,000,000 tons, at 8c, and lignite, 50,000,000,000 tons, at 5c aggregating..................	5,900,000,000
Royalty value of 700,000,000 barrels of oil at 12½ per cent...........	175,000,000
Royalty value of 50,000,000,000 barrels of shale oil, at 5 per cent...	5,000,000,000
Royalty value of 3,500,000,000 tons of phosphate at 2 per cent.......................................	280,000,000
Royalty value of 20,000,000 tons of potash, at 2 per cent..	30,000,000
Royalty value, Alaska:	
Coal of all grades, 20,000,000,000 tons at 5 cents	1,000,000,000
25,000,000 barrels of oil at 10 per cent..............	2,500,000
Total estimated royalty and sale value of public lands and resources................................	$13,697,500,000

In addition, he estimated the annual return from water power on the public lands, at 10 cents per horsepower, per year, $1,550,000.

The returns to July 1, 1926, under the general leasing and potash leasing laws, covering a period of something over six years, were $56,400,749. Returns from this source last year were $8,626,465.

In this connection there should be considered the fact that under the general mining laws 5 per cent of total receipts are allocated to the States, and that under the general leasing and potash laws proceeds from royalties, rentals, bonuses, etc., are divided, so that 37½ per cent thereof is payable at the expiration of each fiscal year to the States within the boundaries of which the leased deposits are located, for construction and maintenance of roads or support of public schools or other public educational institutions, as the State legislature may direct. The total amount paid to the States under this provision of law to July 1, 1926, is $18,181,527. Fifty-two and one-half per cent of the receipts under the leasing laws is paid into and appropriated as a part of the reclamation fund, for the irrigation of arid lands in the Western States. The remaining 10 per cent is paid into the Treasury of the United States and credited to miscellaneous receipts.

If, as proposed in this bill, all lands and resources are turned over to the States, it would mean the end of Federal reclamation and Federal conservation.

By the act of June 17, 1902 (32 Stat., 388), all moneys, except the 5 per centum heretofore set aside by law to the States for educational purposes, were set aside and appropriated as a reclamation fund for the examination, construction, and maintenance of irrigation works in the Western States. Since that time $208,217,323 has been expended by the Federal Government from this fund in connection with reclamation projects in the Western States. It is estimated that it will require $90,000,000 to complete the projects heretofore authorized and undertaken.

The conservation of the natural resources of the public domain, and particularly such exhaustible resources as timber, oil, gas, coal, shale, potash, phosphate and sodium, became the subject of widespread interest and discussion during the administration of President Roosevelt, and the importance of the adoption of a general policy with respect thereto resulted in the reservation of timbered areas for the preservation and perpetuation of national forests and the protection of stream flow. This was followed, as the value and necessity of a sensible and uniform policy as to deposits of oil, gas, shale, coal, potash, phosphate and sodium in the public domain became apparent, by the enactment of the potash leasing act and of the general leasing act of February 25, 1920, which enactment was preceded by eight years of thorough consideration by the Congress. The same year Congress adopted a national policy with respect to water power development of the public lands, reservations and navigable streams.

These laws permit of a broad and uniform policy for the care, preservation, development, and use of the resources described. They are designed to procure the maximum of production with the minimum of waste. They permit of development under a uniform policy of skilled supervision, beneficial alike to the individuals engaged in the development and to the public which uses the products. Moreover, such a policy is calculated to prevent monopoly, as well as to prolong the life and use of exhaustible resources.

With exhaustion of soils by continued cultivation, with insufficient fertilization, the necessity for the utilization of the large deposits of phosphate and potash in the public domain becomes increasingly important. It is believed that these resources should be retained, conserved, and developed for the general good, under the policies already adopted and herein outlined.

As indicated herein, and in previous reports, very liberal grants of lands have been made to the western States. The States of Arizona, California, Colorado, Idaho, Montana, New Mexico, Oregon, Utah, Washington, and Wyoming have received grants aggregating 64,420,337 acres. Moreover, as stated herein, I am now preparing a bill to grant the minerals in numbered school sections for the support of common schools, thus increasing the value of the grants heretofore made.

The remaining public lands and resources should, in my opinion, continue subject to use, development, and disposition under existing laws, with such improvements therein as may be from time to time approved by Congress, and I therefore recommend that Senate Bill No. 4605 be not enacted.

Yours very truly,

HUBERT WORK,

Secretary of the Interior.

"Public Domain," as used in the above table, means unreserved and unappropriated lands now open to entry by citizens under the various land laws, 180,-000,000 acres.

"Public Lands" mean all lands under Federal ownership and control, including the reserved areas, 235,-000,000 acres. Total, 415,000,000 acres. These figures vary from day to day, month to month, and, year to year, sometimes enlarging and sometimes diminishing, by reason of failures of entries, withdrawals and restorations.

CHAPTER XXIII.

Recapitulation—The Case in Behalf of the States.

CESSION: The States should be ceded all of the unreserved and unappropriated public land with all the resources contained on or in them. The Forest Reserves should be made over to the States. Water Power Sites should be conveyed to the States. The States should have complete jurisdiction over the Indian Reservations.

The National Parks should remain under federal control. They should not be further enlarged.

SURFACE RIGHTS: There is value in the surface rights of the approximately 180,000,000 acres of unreserved public land, including areas withdrawn but not reserved, with a great potential value in those areas where sub-surface water may be developed, and in those areas possible of dry farming to the amount of perhaps 50 million acres of sagebrush and grass land.

MINERAL RIGHTS: Nevertheless, the states should insist upon the ceding of the minerals as well as the surface. They should not be separated and should both be in the control of the States. Vested interests would not be disturbed. Existing rights, leases, permits, entries and locations would remain intact. The status and province of the Government with relation thereto would simply be transferred to the States.

TERMS OF MINERAL LEASES BY THE STATE: The States, if given the lands and minerals, can and should be more liberal than the federal government, as to minerals now under the mineral leasing law, in the royalties and other terms of permits and leases, including a longer term on leases than is now provided by some of our States. A 10-20 year term the same as present Federal leases, and a reasonable royalty graduated downward on small wells, would aid the oil industry and at the same time bring more into the State treasuries, as they would receive all instead of a portion of the royalties. The same principle of reasonable royalty and long-time should be applied to coal, phosphate, sodium and potash leases.

NEW STATE LEGISLATION, IF CESSION IS MADE: It should be understood that new legislation will have to be enacted by the States and a comprehensive plan put into effect covering the administration of the newly ceded lands. While they cannot change the enabling act and conditions of the old grants, there should not be opposition to State ownership because of present unsuitable State land laws. Changes would doubtless be made to more fitting provisions under a new grant. They should of course oppose any unreasonable conditions imposed on the States in the grant from the Government. The States should be left free to legislate as they desire on sales, prices, period of leases, rentals, royalties, homesteads and mining locations and patents, and to apply the income as they deem wise.

MINERAL LEASING ACT: Until the lands and minerals are ceded to the States, the Public Land States should have in full operation the federal mineral leasing act, as was intended by Congress.

OTHER MINERALS: The grant with minerals when made to the States, should not be conditioned on the State retaining title to all minerals. If required by Congress as a condition, title can be kept in the

States under a lease and royalty system as to the minerals which are now under the federal leasing law; (coal, oil, oil shale, gas, phosphate, sodium, potash, gilsonite) but as to all other minerals the individual or company should have the right to locate and patent so that title may pass entirely to private ownership.

HOMESTEADER AND MINER: Likewise, if the lands and resources are ceded, the poor man who wishes to establish a home must be allowed to homestead under a liberal State Homestead Law. The miner and the homesteader should be protected and encouraged. Opportunity for the poor man to acquire claims or lands and a home must be preserved . Of such and by such the mines have been discovered, the settlements have come, the wilderness has been subdued, civilization and wealth advanced in the great West.

SALE PRICE: The States should not be required in any act of cession to fix a minimum sales price. The lands which would be ceded should be sold for a low figure per acre up to tracts of 2,560 acres to one purchaser. Transfer to private ownership is the fundamental policy and ultimate purpose. This means conservation, development and taxation, all in the interest of the States.

FOREST RESERVES: As long as the Forest Reserves remain under federal control, all unnecessary regulations and restrictions which hamper the stockman in running his stock, or the miner in locating and patenting of claims, should be removed. Prospecting on the Reserves which occupy our mountains where the lode minerals are to be found, although allowed by law, has practically ceased because of impractical conditions.

STATE ADMINISTRATION: The States and their representatives in the legislatures have the intelligence and honesty to enact proper State sale, lease, homestead and mining laws and State officials have the wisdom and integrity to administer them.

Those who express fear of "exploitation," "favoritism," "corruption," or "incapacity" of western people to manage their own affairs and administer our resources, or who state that western lands and resources are "for the benefit of all the States," do these people a great and grave injustice. The President of the United States and the Secretary of the Interior have expressly stated in official documents that these Western States are now better qualified to administer their resources than is the Federal Government. Who in the West will claim less for themselves? The fear that the "big fellow" will receive an advantage in some way over the "little fellow" is not well founded. Legislatures and officials will take care of that. No administration could afford to do otherwise even if there was any inclination which there is no reason to assume.

WATER POWER: The water power sites should belong to the States which now own and control the beds of the streams and the water which gives the power.

NON-TAXATION: Federal non-taxable ownership and control of 55 per cent of their area, and alleged ownership of the waters of these States, should cease in order that Federal bureaucracy may be lessened and Federal dictation shall be entirely withdrawn from the State so far as it relates to our lands, minerals, waters and forests.

FEDERAL AID: The State would still have by right, even though the states owned the lands and resources, their proportionate shares of Federal aid extended to all the States under the policy of national internal improvements. Under the President's plan, the present overproportion of Federal aid in the public land states in the road-building program would continue for at least ten years. U. S. geological, topographical and mineral surveys and research could continue just as such aid is given to agriculture, which is in private ownership. We would not lose these Federal aids.

The States should have, and would have under State ownership, 100 per cent of these proceeds from our resources instead of 25 per cent of forest grazing fees, and 37½ per cent of mineral royalties and public lands sales which they now receive under Federal control. The cost of administration by the States would be a small matter compared to the gain in receipts. The government now retains 10 per cent of mineral royalties and public land sales, a large sum, for the expenses of administration. The States already have the machinery in operation on their present State lands; it will simply need expansion under appropriate legislation.

CONSERVATION: The principle of conservation on which Federal control is based can and will be best applied by the States whose people know that the State's life-blood depends upon the conservation of the range, forests and waters. Further, the States, and not the Federal Government, have the power of regulation of oil and gas production in private ownership as well as on the State lands.

The States will pass appropriate and necessary legislation, if such is needed, to maintain true conservation. Conservation in its true sense does not mean the withdrawal and locking up of resources, but their wise and beneficial development and use.

PUBLIC LAND COMMITTEE: President Hoover for the first time in the history of our country has by active proposal opened the door of opportunity for the States to come into their full inheritance. They can and should now vigorously take advantage of such opportunity and push the door wide open to enter into the full possession and sovereignty through presentation of the facts and equities to Congress. This Public Land Committee was not restricted in its consideration to the proposed transfer of surface rights only, but was free by express instruction to consider and make recommendation upon the whole question of the public domain.

FREE RANGE: Under the accumulated momentum of public opinion, as it has been formed in the populous East, and in parts of the West, some form of regulation based on conservation of the unreserved and unappropriated areas commonly known as the "free range" is inevitable.

Whether it be true or not that the grazing capacity of the range has, because of lack of regulation, been reduced on the average of 50 per cent (and it has not been so reduced), regulation cannot be longer deferred. If western stockmen will be shortly compelled to accept either federal or state regulation, which means, so far as the government is concerned, the imposition of grazing fees under leases or permits, clearly they would naturally prefer paying such fees into the State treasury and have the State thus receive 100 per cent of such fees, also thereby reducing the amount necessary to be raised by taxation, rather than to pay them into the national treasury, from

GRAND CANYON—ARIZONA
Courtesy Chamber of Commerce, Tucson

which the States would be repaid but 25 per cent, if, as contemplated, the public lands are placed under regulation and administration of the Forest Service. The government is committed to the policy of charging the "commercial value" of grazing, hence it must apply that policy to the vast grazing area it now seeks to regulate. The State can do better both for itself and the stockgrower.

STATE SUPERVISION: Sympathetic and understanding State supervision is infinitely preferable to the autocratic, long-distance federal surveillance and dictation. The livestock industry should, therefore, support States ownership of lands and resources.

PROGRESS: In the last few years during which has been advocated the ceding of the public domain to the States many in both parties agreed that it would be a great thing if it could be accomplished.

Today under the direction of the President of the United States and appropriation of Congress a Committee on Conservation and Administration of the Public Domain has studied the whole subject of the public lands and given the President their recommendations.

They suggest and concede, subject to the action of Congress, the ceding of 180,000,000 acres, in fee simple right to the States.

Further, the Committee has recommended the ceding, in time, of mineral resources as well. The Congress has the power to and will, if the proper kind of a fight is made, include minerals without reservations in a cession. The Secretary of the Interior has gone so far as to say that eventually it may prove the wisest course to have the States own and administer the Forest Reserves. Today, then the question is before the nation and before Congress and there is opportunity to win the fight. The States should be of one mind in favor of State ownership of lands and minerals.

ALTERNATIVES: The one complete relief from constantly recurring and permanent restrictions upon State development by the Federal departments is State ownership and control, with the object of disposition by the State of the lands to private ownership under liberal State laws.

There are two alternatives, which could be accepted with profit to the States so far as non-mineral lands are concerned which would comprise the bulk of the 180,000,000 acres in these States, of unreserved area.

The first alternative is a direct sale by the Federal Government to individuals of such lands at a nominal price of 50 cents to $1.25 per acre according to classification with payment extending over a term of years.

The second alternative is to increase the area of a stock raising homestead from 640 acres to 1,280 acres, or 2,560 acres, and permitting present owners of homesteads to increase their holdings to that acreage.

Either of these plans would be good, as far as they go, but we would still have the problem of the mineral lands to be ceded to the States. Either of those alternative plans would also require an act of Congress.

MINERAL WEALTH: The question before us involves the ownership and future income from incalculable riches. The United States Geological Survey and the State Geological Department estimate the known mineral resources of all the public lands at billions of dollars. This is a vast patrimony which the States of the public domain should secure for their children's children and for the future generations.

It will take great private capital and years to produce even an appreciable quantity of these resources but there will be substantial income from the beginning (100 per cent royalties where they have been receiving but 37½ per cent) and greater permanent income as time passes, from sales, leases and royalties all of which will go into the States instead of the federal treasury. Had the States owned the minerals they would have received $80,000,000 in royalties, instead of $30,000,000 since 1920 on the minerals included in the mineral leasing act. Had the States owned the forests they would have received $44,000,000 instead of $11,000,000.

STATES' RIGHTS: The Western States have been and are believers in a strong national, central government. Their people believe in the Union. Washington, Hamilton, Marshall, Webster, Clay and Lincoln are the leaders whose principles they in the main have followed and still follow. They oppose the pre-Civil-war idea of States' rights which was that a State could nullify a Federal law. But there are States' rights provided by the Constitution and specifically reserved by it "to the States or to the people." They uphold such rights and oppose the exercise of rights by the Federal Government not specifically granted to it, in accordance with the Tenth Amendment. Under this principle, they urge State Sovereignty. Permanent Federal ownership, control, or trusteeship over immense areas within a State, unless consented to by its legislature and secured by purchase, are contrary to the letter and spirit of the Constitution, and are an injustice and reflection on the intelligence and character of our people.

PROCEDURE: The Government through Congress must act first. Under the Federal Constitution the United States offers the grant. Under each State Constitution the State accepts or rejects or fails to accept the offer. The States should unite in securing the grant without conditional provisions. The legislature of each State can determine for itself and its people whether to accept or not.

STATE MEMORIALS: The States of Wyoming, Washington, Oregon, California, and others, through the solemn acts and memorials of their Legislatures voted for by members of both parties have gone on record in memorializing Congress to cede all the lands and resources to the State. The petition and arguments of these States, have doubtless been a factor in determining President Hoover in advocating a change of public land policy in favor of the States. The Governors of 22 States have petitioned Congress to cede the unreserved lands.

Reclamation.

STORAGE DAMS: In the readjustment of the Reclamation Act the Western States should strongly support President Hoover by every means in their power in his suggestion submitted to the Western Governors and to his Commission that storage dams should be constructed at every feasible natural dam site by the federal government as a part of the federal program with incidental flood control and then be made over without cost to the States where located, leaving to the States the construction of the distributing system where irrigation is possible and leaving for repayment by the settlers on reclamation projects only the costs of the distributing system.

FLOOD CONTROL: The whole problem of flood control on the Mississippi, under the present act, should be solved by a system of storage dams on all of the tributaries from the highest to the lowest branches rather than by a costly, inefficient, additional system of levees or canals on the lower trunk of the river. Levees have been tried for fifty years and have been found wanting. The present levees should now be supplemented by reservoir impoundment of flood waters on the tributaries. The "run-off" waters should be controlled at or near their sources.

OPPOSITION: The arid States have every right to have every acre susceptible of irrigation put under water. Powerful influences have attacked reclamation and opposed it in Congress on the entirely mistaken theory that it adds to the farm problem by additional production. Irrigation projects do not add to the exportable crops which are alleged to be over-produced. Irrigation projects in the main raise specialized and other crops, of which $800,000,000 worth are imported annually.

Even if the staple crops, hay, wheat, corn, barley and oats, were not all needed and consumed on the projects as they are, and even if they were in competition with other agricultural States, which they are not, since they are needed at home to carry the livestock through the winter seasons, and to fatten them for market, still the arid states have a right to have 5 per cent of their total area (all that can be irrigated) made agricultural land by the application of water in view of the fact that the older, natural rainfall States have 100 per cent of their area capable of producing. They must combat the widespread, untrue and unjust propaganda against reclamation and insist on irrigation to the maximum limit of their irrigable area. This means and needs energetic defense and offense.

FUND: In this connection, let it be understood that if the States are ceded their lands and resources and the States thereby collect and retain all royalties and proceeds of sales which under the present system go in part to the reclamation fund (52½%), federal reclamation will not cease. Areas withdrawn for reclamation projects are not a part of the unreserved and unappropriated public land to be ceded. The present settlers on government reclamation projects are repaying into the revolving fund over $6,000,000 per year. This amount will steadily increase to probably $7,000,-000 or $8,000,000. The revolving fund to be thus repaid will soon be over $240,000,000.

Again, if the government builds all storage dams as a part of flood control, and they are paid for out of flood control appropriations, not nearly so large a federal reclamation fund would be needed; but there would still be a federal reclamation fund.

WATER: The claim of the Department of Justice that the streams and waters of the States belong to the government must be actively resisted and fought until the question is permanently settled in favor of the States.

Compensation.

Because of the change of policy of our government in the last thirty years from the principle of disposition of lands and resources to the private ownership of the people, to that of permanent reservations of more than one-fourth of the area of the public land states and the proposed federal regulation of another fourth of their area under conditions which will forever preclude acquirement by and transfer to the citizens of our country, the States are now entitled to ask and receive from the general government the ownership and complete sovereignty over all lands and resources within their borders, surface and subsurface.

If, however, the Congress of the United States refuses to cede the 235,000,000 acres of reserved lands, principally forest lands, on the mistaken ground that the nation alone can preserve them for "all the people" then the least that can be done in payment and recompense is to cede the 180,000,000 acres of unreserved area (the residue of the billion and a quarter acres sold by the government for over $600,000,000), poor in surface values as compared to that disposed of, with the minerals therein as in part commensurate value with the 150,000,000 acres of Forest Reserves in the West.

If no cession of both or either is made, then since the property within the States which could and would have passed to private ownership and taxation under the wise policy applied for a century, of which the now non-public-land States received the full benefit, is to be permanently held by the Government as nontaxable land, in immense permanent reservations, the States would be justified in asking payment from the general government representing "all the people," for whose benefit the lands are withheld from the States in which they lie or their part of the people; or an annual income on the basis of their value with their resources developed, in lieu of immense sums lost to the States by reason of their inability to tax them. Even this would not be commensurate with the loss of independence, sovereignty, and right to develop.

CHAPTER XXIV.

Reclamation.

From time immemorial the human race has occupied desert lands and builded civilizations upon them. This was possible only through a system of diversion of the waters of streams by means of canals and ditches, thus spreading them out over the arid areas.

The ancient nations of Babylon and Assyria were founded upon lands thus reclaimed by irrigation by the waters of the Euphrates and the Tigris. Egypt erected her civilization upon a system of inundated lands from the waters and silt of the Nile. The remnants of irrigation ditches are found and even used which were built by the ancient Mayan and Aztec races in Mexico and Central America. All the great modern nations having control over alien desert countries have inaugurated and are carrying on vast reclamation enterprises.

In modern times technical engineering has extended irrigation, from the old basis of merely diverting water from the stream bed, through the erection of huge dams at natural dam and reservoir sites to impound enormous quantities of flood waters in the spring of each year when the rains, and snows precipitated through the winter season at high mountainous altitudes flow to and down the streams.

The United States has its arid region extending from the plains east of the Rocky Mountains westward to the Pacific. This arid or semi-arid area comprises one-third of the total area of the United States proper. In this area the annual average moisture precipitation by rain and snow is but eighteen inches.

This is insufficient for cultivation and agricultural crops. Many of the eleven western States covering this area have but twelve to fourteen inches of moisture a year. The average is brought up by the extraordinary rain and snow-fall of the states of Washington and Oregon on and west of the Cascades.

By 1902 the limit of private irrigation from and along the streams and tributaries had practically been reached. The great storage projects were too costly for private capital. There were millions of acres of sage-brush and grass-covered plains upon which the waters could be diverted only by the erection of dams hundreds of feet in height in the canyons and gorges. These lands belonged to the Government. Thereupon the Congress of the United States, in 1902, under Theodore Roosevelt, inaugurated the system of Federal reclamation to make these sterile but fertile lands capable of production. This was in continuance of the highly successful policy of homesteading, begun in 1862. The tide of people seeking homes had reached to the arid regions. Reclamation by the government was legally upheld as the right of the Sovereign to improve its own lands for habitation and acquirement by its citizens.

The financial policy to carry on this beneficial national enterprise was that the receipts from the sale of public lands should be desposited in a fund designated as the Reclamation Fund. This was to be and is a revolving fund, annually restored by the payment by settlers of fixed charges on construction and operation and maintenance costs aggregating yearly an average of about $4.00 to $6.00 per acre, the whole, without interest, payable in a maximum period of 40

years. The fund thus replenished from year to year
is used in the construction of new projects.

In 1902, under the Mineral Leasing act of February 25th, the royalties collected by the Government
on minerals produced under Federal permits and
leases were dedicated and applied to the Reclamation
Fund. These lands and minerals were situated in the
western States so that the fund was provided by the
States themselves. It was not and is not raised by
general taxation.

Under this policy there have been erected since
1902 twenty-nine reclamation projects, with at least
one in each of the western States, at a total expenditure to June 30, 1930, of $239,292,144.27. Under these
projects there is an irrigable acreage of 1,922,330; an
irrigated acreage of 1,483,900; a cropped acreage of
1,512,250. These figures do not include an acreage of
privately owned lands to which the Government sold
water under the Warren Act. Crediting to Warren
Act lands irrigable acreage of 1,480,040; irrigated acreage, 1,234,230; cropped acreage 1,192,990, the grand
totals of the foregoing classifications are respectively
3,402,370; 2,718,130; 2,705,880.

The crop value produced on the Government projects in the year 1929 was $88,459,390. The crop value
produced on Warren Act lands to which waters were
sold by the Federal Government was $72,720,490. The
total value of crops produced by government irrigation
in the single year 1929 was $161,179,880. This was
an average crop value per acre of $58.49 on project
lands, and $60.76 on Warren Act lands; making an
average of $59.72 per acre. The average per acre
crop value of non-irrigated farm lands in the United

States is approximately $27.00. This forcibly illustrates the efficiency and benefit of scientific irrigation.

Since 1906, when the first crops were raised, the total value of crops on government projects up to and including 1929, was $1,037,037,890. The value of crops on Warren Act lands during the period since 1918, when such sales of water began, is $605,229,790. The total of both classes of crop values to and including 1929 was $1,642,267,680.

Thus it is seen that the total crop value of the one year of 1929, $161,179,490, was approximately 70 per cent of the grand total of all expenditures of the Government on twenty-nine projects in twenty-nine years, $239,292,144.27.

There are on all the projects 39,970 farms, 157,088 population on these farms; 214 towns with a population of 473,073; 686 schools, 713 churches; 130 banks, with a total capital stock of $11,180,000; deposits of $145,386,400; number of depositors, 245,181. It is estimated that all the projects consume $600,000,000 a year of manufactured goods and other products. These are shipped from every State in the union.

The character of the crops produced is largely special, not coming in competition with the staple products of the rest of the States. They do not add to the crops of which we are alleged to have an overproduction. Such crops are needed and consumed at home. They do not reach the general markets.

Of the specialized crops and other crops that can be raised in this country we still import from other countries under our tariffs to the value of $800,000,000 per year. Projects are consumers and importers from other States of wheat, corn and cotton, the supposed surplus crops, and are producers of many products needed by our people, of which vast quantities are purchased from abroad. Under such a condition the policy of reclamation should be cordially supported by the North, East and South, instead of mistakenly opposed as has been the case in some quarters. Finally, the total amount produced on all the projects is only ¾ths of 1 per cent of the total production of the United States. Hence, even if it was competitive with general agriculture, the amount is insignificant compared to the total. Yet it is of tremendous importance to the western States.

The total land area of these States is 753,067,000 acres. The farmed and cropped area is only 44,229,000. Of this cropped area 19,600;000 acres, approximately one-half, is irrigated privately or governmentally, the balance being nearly all dry-farm land and cut-over timber lands.

Elwood Mead, Commissioner of Reclamation, estimates that the maximum of new irrigable lands in the arid States is 10,000,000 acres, that being the limit of the water supply. This, added to the present irrigated lands, makes a possible total maximum of 30,000,000 acres, which is but 4 per cent of the total area of the eleven western States. Contrast this with the rest of the States which have 100 per cent of crop productive lands. 19,000,000 acres of the public domain have been withdrawn for existing and proposed reclamation projects.

It is estimated that, with a growth of population 3½ times faster than the whole of the United States, the present population of the eleven States of the West, 10,000,000 to 11,000,000, will increase to 25,000,000 in the next 3 years.

They will need and consume vastly greater amounts of the products raised on irrigated lands. Hence it is apparent that there should be no cessation of reclamation construction. The imperative agricultural development of the West lies in the extension of irrigation. In dry years these additional acres may prove an important and much needed source of supply to drouth stricken areas. In these same western States are now 8 per cent of the population, 65 per cent of the lumber, 9 per cent of the copper, 50 per cent of the lead, 35 per cent of the zinc and 53 per cent of the water power of the nation. These resources will make growth inevitably and at once demand sources of food and living products to the full extent of the irrigation possibilities.

This is not a local problem and need; it is national. The nation will need the West's beef, mutton, wool, and its special crops of fruit, long staple cotton and sugar beets. At the same time the West will thus provide an enormous market for the products, especially manufactures, of the rest of the country.

If the question be asked why these States cannot construct their own reclamation projects without governmental assistance the answer is that they can and will if they or their people owned or could own their lands and resources, or if the Government paid taxes on the vast areas and resources it still holds and controls and withholds from the States and their peoples. The West contains in addition to the minerals heretofore enumerated practically all of the Federal reserves of timber, coal, phosphates, potash, oil and gas. It is the withholding of all these resources and their non-taxation that makes impossible the financing of its irrigation projects by the West.

This brings us to the record of the money which has been expended by the Government in the building of reclamation projects. There have come into the Reclamation Fund since the beginning, June 17, 1902, to June 30, 1930, a total of $240,333,138.02.

Of this amount $110,332,537.76 has been from the sale of public lands and $38,285,947.38 from the mineral royalties under the federal mineral leasing act of 1920. $59,360.35 has been received from Federal water power licenses and $68,296.51 from royalties and rentals from potassium deposits.

The receipts from sale of public lands have steadily reduced until, in the fiscal year ending June 30, 1930, they were only $690,563.36. The receipts into the Reclamation Fund from royalties in the same period were $2,417,000, 3½ times as much, and the repayments from settlers, $6,215,070.24, nearly 9 times as great. Thus 67 per cent of the yearly income to the fund is from project collections, 26 per cent from mineral royalties and 7 per cent from other sources.

The annual sum to be repaid by the settlers on the projects, and they are the real builders and financiers of these great works, will steadily increase. They are the main reliance of the future maintenance of the fund from year to year. They have obligated themselves to pay and will pay back to the fund, and thus to the Government, all of the $240,000,000 expended thus far, except certain amounts charged off because of bad lands included and later excluded from projects, and all that is to be expended in the future activities of the federal policy. They have repaid $39,438,243.93, which is 96 per cent of the amount due under the plan of repayment.

It is thus apparent that reclamation will not cease

even if the mineral resources, from which royalties are now derived for the fund, 26 per cent, should be made over to the States. In addition it is proposed to pay into the Reclamation Fund the net receipts from power plants built in the future. The fund derives no income from the unreserved, unappropriated, vacant 180,000,000 acres, which is now proposed to be granted to the States. Therefore the fund will not be affected by such cession.

One of the incidental sources of income to the Reclamation Fund is from the net proceeds from the 23 power plants which have been built in connection with the projects. These plants were originally constructed to furnish electrical power used in the construction of the projects. They were economically justified for construction purposes alone. But after construction was completed and even before completion it was found that their surplus current could be sold to adjacent towns and industries, after providing electricity on the projects to the settlers. Thus during the fiscal year 1929-30 gross power sales were $3,550,804.46. The net proceeds from power are credited to the account of the settlers on the construction costs, since they obligated themselves to pay for the power plant, as a part of the project. When construction costs are all repaid the Irrigation Districts own the plants or their proceeds as a part of the project or are entitled to all the net proceeds in the future under the provisions of the general reclamation law.

The Reclamation service now desires, and the Committee on Conservation and Administration of the Public Domain has recommended in their Report to the President, that hereafter the law be changed so as to provide for the payment of the net proceeds from

GRAND TETON MOUNTAINS—WYOMING
Grand Teton National Park. Photo by Sheelor

reclamation power plants, after payment of all costs of the plant and dam, into the Reclamation Fund. This clearly cannot be done on those projects heretofore built, where the settlers were compelled to obligate and have obligated themselves to pay for the power plants as a part of their projects. The Reclamation law directs the Secretary of the Interior to require the settlers to obligate themselves for all costs. There is no authority in the Reclamation Law for building a power plant by the Government except in connection with and as a part of the project. Consequently he must also obligate the settlers, individually, or as districts, organized under State laws, to pay for the power plant as well as the rest of the works and construction costs. Having done so the settlers have a vested right under their contracts to the power plant or its proceeds, first to their credit on construction accounts, then for their own use. This cannot be taken from them even by an act of Congress amending the Reclamation Act, and certainly not by a condition attached to a reclamation appropriation.

If it is sought to change the reclamation law in this regard, and provide in the future for the payment of the net proceeds from new reclamation power plants, after repayment of construction costs, on new projects all of which would then come under the changed law, the cost of the plants should not be charged to the settlers or their organized district. The Reclamation Bureau would have to be authorized to build and operate power plants, independent of the project. Even then the power is generated by the water stored in the dam which the settlers are required to pay for. Without the dam there would be no power plant.

But the most serious question in such proposed

change of the reclamation law and change of disposition of the net proceeds, after payment of construction costs of the power plant and the project, dam and reservoir, including lands covered and taken by condemnation, would arise with regard to the rights of the State where plants are located, for the States are the owners of the stream beds where the dams are built, and of the waters that furnish the power. It would seem that when the Government is fully repaid its constitutional powers over the proceeds cease and the rights of the States attach. On this theory the net receipts, after government repayments, would go to the States.

In considering the reasons for carrying on the policy of reclamation by irrigation it should be remembered that the dams and reservoirs of impounded flood waters are an integral part of a general system of flood control, navigation, and transportation. These, together with irrigation and electrical power are wealth conserving and wealth producing agencies, and of national benefit.

Finally, Reclamation is not only a matter of material wealth production. It is not only the creation of taxable wealth to help sustain the Government for all future times. The great thing is the transformation of the wilderness into civilization. It is the occupation and cultivation by the capital and labor of the settler of the unoccupied lands of this country. It is the establishment of homes. It is the strength of manhood and womanhood contributing to the greatness and safety of the Nation. It is the addition to our population of a splendid, enlightened, industrious citizenship which will enhance and enrich the security, the resources, the welfare of our common country.

CHAPTER XXV.

The Issue as to Ownership of Waters.

First let us take note of the physical facts as to water surface areas. The following figures are of interest and importance as showing the proportionate land and water conditions of the eleven Western States, which, because they contain 97 per cent of the remaining public lands, are contrasted with the remaining thirty-seven States, although there are nine of the thirty-seven which contain the other 3 per cent of the public lands.

As will be seen in detail in the proper table at the rear of this volume, of the total land area of the eleven Western States of 761,049,600 acres, 753,420,800 acres are land and 7,628,800 are water. Of the total land area of the other thirty-seven States of 1,168,476,560 acres, 1,142,241,280 are land and 26,235,280 are water. The percentage of water surface to land surface in the eleven Western States is .01, or one-hundredth part, while the percentage of water to land in the remaining States is .023, or two and three-tenths hundredth part.

For every 100 acres of land in the eleven Western States there is approximately one acre of water; while in the remaining States for every 100 acres of land there are 2.3 acres of water.

The non-arid States have therefore nearly two and a third times as much water surface relatively to land surface than the arid States.

The average mean annual rainfall in the eleven western public land States is 18 inches while the remaining 37 States have 40 inches.

It is therefore of the utmost importance to the

eleven Public Land States that their water resources be conserved, the flood waters stored by dams and reservoirs and all used to the utmost of their service. When this is all done there will be but 5 per cent of the area of these States made crop productive compared to practically 100 per cent in the rainfall states.

From the time of the admission of the first of these States in and west of the Rocky Mountain region, and the adoption of their constitutions, consented to by Congress in the enabling acts, the ownership and control of their waters have been claimed by and considered to be in those States.

Of late years, but especially since the Wyoming-Colorado case, (259 U. S. 419, 66 Law. ed. 999) was presented to the Supreme Court of the United States, June, 1922, in which it was first suggested by brief of attorneys for the Government, the Department of Justice has urged the theory and claim of Federal ownership of the non-navigable waters, where the Government owns the land, and has brought suit in the Federal Court of several of these States alleging such ownership. These suits are pending.

Naturally the arid States have strenuously resisted such claim and policy, as involving control of their life's blood and taking from them a fundamental right.

The report of the Committee recommends Interstate agreements covering water control and elimination of theories of Federal ownership and control.

This again calls attention to the fact that the Department of the Interior through its Reclamation Service has advanced the claim that the Government always was the owner of the waters, having received title to lands and waters by cession from other nations; that it now is the owner of the unnavigable water resources

of the country adjacent to the public lands; and that
this is true in the Western States as well as other
States.

The theory is that having thus been the original
owner of the land, and consequently, of the waters in
the lands, by purchase and cession direct to the United States, it could never have been divested of its title
except by grant, and that no single Act of Congress,
nor all acts taken together, whether in recognizing
miners and local customs, Federal statutes or in the
Enabling Acts, the Constitutions of the States, the
Desert Act, the Reclamation Law, the Water Power
Act, constitute such a grant.

Following are quotations from the Government brief
in the case of Wyoming vs. Colorado:

Because of its fugitive nature, the only property rights
which exist in water in its natural state are rights of use, the
corpus being only susceptible of ownership while in possession. This corpus, while in possession, is personal property;
but the right of use of the water in its natural state is a real
property right of the highest dignity and value.

Because of the necessity of protecting the public interests
therein (mainly navigation and fishery), property rights in
navigable waters in England belonged prima facie to the
Crown, and in this country they belong prima facie to the
municipal sovereignties, the states. The Federal government,
though having full control (under the commerce clause) for
purposes of foreign and interstate navigation, has no rights of
property in such waters or their shores or beds except as it
derives it from the states, either by grant or under operation
of state law.

The crux of the question is whether non-navigable waters
are publici juris, like navigable waters. Ownership by the
states depends upon showing that they are. Such waters are
not publici juris, and ownership of usufructuary rights therein
rests upon the same basis and is of the same character as
ownership of land.

Water rights in non-navigable waters, being vested rights
in real property, the state has the same control over them as,
and no greater control than, over vested rights in land. Regulation under the police power should not be confused, as it
often is, with rights of property in the state, or any denial of
property rights in the individual.

Water rights now vested in others derive their existence, like titles to land, from the acts of Congress. All interest in water not so granted necessarily remains in the United States. The acts grant nothing to the states, and ratification of state constitutions asserting state ownership of water does not divest the United States of its property rights therein.

Let it be understood at once that there is no contention on this point as to those States, and this includes practically all of them east of the Missouri River, where the doctrine of riparian rights obtains exclusively, based on the Common Law, and there are no public lands. The contention arises when we consider the semi-arid and arid public land States where the government is still the owner of land and in which the doctrine of prior appropriation is in force, and "riparian rights" are either given only equal status with appropriation, or ignored, rejected by custom, precedent, and by implication, or by express provision in State constitutions or statutes.

By riparian right is meant that the owner of land bordering on a stream or body of water, has the right to have it continue to flow or stand undiminished, unchanged and uncontaminated from its condition at the time the original and first owner took title and to make use of such waters limited only by the similar rights of other owners of land on the stream; that this right followed the title to all subsequent owners.

Two fundamental things in the West demanded a change from the old Common Law Doctrine of riparian rights; these were, first the mining industry, and secondly, agriculture by irrigation. Water was and is essential to both. The necessity for a change arose in mining in California after the discovery of gold in 1848. Later the demands of agriculture by reclamation increased until in most of the arid states it became more important than mining.

Both necessitated the diversion of water from streams and lakes out of and away and considerable distance from the channel or bed, to the place of application and use. Therefore, from sheer necessity, from force of circumstances, from the fact that an immense part of the United States could not develop in its most important basic industries unless diversion of water was permitted the theory of right of use by diversion through prior appropriation was adopted in those States.

It began with the customs and rules adopted by miners in California. Later these were augmented by like practices of diversion of water and rights by priority of use of water by the agriculturists. Then after a few years came Acts of Congress acquiescing in and recognizing these rules and customs. Decisions of the Supreme Courts of the various new Territories and States sustained the whole theory of right by prior appropriation and use. These decisions were later based also on the Enabling Acts by which Territories became States, in which Congress consented to the Constitutions of the Western States containing specific or implied repudiation of the doctrine of riparian rights, and in some cases express provisions asserting the law of appropriation.

This appropriation doctrine, of, by and for the arid and semi-arid States was next recognized and settled by decisions of the Federal Courts:

The water in an unnavigable stream flowing over the public domain is a part thereof, and the national government can sell or grant the same, or the use thereof, separate from the rest of the estate, under such circumstances as may seem to it proper. Howell v. Johnson. 89. Fed. 556.

The California Doctrine, as distinguished from the Colorado Doctrine, which will be analyzed further on, is that an appropriation of water constitutes a grant from the United States to the appropriator. This was originally implied from the silent acquiescence of the United States. See Smith v. Hawkins, 110 Cal. 122; Pac. 453, and cases cited.

And see Pomeroy on Riparian Rights, Sec. 32 and Kinney on Irrigation, Secs. 147, 188, in support of the further proposition that the Grantor, the United States, had the power to and did impose conditions on the grant to the appropriator; that, recognizing the conditions of early customs of miners in California, it imposed those conditions. One of the important conditions was beneficial use.

The California Doctrine further in brief is that the laws of appropriation and of riparian rights can and do exist side by side under the Common Law, and that relative rights under either and both are fixed by priority. The same view is held in Oregon, Washington, Montana, North Dakota, Nebraska, Texas, Kansas, and South Dakota. Lux vs. Huggins, 69 Cal. 255, 10 Pac. 674, restored riparian rights to an equal position with appropriation. It is claimed this view was applied in the Supreme Court of the United States in Sturr v. Beck, 133 U. S. 541.

It will be observed that the first theory is held in semi-arid States, with much developed agriculture, while the second is declared in the arid States with limited agriculture. In the first list of States will be recognized States where natural dry farming exists to a considerable extent. In the second, those States which are dependent for agriculture on extensive storage and diversions of water for large irrigation projects.

Again, there is a geographic difference in the two lists; the first are Pacific Coast and plains States, the second are Rocky Mountain and Valley States. This suggests that the systems are each following different fundamental conditions of necessity, in altitude, topography, climate and aridity, just as in the beginning both groups were and still are united by necessity of diversion of waters in originating the doctrine of appropriation; and both groups to that extent denying the exclusive application of the riparian common law.

Appropriations under the California system hold that they deraign their titles under the Federal Statutes hereinbefore referred to. The Supreme Court of the United States in Broder vs. Natoma Water Co., 101 U. S. 274, held:

We are of the opinion that it is the established doctrine of this court that rights of miners, who had taken possession of mines and worked and developed them, and the rights of persons who had constructed canals and ditches to be used in mining operations and for purposes of agricultural irrigation, in the region where such artificial use of the water was an absolute necessity, are rights which the government had, by its conduct, recognized and encouraged and was bound to protect before the passage of the act of 1866, and that the section of the act which we have quoted was rather a voluntary recognition of a pre-existing right of possession, constituting a valid claim to its continued use, than the establishment of a new one.

The United States Supreme Court has further construed these statutes in Basey v. Gallagher, 87 U. S. 670, 22 L. ed. 452, as follows:

It is very evident that Congress intended, although the language used is not happy, to recognize as valid the customary law with respect to the use of water which had grown up among the occupants of the public land under the peculiar necessities of their condition; and that law may be shown by evidence of the local customs, or by the legislation of the State or Territory, or by the decisions of the Court. The union of the three conditions in any particular case is not essential to the perfection of the right by priority; and in case of conflict between a local custom and a statutory regulation, the latter, as of superior authority, must necessarily control.

The Colorado View, first, denies the doctrine of riparian rights; secondly, does not ground its system of appropriation on the title of the government but on the proposition that the Common Law did not fit and was unworkable under the conditions of the West and that the settlers established only such part of the Common Law as harmonized with their necessities in the new land; thirdly, it questions whether the United States, though the original owner of the land, ever had riparian rights for the simple reason that the local law never recognized riparian rights.

It followed of course, if these propositions were well grounded, that when public lands of the United States passed into private ownership the private owner could not succeed to a right or title from his grantor which did not exist. The conclusion therefore, is that the right of the appropriator comes from the State, which received its right by its constitution and statutes; and that the United States having consented to such constitution which declared ownership of the State in all of its waters, thus waiving all rights it might have had, if any, is not in a position to make any claim whatsoever to the waters.

The cases upholding the above views are presented in the case of Willey vs. Decker, 11 Wyo. 32. 100 Am. St. Rep. 925, 70 Pac. 726, wherein the Court said: "In this State, on the other hand, the Common Law Doctrine concerning the rights of a riparian owner has been held to be unsuited to our conditions, and this Court has declared that the rule never obtained in this jurisdiction" and cited Moyer vs. Preston, 6 Wyo. 308, 71 Amer. St. Rep. 914, 44 Pac. 845.

The Supreme Courts of Nevada, Arizona, Utah, Colorado, and other states of this group declared similar views.

In the Wyoming case above quoted the decisions of these States are reviewed. Among such citations and quotations is the following from the Supreme Court of Arizona:

The leading case in Arizona is Clough v. Wing, 2 Ariz. 371, 17 Pac. 453. In that case it is said that the problem to be solved in the arid portions of the earth has not been how best to drain the water off the land and get rid of it, but how to save it to be conducted upon land in aid of the husbandman. The learned judge who wrote the opinion refers to the antiquity of irrigation in that section of country and in other lands, and remarks: "Thus we see that this is the oldest method of skilled husbandry, and probably a large number of the human race have ever depended upon artificial irrigation for their food products. The riparian rights of the common law could not exist under such systems; and a higher antiquity, a better reason, and more beneficent results have followed from the doctrine that all right in water in non-navigable streams must be subservient to its use in tilling the soil." And further, it is said that the common law, so far as the same applied to the use of water, "has never been, and is not now, suited to conditions that exist here."

A distinction has been suggested that the right of ownership of water does not exist, but only the right of the use, the usufructuary right. The Supreme Court of Idaho, in Boise, etc. Co. v. Stewart, 77 Pac. 25, rested upon this theory.

Against the proposition of the California idea that the United States was the first owner of all the lands and waters, and therefore its grantees took its title to the waters with the lands and that no State law or custom could take away such right, the Wyoming Court answered that the State's Constitution declared the State's ownership of its waters and denied riparian rights; that the Congress ratified that constitution, thus irrevocably consenting to the system of State ownership and appropriation. Again, the exclusively appropriation States meet the proposition that grantees from the United States took title to water from the Government with the statement that federal sanction of the claims of the States, and waiver of any rights it may have had are contained in Sections 2339 and 2340 of the Revised Statutes of the United States (Acts of 1866 and 1870). It is declared by the Courts of those States holding the Colorado viewpoint that those sections negative all other rights except those in the State and derived from the State.

It is claimed on behalf of the California view that the Supreme Court of the United States has applied their construction in Sturr vs. Beck, 133 U. S. 541; but on the other hand there is nothing in that case to preclude the Supreme Court from also applying the Colorado system and construing the federal statutes referred to as following and ratifying the local customs, laws and decisions of the Courts in the jurisdictions of that group; that the United States in handling certain tracts of arid lands supported the laws of appropriation, as stated in Farm etc. Co. vs. Carpenter, 9 Wyo. 110, 61 Pac. 747:

If any consent of the general government was primarily requisite to the inception of the rule of prior appropriation, that consent is to be found in several enactments by Congress, beginning with the act of July 26, 1866, and including the Desert Land Act of March 3, 1877. Those acts have been too often quoted and are too well understood to require a restatement at this time at the expense of unduly extending this opinion."

In order that the reader may have the benefit of the federal statutes referred to they are here inserted:

Rev. Stats., sec. 2339: "Whenever, by priority of possession, rights to the use of water for mining, agricultural, manufacturing or other purposes, have vested and accrued, and the same are recognized and acknowledged by the local customs, laws, and decisions of courts, the possessors and owners of such vested rights shall be maintained and protected in the same; and the right of way for the construction of ditches and canals for the purposes herein specified is acknowledged and confirmed; but whenever any person, in the construction of any ditch or canal, injures or damages the possession of any settler on the public domain, the party committing such injury or damage shall be liable to the party injured for such injury or damage."

Rev. Stats., sec. 2340: "All patents granted, or premption or homesteads allowed, shall be subject to any vested and accrued water rights, or rights to ditches and reservoirs used in connection with such water rights, as may have been acquired under or recognized by the preceding section."

Compiled Statutes Section 4674. Proviso to Desert Act. "the right to the use of water by the person so conducting the same, on or to any tract of desert lands of six hundred and forty acres shall depend upon bona fide prior appropriation; and such right shall not exceed the amount of water actually appropriated, and necessarily used for the purpose of irrigation and reclamation: and all surplus waters over and above such actual appropriation and use, together with the water of all lakes, rivers and other sources of water supply upon the public lands, and not navigable, shall remain and be held free for the appropriation and use of the public for irrigation, mining and manufacturing purposes subject to existing rights."

The position of the strictly appropriation States under said federal acts is thus stated by Wiel in "Water Rights in the Western States"; page 65:

The purpose of the Colorado, Wyoming, and similar courts seems to be as follows: That those sections broadly sanctioned a new system. If the local customs, laws and decisions considered waters as owned by the State and ignored riparian rights, then such was the system sanctioned by the Federal government, and such is consequently binding on the government's grantees of land who would otherwise have had riparian rights. That whether riparian rights are abolished depends on the local decisions of each State where local customs, laws, and decisions were sanctioned.

But he further states on page 66:

* * * the California view has this advantage—that it favors the rights of the United States as landowner, and has

been applied by the Supreme Court of the United States, whereas the Colorado view is in derogation of the rights of the United States, and has not been directly passed upon by the Supreme Court of the United States.

However, the following language of Chief Justice White in Gutierres vs. Albuquerque etc. Co., 188 U. S. 545, would seem to indicate that the Supreme Court, if the question comes before it for decision, will support the purely appropriation theory, State ownership and State title of and to waters:

The contentions urged upon our notice substantially resolve themselves into two general propositions: First, that the territorial act was invalid, because it assumed to dispose of property of the United States without its consent; and second, that said statute, in so far, at least as it authorized the formation of corporations of the character of the complaint, was inconsistent with the legislation of Congress and therefore void. These propositions naturally admit of consideration together.

The argument in support of the first proposition proceeds upon the hypothesis that the waters affected by the statute are public waters, the property, not of the Territory or of private individuals, but of the United States; that by the statute private individuals, or corporations, for their mere pecuniary profit, are permitted to acquire the unappropriated portion of such public waters, in violation of the right of the United States to control and dispose of its own property wheresoever situated. Assuming that the appellants are entitled to urge the objection referred to, we think, in view of the legislation of Congress on the subject of the appropriation of water on the public domain, particularly referred to in the opinion of this court in United States v. Rio Grande Dam and Irr. Co., 174 U. S. 704-706, 43 L. ed. 1142, 1143, 19 Sup. Ct. Rep. 770, the objection is devoid of merit. As stated in the opinion just referred to, by the act of July 26, 1866 (14 Stats. at L. 253, c. 262. sec. 9; Rev. Stats. 2339; U. S. Comp. Stats. 1901, p. 1437), Congress recognized, as respects the public domain, "so far as the United States are concerned, the validity of the local customs, laws, and decisions of courts in respect to the appropriation of water."

Let it be noted that the California view does not repudiate but asserts the right of appropriation, the same as the Colorado group, but regards riparian rights as co-existent where the Colorado view declares them abolished.

It would seem clear that inasmuch as the right of appropriation is thus recognized by California and the Courts riparian right doctrines must give way as the two are fundamentally inconsistent, in the judgment of the writer. No stream or body of water once subject to the law of prior appropriation, can remain unchanged in volume, flow, channel, and height, and therefore in use, which is the principle of riparian rights. Once admitted, appropriation replaces and supersedes riparianism.

In either view, in our opinion, the Western States comprising both groups are, we believe, united for State control of all waters and in the belief that it is best for all that the question be finally and forever settled by Act of Congress in favor of the State ownership and jurisdiction of its water and therefore commend and support the recommendation of President Hoover's Committee: That the Federal government abandon its doctrine of federal ownership of the waters of the public land States and retire to its own undisputed constitutional rights relative to water-way inter-state commerce and navigation.

It seems apparent that the ownership and control of the waters should remain in the States in the arid regions where there is public land in vast areas especially now that it is proposed to make the States owners of the public land as well. The foregoing discussion applies even though the surface rights only of the public domain should be ceded.

WILD GAME—UTAH AND WYOMING
Elk Photo by Belden

CHAPTER XXVI.

The Boulder Dam Bill and the Colorado River Compact.

The various questions involved in the construction of dams, particularly on navigable streams by the Federal Government are nowhere more numerously and variously presented and exemplified than in the famous Boulder Dam Bill, under which construction has begun by the Reclamation Service on the $165,000,-000 project, including and incorporating as it does the Colorado River Compact. This legislation involves inter-national relations as the Colorado River flows for ninety miles through Mexico before it empties into the Gulf of California; it includes inter-state relations as seven States are divided or bisected by this mighty stream and its tributaries; it presents relations between the United States and the seven States of Arizona, California, Nevada, comprising the "Lower Division" States, and Colorado, New Mexico, Utah and Wyoming, comprising the "Upper Division" States; it involves compacts between and among States, and consent of Congress thereto; it goes back to the Interstate Commerce Clause as the basis of the Federal function and power delegated by the people in the United States Constitution; (Article 1 Section 8) "The Congress shall have power * * * to regulate Commerce with foreign nations and among the several States and with the Indian tribes."

From that express provision flow the implied powers to maintain navigation, control floods, to prevent floods, (which waste water and destroy life and property and affect navigation) through flood water storage by means of dams and reservoirs on the main stream or on the tributaries, to regulate the flow of water throughout the seasons, keeping it equable and average for water transportation; and incidentally providing power and irrigation as the stored waters are released. Lastly, irrigation projects themselves constitute great underground reservoirs, comprising automatic conservation of water and stabilization of flow as the waters return to the stream bed after use.

Add to these functions those resident in the general Government by reason of its duty "to promote the general welfare" and great Federal Power is apparent.

All of the above named questions of international, national, and State jurisdiction are involved and a discussion of the Bill and Compact may help to clarify the subject of respective rights and powers of the co-operation of the United States—and the several States —under which the magnificent development which has been suggested can go forward, notwithstanding the Government may cease to be owner, holder, controller, landlord, guardian, or trustee over the areas in the public land States; and those States come into full authority and sovereignty by grant of Congress. The subject matter is pertinent to and inseparable from the entire subject of the public lands and their disposition. The principles to be considered are, as to navigable streams, applicable to all projects and developments wherever situated in the United States.

It is not the purpose here to show the physical conditions, length, and volume of the river; the number of States involved; the area of drainage; the need of flood protection; the conditions of the river as to navigability and improvement thereof; the needs of the Imperial Valley for protection from flood and the future reclamation of great additional areas of fertile lands; the needs of the cities of southern California for a supply of stored water from the Colorado, first for domestic use and electrical energy for commercial uses, or the engineering features, and the economic soundness. All these elements have been presented in previous publications.

The bill involves international relations, interstate relations and relations between the United States and the States of the Colorado River Basin.

The right of the United States to build a structure on the Colorado River rests primarily on the interstate-commerce clause of the Constitution, which authorizes the Federal Government by giving it the power of regulating interstate and foreign commerce, to do whatever is necessary to maintain or improve navigation. This may be accomplished by regulating the flow. Regulation of flow is secured by storing flood waters by means of a dam and discharging them in a low-water season.

There is no express provision in the Constitution authorizing the Government to engage in flood control per se, but it is assumed that such a right and duty is included in the power to regulate the flow to benefit navigation to assist interstate commerce.

In the case of the Colorado River, if the Boulder Dam be built it will eventually and permanently regulate the flow and improve navigability from the dam 200 miles south, to the Gulf of California and thus to the Pacific. North of the dam it will create a deep navigable body of water approximately 115 miles in length. At present the River, while practically unnavigated, is navigable in fact and in law. This may be denied, but only a Court can ultimately answer the question.

The question is not whether navigation is actually taking place on the stream. The question is simply and clearly whether it is a navigable stream in fact and in law.

The bill, then, is founded upon the theory, which can not be denied or overthrown, that the Government may proceed, build the Boulder Dam, because: First, an international stream and treaty relations are involved; second, improvement of navigation; third, flood control for protection of life and property.

No matter how much these matters may be minimized, they have been admitted to be in this proposition. Therefore the power and the right and authority of the United States Government to proceed for these purposes can not be questioned. Men might differ and argue as to the amount of money the United States Government ought to invest for these purposes, but they can not question the authority of the Government to do these things in the exercise of these functions.

Thus the dam may be built for the above purposes without the consent of the States of Arizona and Nevada, on whose soil the dam is to be built, or any other State on the river. As amended the title of the bill expressly includes the improvement of navigability.

Much was made of the fact that this had not been in the title of the bill during all of the years this bill was before the committee in Congress. That is immaterial. The question is simply whether or not this stream is a navigable stream at the place where it is proposed to erect the structure. If it is, the Government can proceed, and there is constitutional basis for its action. As passed, it includes protection of the lower Colorado River Basin of flood control.

Next, as to the building of a dam to impound waters for irrigation, the Supreme Court has decided that question and held that it is a constitutional right of the Government to improve its own lands for settlement.

This brings us, however, in contact with the rights of the States. Under the Reclamation Law the Secretary of the Interior complies with the laws of the States regarding the appropriation of water in those States. He obtains a permit from the State to build a dam and create a reservoir within its borders. This is true of the arid States, because the doctrine of riparian rights is abolished and superseded by the doctrine of prior appropriation.

This was provided for in the enabling acts of Congress and the Constitutions of those States and has been recognized by the Congress since 1866 when it conceded and consented to and provided for the regulation of the use of water for mining and irrigation purposes by the local laws and district or State government. Repeatedly, the Congress has recognized this principle with respect to those States and the use and control of the waters within a State by that State has been recognized, together with the principle of prior appropriation, by the United States Supreme Court.

If, then, the Boulder Dam were to be merely a reclamation dam, compliance with the reclamation law and the decisions of the courts would be required. That is, compliance with the laws of those States with reference to the acquiring of a water, dam and reservoir right by the issuance of a permit would be a condition precedent.

Likewise, if the proposed dam was one solely for power and was to be built under the provisions of the Federal water power act, under the provisions of that act, the parties applying for a license from the Federal Power Commission are required to first secure the permit from the State. Thus we have the rights of the States with reference to the use of the waters of the States firmly established in the reclamation law, in the Federal water power act, and in the decisions of the Supreme Court.

The proposed Boulder Dam is a project on which the Government can proceed under its constitutional functions of navigation and flood control without the consent of the States of Arizona or any of the States of the Colorado River Basin.

There is a contrary theory which absolutely ignores and denies the rights of the States to the use and control of waters of the State, except the ownership of the State to the bed of a navigable stream. The right of arid States respecting the use and control of the waters of the States, applies both to navigable and non-navigable streams and is expressed in the organic laws of the Western States.

Again, under the Constitution, the States of Arizona and Nevada own the bed of this navigable stream at the point where the dam is to be built, but that ownership and right we have seen is subordinated in this case to the right of the Federal Government to build the dam and operate it and use it for the purposes granted by the Constitution.

However, the Government's superior right ceases with the doing of those things which are necessary in and to the exercise of its constitutional functions.

Further, it can constitutionally make use of any

benefits created which are incident to or flow out of the exercise of its main power or function to improve navigation.

One of these incidents is power. When power is created as an incident of the building of a dam and the storing of waters for the constitutional purpose of navigation or flood control that power may be used and controlled by the United States.

The real problem arises, however, when we come to the question of the creation of power in an amount beyond that which can be used for the construction, operation, and maintenance of the dam or construction, operation, and maintenance of an area irrigated therefrom. The question then is, can the Government after it has fulfilled every constitutional function operate further with the power and sell the use of the water or sell or lease such excess hydro-electric energy for a profit?

The element of power is almost necessarily present in every dam that has been constructed in our western country. The fact is that 23 out of the reclamation dams erected by the Reclamation Service today have power plants built by the Government in connection with the projects and are serving, first, for the construction of the projects, and second, for their operation, and third, for the use of the settlers upon the projects, who, by their hard-earned dollars, in time pay for the projects and plants and will ultimately own them though legal title remains in the United States.

The Chandler-Dunbar decision by the Supreme Court held that where the Government built a navigation dam, any incidental power that might be developed at that dam could be leased, but it is here pointed out and emphasized that in regard to the word "incident" or "incidental" there is a limit to the extent that the Government can proceed with governmental operations as an incident to the exercise of its main power or function.

Again, if it can do so for a profit for the purpose of repaying the Government its expenditure, can it go further and after such repayment engage in and remain in the business of selling power purely for profit? Further, if it does so purely for the profit, after the cost of the structure with interest has been repaid, can it ignore and refuse to recognize the claims of the States where the structure is located in view of the fact that the use of the water and the ownership of the bed of the stream on which the dam and the reservoir rest are unquestionably in the States?

The following resolution was adopted at a conference of the Governors of the States of the upper division on the Colorado River, to-wit, Wyoming, Utah, Colorado, and New Mexico, August 29, 1927:

Whereas, it is the settled law of this country that the ownership of and dominion and sovereignty over lands covered by navigable waters within the limits of the several States of the Union belong to the respective States within which they are found, with the consequent right to use or dispose of any portion thereof, when that can be done without substantial impairment of the interests of the public in the waters, and subject always to the paramount right of Congress to control their navigation so far as may be necessary for the regulation of commerce with foreign nations and among the States; and

Whereas, it is the settled law of this country that, subject to the settlement of controversies between them by interstate compact or decision of the Supreme Court of the United States, and subject always to the paramount right of Congress to control the navigation of navigable streams so far as may be necessary for the regulation of commerce with foreign nations and among the States, the exclusive sovereignty over all of the waters within the limits of the several States belongs to the respective States within which they are found, and the sovereignty over waters constituting the boundary between two States is equal in each of such respective States; and

Whereas, it is the sense of this conference that the exercise by the United States Government of the delegated constitutional authority to control navigation for the regulation of interstate and foreign commerce does not confer upon such Government the use of waters for any other purposes which are not plainly adapted to that end and does not divest the States of their sovereignty over such waters for any other public purposes that will not interfere with navigation: Therefore be it

RESOLVED, That it is the sense of this conference of governors and the duly authorized and appointed commissioners of the States of Arizona, California, Colorado, New Mexico, Nevada, Utah, and Wyoming, constituting the Colorado River Basin States, assembled at Denver, Colo., this 23rd day of September, 1927:

The rights of the States under such settled law shall be maintained.

The States have a legal right to demand and receive compensation for the use of their lands and waters, except from the United States for the use of such lands and waters to regulate interstate and foreign commerce.

The State or States upon whose land a dam and reservoir is built by the United States Government or whose waters are used in connection with a dam built by the United States Government to generate hydro-electric energy are entitled to the preferred right to acquire the hydro-electric energy so generated or to acquire the use of such dam and reservoir for the generation of hydro-electric energy upon undertaking to pay to the United States Government the charges that may be made for such hydro-electric energy or for the use of such dam and reservoir to amortize the Government investment, together with interest thereon, or in lieu thereof agree upon any other method of compensation for the use of their waters.

We, the under signed committee, to which has been referred the foregoing resolution, as presented to the conference on August 29, 1927, by Senator Key Pittman, having adopted certain amendments unanimously, which are now incorporated therein, we recommend that the resolution set out above be adopted.

KEY PITTMAN,
FRANCIS C. WILSON,
WM. R. WALLACE,
CHARLES E. WINTER,
A. H. FAVOUR,
DELPH E. CARPENTER.

It might be claimed with considerable reason and force that the right of the State, suspended for and to the extent of the exercise of the constitutional Federal function, again attaches at the point when and where the Government ceases to operate for that purpose. If the rights of the States do not fully obtain at such point, completely and as a matter of legal right so that it could demand either all of the benefits of the structure or a reasonable compensation, at least certain equities arise. As a matter of fact, these equities arise in point of time coincident with the operation for profit to be applied to the repayment of the Government and will not be removed in point of time in this case from 30 to 40 years to the time when the Government has been fully repaid with interest.

It is on the basis of such equity that the following provisions as committee amendments were adopted:

On page 8, line 7, change the word "license" to "Licenses" and add "except that preference to applicants for the use of water and appurtenant works and privileges necessary for the generation and distribution of hydro-electric energy, or for delivery at the switchboard of a hydro-electric plant, shall be given, first, to a State for the generation or purchase of electric energy for use in the State, and the States of Arizona, California, and Nevada shall be given equal opportunity as such applicants.

"The rights covered by such preference shall be contracted for by such State within six months after notice by the Secretary of the Interior and to be paid for on the same terms and conditions as may be provided in other similar contracts made by said Secretary."

Page 6, line 6, after the period, add the following paragraph: "If during the period of amortization the Secretary of the Interior shall receive revenue in excess of the amount necessary to meet the periodical and or accrued payments to the United States as provided in the contract or contracts executed under this act, then immediately after the settlement of such periodical and or accrued payments he shall pay to the State of Arizona 18¾ per cent of such excess revenues and to the State of Nevada 18¾ per cent of such excess revenues."

If it be conceded that the Government in building a dam for navigation or flood control may build a dam much higher than necessary for such purposes, plus irrigation, and create power beyond those purposes with the object of selling water for power or creating and selling power to repay the cost of the structure, the question will eventually arise as to what are the rights of the States whose waters and lands are used during and after Government repayment. The bill does not provide for that contingency. Hence, there need not be particular concern as to that, but there might well be a surplus of receipts, and there will be under a wise and proper administration of the act, from the sale of power above that necessary to meet the fixed annual return to the Government. It would seem clear that the States should receive such surplus as compensation annually during the period of amortization of the Government costs, in view of all of the foregoing and the further fact that these great Government structures can not be taxed; whereas, if built by private capital, under the Federal water power act, there would be a substantial income in taxes to the State or States where the structure is located.

As to the States of the Colorado River Basin comprising the upper division, namely, Wyoming, Utah, Colorado, and New Mexico, a practical situation confronts them. As matters stood before the adoption of the Bill the upper division States were subject to the law of prior appropriations. This meant the loss of the use of the waters of the Colorado and the ultimate failure to make productive by the beneficial use of those waters probably a million acres in each of those States. This is so because of the certain prior development and use of the waters in the lower division of States, particularly Arizona and above all California.

When California and Arizona 13 years ago began the advocacy of a Government dam for flood control for protection of life and property in both of those States, the upper States were sympathetic and entirely willing that such a project might go forward, but recognized that water rights initiated for flood protection, reclamation, domestic use or power in the lower reaches of the river would gradually appropriate all of the volume of the flood waters of the river and leave the upper States waterless. This means ultimately billions of dollars of loss and failure to develop and settle those States.

Hence negotiations then began for an interstate compact which, if signed by all of the seven States, would substitute for the law of prior appropriations the principle of equitable division. This was done, and the Colorado River compact was written and on the 24th day of November, 1922, at Santa Fe, New Mexico, was signed, providing for a division of the waters of the river—7,500,000 acre-feet to the upper division and 7,500,000 acre-feet to the lower division.

All of the States excepting Arizona have at one time or other ratified, either conditionally or unconditionally, the seven-State compact and later the six-State compact, which was an agreement among six States to be bound by the terms of the seven-State compact and waiving that portion of that compact which required ratification by seven States. Arizona has seen fit to refuse to enter the Compact. Her right to do so is recognized. Her right to prohibit the other six States of the Colorado River Basin or other five States or any number of States to enter into a compact and support in Congress a bill which incorporates, recognizes and will put into operation such compact is denied. Arizona will not be bound by any compact to which she is not a party. That is the limit of her right.

Every State of the upper division was in daily peril of the acquirement of water rights for irrigation and power on the lower Colorado. By act of their legislatures and by reason of the refusal of Arizona for six years to enter the compact, they ratified a six-State compact.

The upper division States secured their future by the passage of the bill, as it requires the ratification of the compact by the State of California.

Their danger of the rapid and prior appropriation of all waters of the Colorado River for irrigation and power lay in the geographic position, topography, wealth, and command of financial resources, of California.

It was perfectly natural, on the other hand, for California, which had already acquired the right by appropriation to nearly all of the natural flow of the stream, to refuse to enter into a compact unless and until provision was made by legislation for the storage of flood waters from which she could guarantee by her signature to and membership in the compact the use of 7,500,000 acre-feet to the upper States.

Thus was necessitated a compact involving flood protection and new storage by legislation incorporating and subject to the terms of the compact.

Arizona has certain rights as a State, which as legal propositions are inherently hers and which belong to each and every Western State in the arid region, and which, involving the beds of navigable streams, belong to every State in the Union. She may begin litigation, delay the operation of the act and the construction of the dam, not for a long term of years but only for the shortest time that would be consumed with the Court expediting the case. Those State rights should be ultimately determined and declared by the Court of last resort. The time has come when they should be defined.

From the practical viewpoint, the division of water and the preferential right to the use of power, the recognition of the right of the State to receive compensation for the use of its land and water in lieu of taxation, being recognized in the Bill, Arizona might well now under this bill and with the provision for the compact, support the measure and complete a full seven-State compact.

Her demands for years have now practically been met. To resist and refuse further is following the shadow rather than the substance. It is emphasizing legal technicalities instead of securing a substantial and practical right and development of the State. Arizona is asserting a legal or constitutional right or principle, which after all, if sustained, will bring her no practical benefit, but, on the contrary, delay for a generation the upbuilding of her area and development of her resources. For even though the Supreme Court of the United States would ultimately sustain certain propositions with reference to the rights of the State, the practical situation is such with navigability involved, with flood control involved, with an international treaty involved, and under the circumstances of the ownership of the Government of the public lands on her side of the river above high-water line and the land to be submerged by the reservoir and the land over which canals will run for reclamation and the lands to be reclaimed, that, first, the technical claims of Arizona may not be sustained as not involved in the controversy, or if sustained, will leave her helpless to proceed to the appropriation of water resources for irrigation and power within her borders for the reason that while she may be the master and arbiter as to the use of the waters, the fact remains that the Government by its ownership of the public lands may make the water rights of the State futile and unavailable.

It is therefore questionable whether substantial results be obtained by Arizona, even though she be right on certain abstract principles; abstract for the reason that though maintained and substantiated they can not be applied by reason of surrounding conditions. She is not independent, and can not be, where the rights of other States and the rights of the General Government are also involved.

The order or precedence of the different causes or purposes in the use of waters involved in the bill is legally as follows:

Flood control; in other words, the preservation of property and of life is given first consideration in the States and by the Federal Government. It requires no argument to show that that is a point upon which there is no disagreement. All consider that the salvation and protection of life first and of property second is a first essential and a proper function in the business of the Government and of the State.

The second use recognized by the statutes of the States is domestic use; where there are different applications for use of a given amount of water, the statutes of the States place the necessity of that use and preference in granting the use, first, to domestic purposes; second, to irrigation or reclamation, and lastly to power.

So there are these four elements in this order— flood control, domestic use, reclamation and power.

Regardless of the amount of power involved in this bill, this order and precedence are present in the bill. Looking into the history of the Colorado River compact, which is incorporated in the bill, it is found that it originated in and was caused by the appeals years ago by the inhabitants of California and of Arizona for protection from the floods of the Colorado River. This was the origin and the genesis of the matter.

The history of the compact shows it originated and was joined in by the upper States, meaning Wyoming, Colorado, Utah, and New Mexico, because of these very appeals from California and Arizona. They recognized the danger and were willing that not only flood protection should proceed in the lower reaches of the river but also developed for other purposes, because they recognized that they were immediately involved; that they were face to face at once with the further needs of reclamation, domestic use, and of power, along with flood control.

The power is last in the order of necessity and legal precedence and therefore and in that sense it is incidental. Because of its volume, importance, and as a source of revenue to repay the cost of the structure, the power feature is apt to be looked upon as dominant. It will be improvident and unreasonable with the erection of a dam necessary to flood control and reclamation and to provide water for domestic use, to stop at that point when under the same operation and the same machinery, the same system and organization, the dam can be built 100 or 200 feet higher, particularly when the canyon structure and dimensions make it easily possible and beneficial; a condition of which advantage should be taken.

INDIAN SCENE, CROW RESERVATION—MONTANA

Photo by Belden

Much is said of the Nation going into the realm of Government ownership and operation of the public utilities because in the bill it is proposed, while constructing the rest of the project, to build at the one available site a power plant through which discharge water will create electrical energy. The fact is that the bill does not require construction of the power plant, but it does give the Secretary of the Interior discretion to do so if deemed advisable. Such discretion should be given the Secretary as a matter of protection to the United States and the public interest.

What is the difference essentially between the Government erecting a dam and selling the water therefrom to municipalities and private corporations to create power for retail distribution, and selling them the power at the switchboard? That should be in the bill if for no other purpose than to give the Government the means of protection of that feature in case it should be found necessary to use it in the public interest. The object, if the right is exercised, is the sale of power at the switchboard wholesale, and not retail distribution.

Starting from the basis that there is no disagreement as to the necessity of the dam for flood control, the only question presented is whether the Government shall stop at the completion of the dam, which necessarily includes a tunnel for the discharge of the waters, or finish the job by putting up the power plant and wholesaling the power at the switchboard.

The Government can build the power plant in connection with the other features and build it cheaper than could any private corporation.

This estimate for the Boulder Dam is not a lump

sum, but separate estimates have been made on every portion of this project, even including a 20-mile railroad from the nearest railroad point to bring in the supplies and material. In the event that this project costs ten, twenty, or even thirty million dollars more than the estimates, the only result is that it will take a few years longer under the contracts to pay out the entire sum. There is no possibility of loss to the Government because these estimates may be exceeded by a few million dollars. The demands for power upon which contracts have been entered into by the Secretary, before begining construction or expanding one dollar, are sufficient so that in the course of 45 or 50 years the entire cost of the project will be repaid, and the only effect of a possible excess over the $165,000,-000 estimated would be a few years longer to complete the entire repayment.

The Government will later on want to use some of the power itself in the construction of the all-American and later other canals.

The American people are inherently opposed to Government ownership and operation. They favor private enterprise. But sometimes the Government is bound, in the public interest, to reserve the right to enter to a certain protective extent.

Are the upper States protected? The bill gives these upper States very substantial protection. They were, without the passage of the bill, without a compact, in view of the decisions of the United States Supreme Court with reference to prior appropriations of water, absolutely without protection; they needed the protection of the compact.

This bill gives them substantial if not complete protection, even though but six States are bound and one, Arizona, is not.

The passage of the bill completed and fulfilled the condition which California attached, and she became bound absolutely with six States. That accomplished the purpose of the six States which agreed that the terms of the seven-State compact should be binding upon six States so agreeing, if California be one of the six.

Regardless of the theories of State rights as to the bed of the stream and control of the use of the water of this stream by the States, it being navigable, the Government controls the public lands above high-water marks, where the dam will be built and the land flooded by a storage of the water, and the public lands over which the canals must run to divert the water around the dam for power, or to distant areas for reclamation in California and Arizona. Hence the Government can require Arizona, before she perfects any water rights, even though she is out of and not bound by the compact, to conform therewith, which means that the rights of the upper States to their equitable division of the water will be protected. Moreover, an amendment to the bill which will make the Federal Power Commission subject to its provisions and to the compact thereby protecting the upper-division States, is provided. This insures against appropriation by Arizona. The upper-division States remained in the compact and supported the bill for the reason that they believed that the rights of the upper-division States are protected therein and that the six-State compact would be perfected by the passage of the bill, which would fulfill the condition of California's entrance.

It is still hoped that Arizona will yet ratify and

complete the seven State Compact notwithstanding she filed suit in the Supreme Court of the United States. In June, 1931, the Supreme Court dismissed the action of the State of Arizona on the ground that as yet no right of the State had been invaded.

CHAPTER XXVII.

Authorities on the Relation of the Federal and State Governments.

The following additional matter bears upon the legal relations of the Federal and State Governments as to lands, waters, resources, stream beds, dams, navigation, power and irrigation.

The Federal Government has no jurisdiction over water resources as such in the States. The jurisdiction belongs to the States. This jurisdiction has been asserted by the States themselves, both in their constitutions and in their statutes. For example:

The water of every natural stream, not heretofore appropriated * * * is hereby declared to be the property of the public and the same is dedicated to the use of the people of the state.—Constitution of Colorado.

Water being essential to industrial prosperity, of limited amount, and easy of diversion from its natural channels, its control must be in the state * * *. The waters of all natural streams * * * are hereby declared the property of the state.—Constitution of Wyoming.

The right of the United States in the navigable waters within the several states is limited to the control thereof for the purposes of navigation. Subject to that right, Washington became upon its organization as a state the owner of the navigable waters within its boundaries and of the land under the same—Port of Seattle v. Oregon So., 225 U. S. 56.

These quotations relate to States formed out of the former public domain, i. e., States the lands and waters of which were originally purchased by the Federal Government. The assertions of rights in the constitutions of western States were made with the assent of Congress, which accepted the constitutions of States set up in the west.

The Governor of Tennessee, in April, 1930, addressed the Federal Power Commission, saying:

We believe in the principle that the waters of the state belong to the state and that the federal government has no jurisdiction excepting insofar as the operation of such projects (for the generation of electric power) might prove somehow to injure navigation on streams to which the project streams are tributary. In any event, I am confident that the laws of this state are adequate to accomplish that purpose.

In 1925, when under the water-power conservation law of the state of New York, a permit had been issued with respect to a project in Niagara river at a point where navigation would not be affected, the position of the State was expressed by its counsel in a letter addressed to the federal commission, as follows:

It is unquestionably appropriate that there should be supervision of construction of the project works and suitable provision for the approval of original plans and alterations, but except so far as Federal authority is directed to the protection of navigation and the enforcement of Federal right, that supervision and control of construction are believed to rest with the State of New York, and in case of any conflict of views with respect to such construction, where the protection of navigation and the enforcement of Federal right are not involved, it is submitted that the determination of the competent authorities of the state must control.

Under the provisions of Article 1, Section 8, Clause 3, of the Constitution of the United States, which empowers Congress to regulate commerce with foreign nations and among the several states, Congress has power to control and protect navigation on streams suitable for interstate and foreign commerce, and in the exercise of that power it is settled * * * that Congress has the right to prevent or abate dams or other structures on the upper non-navigable reaches of rivers, the effect of which is to impair the navigable capacity of the lower navigable portions of the stream. It also has power to provide for the erection of dams in the upper non-navigable portions of a stream for the purpose of improving navigation on the lower reaches, when the navigable portions of the stream are available for interstate or foreign commerce.

Opinion rendered on July 1, 1930, by the Attorney General of the United States.

The Federal Power Commission had jurisdiction to impose upon the project only conditions as to a very minor part of the project, i. e., insofar as the project, and the operation of its works would affect the flow of the stream below the dam.

Opinion from the Attorney General of the United States on September 22, 1930, with respect to the Power Commission's authority as to power projects on non-navigable streams.

The Attorney General said he was using an interpretation of the Federal Water Power Act which appeared "necessary in order to avoid serious questions regarding the constitutionality of the Act if its general provisions were made applicable to projects on nonnavigable streams" which only remotely and indirectly affect the navigability of waters in the lower reaches of streams to which they are tributaries.

A navigable river in this country is one which is used, or is susceptible of being used, in its ordinary condition, as a highway of commerce over which trade and travel are or may be conducted in the customary modes of trade and travel by water. Brewer-Elliott Co. v. U. S., 260 U. S. 77.

The Federal Water Power Act attempts to extend Federal jurisdiction over water resources belonging to and under the jurisdiction of the State in that it defines "navigable waters" as including all falls, shallows and rapids between navigable portions of streams, and in that act provides for a "recapture" (by purchase) after fifty years, of the whole project. A part only of the project could be licensed by the Federal Power Commission; the remainder is subject to State jurisdiction.

This situation is bound in time to come into conflict with the principles and decisions which hold that not only States, by compacts with the government, but individuals by contract cannot confer upon the Government powers not delegated to it by the Constitution. The Act should be revised so as to recognize and adhere to the principle that the use of water for all purposes except navigation is under the jurisdiction of the States.

It has been stated and the fact appears that:

The Constitution in reality contains two provisions with respect to formal arrangements between States. One provision appears in Article 1, section 10, in a prohibition against any State entering into an alliance or a confederation. Subsequently, in the same section the second appears, in the words "No State shall, without the consent of Congress, * * * enter into an agreement or compact with another State."

The first of these two prohibitions, clearly intended to reinforce the grant of the treaty-making power made by each state to the Federal Government, relates, of course, to matters of a political nature, i. e., to the subjects with which governments commonly deal through treaties. The second of the prohibitions has likewise been understood from early times as relating to compacts and agreements with respect to subjects of a political nature, e. g., the boundaries between states, the setting up of a joint agency with jurisdiction over development of a harbor common to the contracting states, the jurisdiction of the state courts over boundary waters, and the division of the public debt between a state and a new state created out of it.

These are all matters as to which the Federal Government under the powers expressly granted to it has something to do. The requirement of the Constitution for approval by Congress of compacts and agreements was obviously intended to enable Congress to see that by action of the states among themselves the authority given through the Constitution to the federal government was not impaired. Where the subject was such as to bear no possible relation to powers granted by the states to the federal government it has never been understood that agreements between the states require for their validity the consent of Congress or of any other part of the Federal Government. The water resources of the states and the utilization of these resources for generation of electric power are subjects as to which the Federal Government received no grant of authority through the Constitution. In the great case of Wyoming v. Colorado, in which the two states engaged in litigation before the Supreme Court over use of the waters of an interstate stream for irrigation, and which raised such questions that the Supreme Court had the case argued before it three times, the position taken without challenge by counsel for Colorado was:

All users of water for navigation, fisheries, power, domestic, irrigation and other beneficial purposes, have been treated as within the sovereign jurisdiction and control of the several States of the Union (save alone for the paramount right of Congress in its control of navigation.)

In the case of Kansas v. Colorado, in which the Government counsel took the position that its ownership of arid lands within western States gave it an interest in waters which might be used for irrigation, the Supreme Court of the United States, concerning the provision of the Constitution that Congress has power to dispose of and make all needful rules and regulations respecting the territory or other property, belonging to the United States, said:

Clearly it does not grant to Congress any legislative control over the states and must, so far as they are concerned, be limited to authority over property belonging to the United States. Appreciating the force of this, counsel for the Government relies upon "the doctrine of sovereign and inherent power." * * * His argument runs substantially along this line: All legislative power must be vested in either the state or national government; no legislative powers belong to a state government other than those which affect solely the internal affairs of that state; consequently, all powers which are national in their scope must be found vested in the Congress of the United States. But the proposition that there are legislative powers affecting the nation as a whole which belong to, although not expressed in, the grant of powers is in direct conflict with the doctrine that this is a government of enumerated powers. That this is such a government clearly appears from the Constitution, independently of the Amendments, for otherwise there would be an instrument granting certain specified things made operative to grant other and distinct things. This natural construction of the original body of the Constitution is made absolutely certain by the 10th Amendment, which was seemingly adopted with prescience of just such contention as the present, disclosed the widespread fear that the national government might, under the pressure of supposed general welfare, attempt to exercise powers which had not been granted. * * * The framers intended that no such assumption should ever find jurisdiction * * * and that, if in the future further powers seemed necessary, they should be granted in the manner they had provided for amendment. It (the 10th Amendment) reads: "The powers not delegated to the United States by the Constitution, nor prohibited by it to the states, are reserved to the states, respectively, or to the people." The argument of counsel ignores the principal factor in this article, to wit, "the people." Its principal purpose was not the distribution of power between the United States and the States but a reservation to the people of all powers not granted. * * * The powers affecting the internal affairs of the states not granted to the United States by the Constitution, nor prohibited by it to the states, are reserved to the states, respectively, and all powers of a national character which are not delegated to the national government by the Constitution are reserved to the people of the United States.

Exclusive right to regulate all commerce on the navigable waters of the realm was an element of title and under the common law of England title was in the Sovereign in trust for the people. This doctrine applied to the Colonies. The Courts extended the principle to navigable rivers as well as tide waters.

The Colonies became States and sovereign themselves and took on sovereign rights. When they formed this nation they surrendered in the Constitution, Section 8, Article 1, the right to regulate commerce to the Federal Government. Thus, under the interpretation of the Courts the United States received plenary power to regulate commerce which includes the right to maintain and improve navigable waterways.

A State law conflicting with the Federal jurisdiction will not stand if Congress has exercised its jurisdiction over a navigable stream. But the States have concurrent jurisdiction over such stream and improvements.

If Congress has not acted as to any given waterway the State has the power to improve navigation and regulate commerce thereon. Even if Congress has exercised its jurisdiction the State still may act so long as it does not conflict with the Federal activities. The Courts have stated the jurisdictional principles as follows:

All rights over the navigable waterways within a particular State not surrendered to the Federal Government by the commerce clause of the Constitution are retained by the State government; but it is the exercise and not the mere possession of the powers conferred upon the Federal Government that limits the freedom of action by the State. Jurisdiction over the navigable waters within the State is concurrent in

the State and Federal Government's, but that of the Federal
Government, when exercised, is supreme. No action can be
taken by the State which conflicts with any action taken by
the Federal Government, and any action taken by the State
is subject to change or nullification by any subsequent action
that may be taken by the Federal Government in the exercise
of its supreme jurisdiction.

Under the Constitution of the United States a State has
the right, if its legislation does not conflict with the action
of Congress upon the same subject, to authorize bridges and
dams across the navigable waters within its limits; to license
wharves, piers and docks intruding upon such waters; to
establish harbor lines to which wharves may be extended; to
prescribe the places and manner in which vessels may lie in
a harbor, what lights they are to carry at night, or what
course they shall pursue in navigating a river; to pass reasonable quarantine and inspection laws, and pilotage or port regulations; to regulate harbor beacon, buoys, salvage and similar
matters of a local and limited nature; to improve the navigability of its waters, and to authorize the collection of tolls
in consideration of such improvements. Gould on Waters,
Third Edition, Page 80.

Calumet River, it must be remembered, is entirely within
the limits of Illinois, and the authority of the State over it
is plenary, subject only to such action as Congress may take
in execution of its power under the Constitution to regulate
commerce among the several States. That authority has been
exercised by the State ever since it was admitted into the
Union upon an equal footing with the original States. Cum-
mings vs. Chicago, 188 U. S. 410.

If the Act of 1890 did not affect the power of the State
to require the removal of an obstruction placed in the stream
unlawfully, we do not see how it could affect the authority of the
State to require the removal of a structure lawfully placed in
a navigable stream, but which has since, become an unreasonable obstruction. The subsequent amendatory acts of Congress, including Section 18 of the Act of March 3, 1899, do
not restrict or encroach upon the power the State had, previous
to those enactments, been authorized to exercise. Conceding
Congress has the power to take sole and exclusive jurisdiction over navigable waters wholly within a State, it has not
done so. People vs. Metropolitan Railway Co., 285 Ill. 246.

The Secretary of War and Chief of Engineers in the
first instance determine the question of fact as to
whether a waterway is navigable or not. The Courts
say such question of fact is to be ascertained by the
history of conditions on a given stream. If the conclusion of the Secretary and Engineer is questioned

the Courts determine the issue upon all the facts submitted to it. The early use of upper reaches of some of our rivers by the pioneers by canoe or boat or for the floating of logs or any kind of primitive transportation makes them, possibly, navigable waters of the United States. They are susceptible of improvement. Modern transportation may be developed thereon.

CHAPTER XXVIII.

Co-operation of Federal and State Government.

In national reclamation by irrigation the plan of tributary storage, primarily for flood control, the true economic method of preventing the destruction of life and property in and near the main channel of the Mississippi, works harmoniously and beneficially to all concerned. President Hoover has tentatively proposed that the dams be built by the Government by the reclamation service, including flood control purposes, and then turned over to the States to be used by the States where located both for power and irrigation. The States could well afford, if the public lands and resources are ceded to them, to build the distribution systems for irrigation projects and thus gradually substitute State reclamation for Federal reclamation. In any event reclamation would proceed. The settlers upon the projects relieved of the burden of repaying dam construction would successfully and easily meet the cost of the distribution system back to the State or Federal Government. In fact the profits from the power alone in many cases would in reasonable time pay the whole cost of the entire project, including both storage and distribution, as it is now doing in some of our Federal reclamation projects. It is well to remember that under the homestead policy, our settlers received their productive lands for a nominal price or entirely free by virtue of residence and improvement. The reclamation homesteader would be the like beneficiary if thus relieved of all repayment for construction charges.

There will come a time when every acre susceptible of irrigation must be brought under cultivation in order to have one source of sure food supply, which may be of the highest importance to the whole American people in seasons of drouth. With all available natural dam and reservoir sites employed and every acre reached with water which can be covered, and every drop of water economically used, the acreage which can be irrigated in the arid or semi-arid states does not exceed an average of five per cent of the area of each of such States. They are entitled to that.

Finally, as to reclamation in the Western States, the new policy may be the salvation of reclamation in view of the fact that government lands capable of irrigation are becoming greatly reduced and in view of the fact that the Supreme Court of the United States upheld the Reclamation Act on the theory that the Government had the right to improve its lands. Much of the land which might be irrigated and for which there is water available, both arid and semi-arid, is in private ownership. Without the basis of a reasonable amount of public land in a project it is a grave question as to how long Federal reclamation can constitutionally continue.

By the cession of the lands and minerals to the States and the building of dams by the Government under its power of flood control and maintenance and improvement of navigation, State reclamation can be successfully substituted, and development by irrigation proceed with safety and great benefit to the States and to the Nation.

If all the public lands or the unreserved and unappropriated public domain are ceded to the Western States in which they lie, the question has been raised as to the effect on subsequent Federal activities which heretofore have been exercised by the Government, owing to its position as landlord or trustee, most notably its control over the public lands.

If at this time the unreserved land only, approximately 180,000,000 acres, are ceded the governmental authority and activities will continue to function as heretofore as to the approximately 235,000,000 acres of reserved lands, comprising national forests, national parks, and monuments, Indian reservations, and water power sites, naval reserves and mineral withdrawals.

It has been suggested that if any cession is made, Federal aid for highways might be reduced to the 50-50 basis which now prevails under the Federal Aid Highway Act as to all non-public land States. The present arrangement rightfully secures a greater government contribution in proportion to the area of public lands remaining in each state under Federal control.

President Hoover has met this situation with a statement, in his letter addressed to Assistant Secretary of the Interior for communication to the Conference of Western Governors at Salt Lake City in August, 1929, that he favored a continuation of the present Federal Aid proportion for a period of ten years, even though there is a cession to the States. This period should see the Highway Program practically completed. Therefore the Western States would incur no disadvantage by a cession of all or a part of the public domain to the States. The most that could happen at the end of the 10 year period would be to take their position with the rest of the States on a 50-50 basis as to future highway construction under the Federal Aid system.

In the interest of all the people therefore, the Government can and should constitutionally proceed, though ceding the lands to the States, in full co-operation with the States to bring to a reality the splendid and universally beneficial system of Inland Waterways, involving and including, as it does, tributary storage, flood control, regulation of flow, water transportation, hydro-electric power and irrigation reclamation.

All this would be true if the reserved as well as the unreserved lands and resources, surface and subsurface, were ceded the States.

Under the complete control of a part or all of their lands and resources by the States there still remain, under the Federal Constitution, room and jurisdiction for Federal participation under the inter-state commerce clause with respect to flood control and preservation or improvement of navigation on navigable streams.

Under this right the Government can proceed with the development of a great inland waterway system, including deepening of channels, levees and flood control and regulation of flow by storage dams on the tributaries of the Mississippi. It can appropriate the necessary funds for the building of such dams, construct them, and turn them over to the States where located, for the purpose of extending and facilitating water transportation, power and irrigation.

The incidental benefits and profits derived by the creation and sale of power and the wealth created by the application of the same stored waters for irrigation would in a reasonable time pay for the entire system, simultaneously give some annual compensation to the States and eventually, after repayment to the United States, be a source of income to the various

HORSES ON RANGE—NEVADA
Photo by Belden

States where such storage dams and reservoirs were located.

This is a magnificent conception of industrial development and general welfare for the entire area between the Alleghanies and the Rockies. It would also apply to the Atlantic and Pacific coast States. The greatest economic sentence in President Hoover's speech of acceptance was that in which he pointed out that "every drop of water that runs unused to the sea is an economic waste." "From headwaters down" is the true principle of the development and use of our water resources. It is an economic crime to allow water to pass any given point from its source on down to the ocean, especially as it entails destruction, when it can be used, returned in major part to the stream bed and used over and over again as it flows on its course to sea level.

In all this splendid development the Federal Government can proceed, exercising its constitutional powers, by either appropriation in aid of or in actual construction, leaving to the States the management of the structures and the exercise of their constitutional rights, to the great benefit of all the people, which is the Federal function, and to the advancement of the welfare of the people of the various States, which is the State function. Under the great policy of national internal improvements and inter-state commerce powers, avoiding friction and without invasion of the rights of the States, the United States can carry on with the States in these great works although not a landlord, landowner, or trustee within the States.

A MEMORIAL

To the Congress of the United States.

WHEREAS, the government records show that the public lands states, to-wit: Alabama, Arkansas, Florida, Louisiana, Mississippi, Missouri, Wisconsin, Michigan, Minnesota, North Dakota, South Dakota, Nebraska, Kansas, Oklahoma, but more particularly, the states of Montana, Wyoming, Colorado, New Mexico, Arizona, Utah, Idaho, Washington, Oregon, Nevada, and California, contain over two hundred and twenty-two million acres of unreserved, unappropriated public lands, in addition to over one hundred and fifty million acres of reserved public lands, making a total of more than three hundred and seventy-two million acres of land, which are not taxed; and,

WHEREAS, the reservation and exemption from taxation of such a large body of land by the Federal Government, cripples the states wherein they are respectively situated, in their efforts looking to the progressive development of said states, principally the states situated in the wholly arid belt, being the last eleven states above mentioned, which are now facing the most critical and important reconstruction and development era in their history; and believing that all considerations of justice demand that these states should own the unreserved and unappropriated public lands within their respective boundaries;

NOW, therefore, we, the undersigned Governors, respectfully ask the Congress of the United States to enact such legislation as will result in the transfer of the ownership and possession, without any mineral or any other reservation, except such, if any, as the Congress may deem proper to provide against possible misuse or misappropriation, of all the unreserved and unappropriated public lands of the United States, to the States wherein such lands are respectively situated, to the end that such states may utilize said lands in the internal improvement and development of said states; that these States may have a permanent fund, other than that derived from direct taxation, which even now is quite heavy and burdensome on the people, upon which they may draw for the support and maintenance of public schools, state institutions of learning and highways, and for the acquisition by the States of good farming lands, fit for such of our returned soldiers, as may desire to make their homes thereon, with a reasonable expectation of finding a fortable living; and for such other uses as may contribute to the upbuilding of said states.

Very respectfully submitted,

O. A. Larrazola, Governor of New Mexico.
Henry J. Allen, Governor of Kansas.
Samuel V. Stewart, Governor of Montana.
John G. Townsend, Governor of Delaware.
Thomas E. Campbell, Governor of Arizona.
Ben. W. Olcott, Governor of Oregon.
Samuel R. McKelvie, Governor of Nebraska.
Robert D. Carey, Governor of Wyoming.
J. B. A. Robertson, Governor of Oklahoma.
Wm. C. Sproul, Governor of Pennsylvania.
Simon Bamberger, Governor of Utah.
Oliver H. Shoup, Governor of Colorado.
Lynn J. Frazier, Governor of North Dakota.
Thomas F. Kilby, Governor of Alabama.
Emanuel L. Philipp, Governor of Wisconsin.
J. A. A. Burnquist, Governor of Minnesota.
Peter Norbeck, Governor of South Dakota.
F. D. Gardner, Governor of Missouri.
Theo. G. Bilbo, Governor of Mississippi.
Albert E. Sleeper, Governor of Michigan.
D. W. Davis, Governor of Idaho.
Ruffin G. Pleasant, Governor of Louisiana.

RESOLUTION ADOPTED AT THE WESTERN GOVERNORS' CONFERENCE

October 29, 1931
Portland, Oregon

RESOLVED, that this Conference of Western Governors expresses its appreciation of the work and recommendations of the Committee on Conservation and Administration of the Public Domain appointed by President Hoover, as a great step in forwarding the interests and equities of the Western States, and in many respects meeting the requirements of justice in the arid regions; that we pledge our support to a Bill embodying its principles and substance as to disposition of the lands.

STATISTICS

STATISTICS RELATING TO THE DISPOSITION OF THE PUBLIC DOMAIN
AREA OF STATES AND TERRITORIES
(Based upon careful joint calculations made in the General Land Office, the Geological Survey, and the Bureau of the Census)

State or Territory	Land Surface		Total Areas	
	Sq. miles	Acres	Acres	Acres
Alabama	51,279	32,818,560	460,160	33,278,720
Arizona	113,810	72,838,400	93,440	72,931,840
Arkansas	52,525	33,616,000	518,400	34,134,400
California	155,652	99,617,280	1,692,800	101,310,080
Colorado	103,658	66,341,120	185,600	66,526,720
Connecticut	4,820	3,084,800	92,800	3,177,600
Delaware	1,965	1,257,600	259,200	1,516,800
District of Columbia	62	39,680	5,120	44,800
Florida	54,861	35,111,040	2,435,200	37,546,240
Georgia	58,725	37,584,000	345,600	37,929,600
Idaho	83,354	53,346,560	341,760	53,688,320
Illinois	56,043	35,867,520	398,080	36,265,600
Indiana	36,045	23,068,800	197,760	23,266,560
Iowa	55,586	35,575,040	359,040	35,934,080
Kansas	81,774	52,335,360	245,760	52,581,120
Kentucky	40,181	25,715,840	266,880	25,982,720
Louisiana	45,409	29,061,760	1,982,080	31,043,840
Maine	29,895	19,132,800	2,012,800	21,145,600
Maryland	9,941	6,362,240	1,527,040	7,889,280
Massachusetts	8,039	5,144,960	145,280	5,290,240
Michigan	57,480	36,787,200	320,000	37,107,200
Minnesota	80,858	51,749,120	2,447,360	54,196,480
Mississippi	46,362	29,671,680	321,920	29,993,600
Missouri	68,727	43,985,280	443,520	44,428,800
Montana	146,201	93,568,640	509,440	94,078,080
Nebraska	76,808	49,157,120	455,680	49,612,800
Nevada	109,821	70,285,440	556,160	70,841,600
New Hampshire	9,031	5,779,840	198,400	5,978,240
New Jersey	7,514	4,808,960	454,400	5,263,360
New Mexico	122,503	78,401,920	83,840	78,485,760
New York	47,654	30,498,560	992,000	31,490,560
North Carolina	48,740	31,193,600	2,359,040	33,552,640
North Dakota	70,183	44,917,120	418,560	45,335,680
Ohio	40,740	26,073,600	192,000	26,265,600
Oklahoma	69,414	44,424,960	411,520	44,836,480
Oregon	95,607	61,188,480	698,880	61,887,360
Pennsylvania	44,832	28,692,480	188,160	28,880,640
Rhode Island	1,067	682,880	115,840	798,720
South Carolina	30,495	19,516,800	316,160	19,832,960
South Dakota	76,868	49,195,520	478,080	49,673,600
Tennessee	41,687	26,679,680	214,400	26,894,080
Texas	262,398	167,934,720	2,238,720	170,173,440
Utah	82,184	52,597,760	1,795,840	54,393,600
Vermont	9,124	5,839,360	281,600	6,120,960
Virginia	40,262	25,767,680	1,513,600	27,281,280
Washington	66,836	42,775,040	1,466,240	44,241,280
West Virginia	24,022	15,374,080	94,720	15,468,800
Wisconsin	55,256	35,363,840	518,400	35,882,240
Wyoming	97,594	62,460,160	204,800	62,664,960
	2,973,892	1,903,290,880	33,854,080	1,937,144,960
Alaska				378,165,760
Guam				131,840
Hawaii				4,099,840
Canal Zone				351,360
Philippine Islands				73,216,000
Porto Rico [1]				2,198,400
American Samoa				48,000
Virgin Islands				85,120
Total				2,395,441,280

1 Including adjacent islands.
Owing to their location adjoining the Great Lakes, the States enumerated below contain ap-

proximately an additional number of square miles as follows: Illinois, 1,674 square miles of Lake Michigan; Indiana, 230 square miles of Lake Michigan; Michigan, 16,653 square miles of Lake Superior, 12,922 square miles of Lake Michigan, 9,925 square miles of Lake Huron, and 460 square miles of Lakes St. Clair and Erie; Minnesota, 2,514 square miles of Lake Superior; New York, 3,140 square miles of Lakes Ontario and Erie; Ohio, 3,443 square miles of Lake Erie; Pennsylvania, 891 square miles of Lake Erie; Wisconsin, 2,378 square miles of Lake Superior and 7,500 square miles of Lake Michigan.

In addition to the water areas noted above, California claims jurisdiction over all Pacific waters lying within 3 English miles of her coast; Oregon claims jurisdiction over a similar strip of the Pacific Ocean 1 marine league in width between latitude 42° north and the mouth of the Columbia River, and Texas claims jurisdiction over a strip of Gulf waters 3 leagues in width adjacent to her coast and between the Rio Grande and the Sabine Rivers.

Summary of Disposition of the Public Domain

	Acres	Acres
Land grants:		
Canal construction		4, 597, 668
Railroad construction—		
To corporations direct	93, 968, 521	
To States	38, 204, 704	
		132, 173, 225
River improvement		2, 245, 252
States—		
Agricultural college scrip	7, 830, 000	
Schools	78, 179, 737	
Swamp lands	64, 805, 651	
Miscellaneous	30, 667, 182	
		181, 482, 570
Wagon-road construction		3, 296, 658
Other disposals:		
Allotments to individual Indians		27, 062, 933
Bounty land warrants located		64, 002, 374
Cash sales under timber and stone acts		13, 838, 564
Cash sales under various other acts—		
To June 30, 1880	[1] 196, 755, 216	
July 1, 1880, to June 30, 1904	[1] 79, 803, 004	
July 1, 1904, to June 30, 1930	34, 812, 116	
		307, 250, 599
Coal entries		604, 443
Desert entries		9, 827, 299
Homestead entries		233, 630, 253
Mineral entires		3, 113, 372
Miscellaneous dispositions, fiscal years 1905–1930, inclusive		4, 182, 777
Private land claims confirmed		34, 772, 471
Scrip locations		1, 621, 612
State reclamation land grants (Carey Act) patented		1, 174, 903
Timber culture entries		9, 856, 264
Reservations and withdrawals:		
Indian reservations		70, 993, 326
National forests, net area		135, 982, 603
National parks and monuments in public-land States		6, 066, 511
Federal reclamation projects		19, 034, 330
Miscellaneous withdrawals and reservations		22, 275, 760
Pending entries		22, 533, 574
Vacant, unappropriated, and unreserved land, including Alaska [2]		557, 145, 206
Total		[3] 1, 868, 764, 547
Total land surface in public-land States and Alaska [2]		[3] 1, 820, 366, 080

1 Includes 4,119,737 acres of desert land and coal entries.
2 The greater portion of Alaska being unsurveyed, the entire area of the Territory, land and water, 378,165,760 acres, has been used.
3 The 48,398,467-acre discrepancy between this total and the total surface in the public-land States and the land and water area of Alaska is due to the fact that in the very early days no record was kept by acreage but only by the number of the various classes of entries, and for the purpose of compiling the statistics from which this table was prepared each entry was considered

as having been made for the maximum area; there is also some overlap in withdrawals; some of the land disposed of was afterwards reacquired either by cancellation of the entry and final certificate before patent was issued or by suits in the Federal courts to cancel patent; and also to the fact that within the exterior limits of withdrawals under the general reclamation act and in Indian reservations, private holdings are scattered; and at this late date it is impracticable to attempt an adjustment of the apparent discrepancy.

The above and all other statistics given are the official figures of the General Land Office of the United States.

We deduce the following as to land areas, which agrees with prior table issued by the Department:

	Acres
Vacant, unappropriated and unreserved land, excluding Alaska	178,979,446
Land area Original States and States formed from their areas, Maine, Vermont, West Virginia, District of Columbia	262,402
All dispositions, excluding Alaska	1,461,909,434
Total land area, excluding Alaska	1,903,290,880

DISPOSITION OF UNITED STATES' LANDS

Land Area, Balance Sheet, Round Numbers

Based on Report of Committee on Conservation and Administration of the Public Domain.

Total Land area of United States proper, exclusive of Alaska and Island Possessions		1,903,000,000
Original States and States formed from them, Kentucky, Tennessee, Virginia, Maine, District of Columbia	300,000,000	
Texas	167,000,000	
Disposed of by grant, sale, homestead, mining location	995,000,000	
Disposed of by permanent reservations	213,000,000	
Withdrawals, mineral and otherwise	70,000,000	
Total	1,725,000,000	1,725,000,000
Balance public domain, unreserved, unappropriated, vacant		178,000,000

Patents issued annually under the stock-raising homestead acts from June 30, 1919, to June 30, 1929

Year	Area	Year	Area
	Acres		*Acres*
1919	4,938.00	1926	2,513,675.87
1920	376,065.71	1927	2,400,604.81
1921	1,249,592.63	1928	1,387,277.80
1922	2,919,819.67	1929	1,350,384.6:
1923	2,590,758.70		
1924	2,952,158.49	Total	20,232,398.44
1925	2,507,122.12		

Final homestead entries from passage of homestead act to June 30, 1929 (commuted homesteads are not included)

Fiscal year ended June 30—	Acres	Fiscal year ended June 30—	Acres
1868	355, 086. 04	1900	3, 477, 842. 71
1869	504, 301. 97	1901	5, 241, 120. 76
1870	519, 727. 84	1902	4, 342, 747. 70
1871	629, 162. 25	1903	3, 576, 964. 14
1872	707, 409. 83	1904	3, 232, 716. 75
1873	1, 224, 890. 93	1905	3, 419, 387. 15
1874	1, 585, 781. 56	1906	3, 526, 748. 58
1875	2, 058, 537. 74	1907	3, 740, 567. 71
1876	2, 590, 552. 81	1908	4, 242, 710. 59
1877	2, 407, 828. 19	1909	3, 699, 466. 79
1878	2, 662, 980. 82	1910	3, 795, 862. 89
1879	2, 070, 842. 39	1911	4, 620, 197. 12
1880	1, 938, 234. 89	1912	4, 305, 068. 52
1881	1, 928, 204. 76	1913	10, 009, 285. 16
1882	2, 219, 453. 80	1914	9, 291, 121. 46
1883	2, 504, 414. 51	1915	7, 180, 981. 62
1884	2, 945, 574. 72	1916	7, 278, 250. 60
1885	3, 032, 679. 11	1917	8, 497, 389. 68
1886	2, 663, 531. 83	1918	8, 236, 438. 18
1887	2, 749, 037. 48	1919	6, 524, 759. 68
1888	3, 175, 400. 64	1920	8, 372, 695. 79
1889	3, 681, 708. 80	1921	7, 726, 740. 44
1890	4, 060, 592. 77	1922	7, 307, 034. 42
1891	3, 954, 587. 77	1923	5, 594, 258. 69
1892	3, 259, 897. 07	1924	4, 791, 436. 44
1893	3, 477, 231. 63	1925	4, 048, 910. 56
1894	2, 929, 947. 41	1926	3, 451, 105. 51
1895	2, 980, 809. 30	1927	2, 583, 627. 48
1896	2, 790, 242. 55	1928	1, 815, 549. 31
1897	2, 778, 404. 20	1929	1, 700, 950. 01
1898	3, 095, 017. 75		
1899	3, 134, 140. 44	Total	232, 259, 180. 24

Timber and stone entries from passage of act June 3, 1878, to
June 30, 1929

States	Acres	Amount
Alabama	43, 734. 95	$147, 169. 55
Arizona	2, 942. 80	9, 311. 07
Arkansas	361, 472. 79	852, 037. 55
California	2, 896, 514. 65	7, 403, 701. 41
Colorado	400, 704. 27	1, 045, 978. 44
Florida	108, 996. 01	314, 726. 79
Idaho	1, 014, 678. 52	2, 693, 123. 27
Iowa	119. 36	298. 46
Louisiana	150, 277. 20	396, 292. 39
Michigan	149, 666. 91	377, 356. 84
Minnesota	1, 403, 865. 85	3, 553, 971. 66
Mississippi	19, 818. 16	73, 476. 20
Montana	664, 004. 57	1, 728, 965. 52
Nebraska	97. 33	268. 00
Nevada	6, 542. 14	16, 305. 74
New Mexico	80. 00	570. 00
North Dakota	8, 646. 31	22, 005. 78
Oklahoma	40. 00	100. 00
Oregon	3, 815, 894. 24	9, 811, 885. 46
South Dakota	63, 908. 73	165, 187. 80
Utah	3, 195. 85	8, 018. 08
Washington	2, 168, 008. 67	5, 524, 680. 16
Wisconsin	80, 362. 04	202, 755. 64
Wyoming	454, 383. 43	1, 135, 645. 50
General Land Office	4, 560. 78	19, 621. 21
Total	13, 827, 515. 56	35, 503, 452. 52

Coal-land entries from passage of act March 3, 1873, to June 30, 1929

State or Territory	Acres	Amount
Alabama	239. 40	$2, 394. 00
Arizona	6, 693. 35	74, 997. 00
California	5, 535. 06	81, 531. 30
Colorado	156, 113. 38	2, 385, 693. 75
Colorado [1]	58, 495. 65	891, 219. 55
Dakota Territory	583. 57	5, 835. 70
Idaho	3, 277. 41	37, 911. 80
Montana	64, 758. 47	1, 219, 419. 39
Nevada	1, 661. 01	20, 442. 20
New Mexico	26, 613. 38	441, 323. 75
North Dakota	9, 543. 59	150, 880. 20
Oregon	10, 571. 96	125, 552. 90
South Dakota	3, 623. 64	39, 764. 80
Utah	75, 828. 02	2, 531, 661. 95
Washington	64, 893. 51	1, 044, 525. 20
Wyoming	113, 923. 87	2, 867, 689. 36
General Land Office	7. 95	159. 00
Total	604, 363. 22	11, 921, 001. 85

1 Within the Ute Reservation.

Desert-land entries from passage of act March 3, 1877, to
June, 30, 1929

State or Territory	Acres		Amount		
	Original	Final	Original	Final	Total
Arizona	2, 573, 791. 35	353, 051. 00	$646, 006. 19	$384, 432. 20	$1, 030, 438. 39
California	5, 166, 441. 03	882, 902. 44	1, 307, 722. 49	904, 938. 40	2, 212, 660. 89
Colorado	3, 224, 868. 99	709, 031. 20	906, 754. 86	702, 736. 47	1, 609, 491. 33
Dakota Territory	20, 021. 00	300. 00	5, 005. 25	300. 00	5, 305. 25
Idaho	3, 110, 544. 67	1, 028, 327. 80	779, 006. 01	980, 746. 24	1, 759, 752. 25
Montana	5, 981, 763. 12	2, 765, 156. 15	1, 501, 991. 90	2, 760, 360. 20	4, 262, 352. 10
Nevada	647, 573. 84	160, 956. 79	152, 303. 59	160, 624. 77	312, 928. 36
New Mexico	2, 158, 836. 23	232, 454. 68	541, 850. 42	330, 924. 52	872, 774. 94
North Dakota	85, 278. 51	20, 094. 18	21, 321. 09	20, 118. 92	41, 440. 01
Oregon	1, 111, 878. 46	297, 881 03	277, 546. 19	294, 209. 47	571, 755. 66
South Dakota	609, 290. 58	101, 921. 12	151, 917. 37	99, 608. 85	251, 526. 22
Utah	1, 500, 190. 29	454, 562. 41	381, 866. 66	459, 759. 01	841, 625. 67
Washington	997, 954. 13	70, 864. 94	260, 408. 98	83, 141. 55	343, 550. 53
Wyoming	5, 535, 860. 24	1, 513, 692. 83	940, 888. 00	1, 517, 752. 66	2, 458, 640. 66
Total	32, 724, 292. 44	8, 591, 196. 57	7, 874, 589. 00	8, 699, 653. 26	16, 574. 242. 26

Estimated area of existing national forests, June 30, 1929 (a little over 80 per
cent is public)

	Acres		Acres
Alabama	198, 385	New Mexico	9, 915, 383
Alaska	21, 397, 515	North Carolina	1, 690, 252
Arizona	12, 266, 923	Oklahoma	61, 640
Arkansas	1, 690, 224	Oregon	15, 520, 528
California	23, 987, 009	Pennsylvania	739, 277
Colorado	14, 774, 106	Porto Rico	65, 950
Florida	620, 228	South Carolina	137, 216
Georgia	672, 094	South Dakota	1, 269, 812
Idaho	20, 648, 230	Tennessee	876, 056
Illinois	10, 710	Utah	7, 981, 730
Maine	115, 558	Virginia	1, 237, 800
Michigan	589, 004	Washington	11, 262, 495
Minnesota	1, 966, 804	West Virginia	819, 100
Montana	19, 086, 317	Wyoming	8, 641, 238
Nebraska	207, 209		
Nevada	5, 245, 606	Total area	184, 564, 953
New Hampshire	870, 554		

	Acres
Area added to national forests during year	1, 121, 258
Area excluded from national forests during year	960, 124
Area within temporary forest withdrawals June 30, 1929	255, 520
Area of existing national forests June 30, 1928	184, 403, 819
Area of existing national forests June 30, 1929	184, 564, 953

Irrigated and cropped acreage and crop values by years, 1906-1929

Year	Federal irrigation projects — Irrigated acreage	Cropped acreage	Crop value — For year	Crop value — Cumulative total	Warren Act land — Irrigated acreage	Cropped acreage	Crop value — For year	Crop value — Cumulative total	Entire area — Irrigated acreage	Cropped acreage	Crop value — For year	Crop value — Cumulative total
1906	22,300	[1] 20,100	$244,900	----	----	----	----	----	22,300	[1] 20,100	$244,900	----
1907	187,600	[1] 169,000	4,760,400	$5,005,300	----	----	----	----	187,600	[1] 169,000	4,760,400	$5,005,300
1908	289,500	[1] 260,500	7,575,800	12,581,100	----	----	----	----	289,500	[1] 260,500	7,575,800	12,581,100
1909	410,600	[1] 369,500	11,920,700	24,501,800	----	----	----	----	410,600	[1] 369,500	11,920,700	24,501,800
1910	465,100	413,000	12,974,600	37,476,400	----	----	----	----	465,100	413,000	12,974,600	37,476,400
1911	541,400	470,100	12,708,600	50,185,000	----	----	----	----	541,400	470,100	12,708,600	50,185,000
1912	588,400	540,000	13,825,400	64,010,400	----	----	----	----	588,400	540,000	13,825,400	64,010,400
1913	699,200	642,200	15,732,200	79,742,600	----	----	----	----	699,200	642,200	15,732,200	79,742,600
1914	761,300	703,400	16,475,500	96,218,100	----	----	----	----	761,300	703,400	16,475,500	96,218,100
1915	814,900	760,000	18,200,000	114,418,100	----	----	----	----	814,900	760,000	18,200,000	114,418,100
1916	923,000	858,300	32,816,000	147,234,100	----	----	----	----	923,000	858,300	32,816,000	147,234,100
1917	1,057,500	966,800	56,462,300	203,696,400	----	----	----	----	1,057,500	966,800	56,462,300	203,696,400
1918	1,141,500	1,051,200	66,821,400	270,517,800	[1] 501,100	[1] 481,600	$35,000,000	----	1,642,600	[1] 1,532,800	101,821,400	305,517,800
1919	1,187,300	1,113,500	88,974,100	359,491,900	916,300	880,600	64,000,000	$99,000,000	2,103,600	1,994,100	152,974,100	458,491,900
1920	1,223,500	1,153,800	66,171,700	425,663,600	981,900	950,900	47,505,800	146,505,800	2,205,400	2,104,700	113,677,500	572,169,400
1921	1,227,500	1,157,900	49,620,300	475,283,900	1,001,300	969,600	44,906,100	191,411,900	2,228,800	2,127,500	94,526,400	666,695,800
1922	1,202,130	1,169,100	50,360,900	525,644,800	983,300	951,300	33,240,800	224,652,700	2,185,430	2,120,400	83,601,700	750,297,500
1923	1,213,700	1,179,870	65,046,300	590,691,100	1,051,400	993,000	37,557,900	262,210,600	2,265,100	2,172,870	102,604,200	852,901,700
1924	1,290,900	1,216,600	66,488,600	657,179,700	930,700	889,500	43,237,500	305,448,100	2,221,600	2,106,100	109,726,100	962,627,800
1925	1,320,300	1,242,800	77,608,900	734,788,600	1,019,200	951,300	53,655,900	359,104,000	2,339,500	2,194,100	131,264,800	1,093,892,600
1926	1,411,000	1,361,500	60,664,900	795,453,500	1,097,200	949,600	49,750,000	408,854,000	2,508,200	2,311,100	110,414,900	1,204,307,500
1927	1,379,000	1,431,600	72,047,200	867,500,700	1,148,100	1,072,500	61,160,000	470,014,000	2,527,100	2,504,100	133,207,200	1,337,514,700
1928	1,442,100	1,489,200	81,077,800	948,578,500	1,255,000	1,192,000	62,495,300	532,509,300	2,677,100	2,681,200	143,573,100	1,481,087,800
1929	1,483,900	1,512,250	88,459,390	1,037,037,890	1,234,230	1,192,990	72,720,490	605,229,790	2,718,130	2,705,240	161,179,880	1,642,267,680

[1] Estimated.

Accretions to the reclamation fund, repayments to the reclamation fund, and expenditures for construction and operation and maintenance of reclamation projects to June 30, 1930

(1)	(2)	(3)	(4)
State and project	Accretions to reclamation fund to June 30, 1930	Collections (repayments to reclamation fund) to June 30, 1930	Total accretions and collections (column 2 plus column 3)
Alabama	$60, 127. 13		$60, 127. 13
Arizona:			
Salt River		$9, 686, 842. 98	
Yuma [1]		[2] 5, 754, 744. 24	
Yuma auxiliary		22, 354. 33	
Total	2, 453, 591. 71	15, 463, 941. 55	17, 917, 533. 26
California:			
Orland		1, 310, 584. 71	
Yuma [1]		[2] 1, 989, 809. 65	
Klamath [1]		[2] 438, 042. 62	
Total	15, 506, 856. 47	3, 738, 436. 98	19, 245, 293. 45
Colorado:			
Grand Valley		829, 758. 12	
Uncompahgre		2, 853, 911. 04	
Total	10, 410, 861. 78	3, 683, 669. 16	14, 094, 530. 94
Idaho:			
King Hill		130, 224. 99	
Minidoka		12, 224, 190. 17	
Minidoka—Gooding division		266, 469. 94	
Boise [1]		[2] 7, 300, 196. 12	
Owyhee [1]		[2] 4, 273. 67	
Total	6, 935, 384. 51	19, 925, 354. 89	26, 860, 739. 40
Kansas: Garden City	1, 032, 764. 48	58, 002. 27	1, 090, 766. 75
Louisiana	20, 413. 71		20, 413. 71
Montana:			
Huntley		1, 203, 682. 09	
Milk River		639, 723. 98	
Sun River		803, 357. 41	
Lower Yellowstone [1]		[2] 546, 507. 08	
Total	16, 025, 369. 79	3, 193, 270. 56	19, 218, 640. 35
Nebraska: North Platte [1]	2, 093, 754. 36	[2] 5, 747, 732. 44	7, 841, 486. 80
Nevada: Newlands	996, 298. 37	2, 682, 824. 91	3, 679, 123. 28
New Mexico:			
Carlsbad		1, 733, 259. 35	
Hondo		34, 956. 70	
Rio Grande [1]		3, 911, 934. 12	
Total	6, 356, 453. 09	5, 680, 150. 17	12, 036, 603. 26

[1] Interstate projects, expenditures for construction and for operation and maintenance partly prorated on an area basis.

[2] Distribution between States of collections on interstate projects partly estimated.

(1)	(2)	(3)	(4)
State and project	Accretions to reclamation fund to June 30, 1930	Collections (repayments to reclamation fund) to June 30, 1930	Total accretions and collections (column 2 plus column 3)
North Dakota:			
Buford-Trenton		17,873.93	
Williston		591,766.47	
Lower Yellowstone [1]		[2] 234,482.48	
Total	12,276,579.13	844,122.88	13,120,702.0
Oklahoma	5,925,274.31		5,925,274.3
Oregon.			
Baker		5,879.29	
Umatilla		1,184,354.76	
Vale		21,020.57	
Klamath [1]		[2] 2,239,981.15	
Owyhee [1]		[2] 9,896.43	
Boise [1]		[2] 53,145.40	
Total	11,883,257.65	3,514,277.60	15,397,535.2
South Dakota: Belle Fourche	7,716,593.30	1,521,168.84	9,237,762.1
Texas: Rio Grande [1]		3,111,433.97	3,111,433.9
Utah:			
Strawberry Valley		2,166,204.22	
Salt Lake Basin		58,476.95	
Total	4,332,325.12	2,224,681.17	6,557,006.2
Washington:			
Okanogan		699,955.58	
Yakima		11,105,546.81	
Yakima—Kittitas division		70,618.77	
Total	7,416,855.95	11,876,121.16	19,292,977.1
Wyoming:			
Riverton		148,898.15	
Shoshone		2,134,648.15	
North Platte [1]		[2] 743,258.27	
Total	37,234,020.79	3,026,804.57	40,260,825.3
All States:			
Secondary investigations		903,759.79	903,759.7
Federal water power licenses	59,360.35		59,360.3
Other collections (including general offices, Indian projects, etc.)		4,401,243.11	4,401,243.1
Grand total	148,736,142.00	91,596,996.02	240,333,138.0

(1)	(5)	(6)	(7)
State and project	Expended for construction of reclamation projects to June 30, 1930	Expended for operation and maintenance to June 30, 1930	Total expenditures to June 30, 1930
Arizona:			
Salt River	$15,106,942.10		$15,106,942.1
Yuma	6,929,700.25	[3] $2,299,391.38	9,229,091.6
Yuma auxiliary		183,651.57	183,651.5
Total	22,036,642.35	2,483,042.95	24,519,685.3
California:			
Orland	2,502,613.70	438,325.15	2,940,938.8
Yuma [1]	3,147,672.82	912,552.48	4,060,225.3
Klamath [1]	2,155,867.04	81,000.00	2,236,867.04
Total	7,806,153.56	1,431,877.63	9,238,031.1

[1] Interstate products, expenditures for construction and for operation and maintenance partly prorated on an area basis.

[2] Distribution between States of collections on interstate projects partly estimated.

[3] Levee maintenance reimbursed by or financed by General Treasury not included.

(1)	(5)	(6)	(7)
State and project	Expended for construction of reclamation projects to June 30, 1930	Expended for operation and maintenance to June 30, 1930	Total expenditures to June 30, 1930
olorado:			
Grand Valley	5, 338, 934. 91	129, 720. 24	5, 468, 655. 15
Uncompahgre	7, 928, 760. 97	1, 020, 544. 89	8, 949, 305. 86
Total	13, 267, 595. 88	1, 150, 265. 13	14, 417, 961. 01
Jaho:			
King Hill	1, 905, 318. 80	156, 734. 25	2, 062, 053. 05
Minidoka	15, 036, 028. 86	2, 137, 206. 72	17, 173, 235. 58
Minidoka—Gooding division	1, 890, 818. 49		1, 890, 818. 49
Boise [1]	16, 030, 428. 76	2, 751, 512. 14	18, 781, 940. 90
Owyhee [1]	762, 350. 55		762, 350. 55
Total	35, 624, 945. 46	5, 045, 453. 11	40, 670, 398. 57
ansas: Garden City	395, 831. 78		395, 831. 78
Iontana:			
Huntley	1, 562, 302. 99	1, 014, 943. 79	2, 577, 246. 78
Milk River	7, 448, 280. 78	217, 611. 55	7, 665, 892. 33
Sun River	7, 187, 721. 71	304, 163. 41	7, 491, 885. 12
Lower Yellowstone [1]	2, 345, 910. 86	827, 664. 95	3, 173, 575. 81
Total	18, 544, 216. 34	2, 364, 383. 70	20, 908, 600. 04
Iebraska: North Platte [1]	14, 953, 360. 92	2, 656, 484. 64	17, 609, 845. 56
Ievada: Newlands	7, 956, 917. 16	1, 453, 490. 54	9, 410, 407. 70
Iew Mexico:			
Carlsbad	1, 464, 522. 57	841, 342. 14	2, 305, 864. 71
Hondo	381, 573. 39		381, 573. 39
Rio Grande [1]	8, 547, 138. 33	1, 610, 779. 50	10, 157, 917. 83
Total	10, 393, 234. 29	2, 452, 121. 64	12, 845, 355. 93
Iorth Dakota:			
Buford-Trenton	223, 423. 06	74, 781. 07	298, 204. 13
Williston	517, 630. 09	904, 662. 04	1, 422, 292. 13
Lower Yellowstone [1]	1, 251, 223. 38	441, 446. 48	1, 692, 669. 86
Total	1, 992, 276. 53	1, 420, 889. 59	3, 413, 166. 12
Iregon:			
Baker	68, 334. 79		68, 334. 79
Umatilla	5, 137, 937. 20	689, 727. 82	5, 827, 665. 02
Vale	2, 638, 738. 61		2, 638, 738. 61
Klamath [1]	3, 715, 708. 82	1, 079, 358. 71	4, 795, 067. 53
Owyhee [1]	1, 765, 472. 63		1, 765, 472. 63
Boise [1]	32, 125. 10	28, 000. 00	60, 125. 10
Total	13, 358, 317. 15	1, 797, 086. 53	15, 155, 403. 68
outh Dakota: Belle Fourche	4, 190, 875. 84	1, 514, 125. 09	5, 705, 000. 93
'exas: Rio Grande [1]	7, 211, 353. 20	1, 332, 796. 46	8, 544, 149. 66
Jtah:			
Strawberry Valley	3, 519, 935. 39	437, 856. 39	3, 957, 791. 78
Salt Lake Basin	2, 363, 024. 31		2, 363, 024. 31
Total	5, 882, 959. 70	437, 856. 39	6, 320, 816. 09
'ashington:			
Okanogan	1, 456, 465. 81	649, 647. 22	2, 106, 113. 03
Yakima	14, 509. 196. 64	4, 236, 112. 29	18, 745, 308. 93
Yakima—Kittitas division	6, 583, 745. 47		6, 583, 745. 47
Total	22, 549, 407. 92	4, 885, 759. 51	27, 435, 167. 43
Vyoming:			
Riverton	3, 835, 484. 30		3, 835, 484. 30
Shoshone	9, 752, 118. 45	911, 740. 50	10, 663, 858. 99
North Platte [1]	5, 206, 657. 03	95, 486. 48	5, 302, 143. 51
Total	18, 794, 259. 78	1, 007, 226. 98	19, 801, 486. 76
Ill States:			
Secondary investigations	2, 900, 836. 52		2, 900, 836. 52
Grand total	207, 859, 284. 38	31, 432, 859. 89	239, 292, 144. 27

[1] Interstate projects, expenditures for construction and for operation and maintenance partly pro- ated on an area basis.

Accretions to the reclamation fund, to June 30, 1930, from receipts under the mineral leasing act of February 25, 1920 (from oil and gas leases, coal leases, phosphate leases, and sodium leases in the public-land States)

State	Oil and gas	Coal	Phosphate	Sodium	Total
Alabama		$60,127.13			$60,127.13
California	$7,536,735.02	12.56			7,536,747.58
Colorado	166,973.10	153,525.09			320,498.19
Idaho		257.25	$5,789.45		6,046.70
Louisiana	20,413.71				20,413.71
Montana	825,936.56	85,009.51			910,946.07
Nevada		12.10	61.00	$3,413.25	3,486.35
New Mexico	85,733.43	32,879.12			118,612.55
North Dakota		64,473.90			64,473.90
South Dakota		381.38			381.38
Utah	17,359.21	204,015.61			221,374.82
Washington		14,486.96		32.01	14,518.97
Wyoming	28,595,279.72	413,040.31			29,008,320.03
Total	37,248,430.75	1,028,220.92	5,850.45	3,445.26	38,285,947.38
Potassium royalties and rentals (California)					68,296.51
Total					38,354,243.89

Irrigation and crop results, Government reclamation projects, 1929—Continued

State and project	Lands on projects covered by crop census					Other lands served by Government works, usually by a partial water supply through private canals under Warren Act or other water-service contracts				
	Irrigable acreage	Irrigated acreage	Cropped acreage	Crop value		Irrigable acreage	Irrigated acreage	Cropped acreage	Crop value	
				Total	Per acre				Total	Per acre
Montana-North Dakota:										
Lower Yellowstone:	[5] 47,450	23,945	23,945	$779,960	$32.58					
District No. 1		17,855	17,855	573,590	32.13					
District No. 2		6,050	6,050	206,370	33.89					
Nebraska-Wyoming:										
North Platte:	238,470	188,450	188,450	7,289,140	39.73					
Pathfinder Irrigation district	111,625	87,995	87,995	3,242,370	36.85	127,590	103,440	102,290	$4,831,900	$47.22
Gering and Fort Laramie Irrigation dist	55,075	49,240	49,240	2,364,940	48.02					
Goshen Irrigation district	55,595	39,830	39,830	1,432,110	35.96					
Northport Irrigation district	16,175	11,385	11,385	249,720	21.93					
Nevada: Newlands	87,500	54,040	51,380	2,057,280	40.07					
New Mexico: Carlsbad	25,655	24,335	24,220	1,847,500	76.27					
New Mexico-Texas: Rio Grande	155,000	144,200	139,775	10,664,670	78.39	71,000	60,000	49,060	1,878,430	37.80
Oregon:										
Umatilla:	18,730	11,340	11,020	286,400	26.00					
East division	11,750	7,680	7,440	177,590	23.88	605	540	435	20,825	50.00
West division	6,980	3,660	3,580	108,810	30.41	605	540	435	20,825	50.00
Oregon-California:										
Klamath:	55,390	45,870	43,765	1,790,670	40.91					
Main division	41,530	34,750	33,975	1,447,160	42.60	63,620	34,700	34,540	1,060,840	30.70
Tule Lake division	13,860	11,120	9,790	343,510	35.10					
South Dakota: Belle Fourche	[6] 61,620	36,195	[4] 47,955	1,206,575	25.16					
Utah: Strawberry Valley	41,030	40,000	38,495	1,305,440	34.00	7,275	7,230	7,230	207,110	29.43
Washington:										
Okanogan	5,850	4,255	3,835	979,220	255.35	166,720	124,390	124,390	18,315,630	147.00
Yakima:	133,280	114,665	101,675	12,431,920	122.27					
Sunnyside division	102,480	87,565	79,075	7,947,570	100.51					
Tieton division	30,800	27,100	22,600	4,484,350	198.42					
Wyoming:										
Shoshone:	73,640	43,390	43,270	1,270,970	29.37					
Garland division	41,650	33,130	33,130	1,092,330	32.97					
Frannie division	20,060	8,070	8,030	160,340	19.96					
Willwood division	11,930	2,190	2,110	18,300	8.68					
Riverton	20,000	1,075	875	10,120	11.56					
Total with irrigation	1,922,330	1,483,900	1,420,070	87,559,670	61.66	1,480,040	1,234,230	1,192,990	72,720,490	60.94

Irrigation and crop results, Government reclamation projects, 1929 [1]

State and project	Lands on projects covered by crop census					Other lands served by Government works, usually by a partial water supply through private canals under Warren Act or other water-service contracts				
	Irrigable acreage [2]	Irrigated acreage	Cropped acreage	Crop value Total	Crop value Per acre	Irrigable acreage	Irrigated acreage	Cropped acreage	Crop value Total	Crop value Per acre
Arizona: Salt River	245,660	[3] 245,660	214,750	$25,423,030	$118.39	90,280	67,800	67,800	$6,475,000	$95.50
Arizona-California:										
Yuma:										
Valley division	64,430	55,695	54,065	4,369,560	80.82	230	210	150	35,255	232.70
Reservation division	47,930	42,450	42,450	3,603,800	84.89					
California: Orland	14,215	11,065	10,905	644,360	59.08					
Yuma auxiliary (Mesa)	2,285	1,160	710	121,400	171.89					
Colorado:										
Grand Valley	20,770	13,490	12,370	503,490	40.70	18,400	13,800	13,400	1,891,000	141.11
Uncompahgre	30,380	15,160	14,435	634,985	44.00	1,650	1,550	1,545	61,800	40.00
Idaho:	75,655	60,520	60,380	2,212,710	36.65					
Boise:	171,550	164,770	150,180	5,389,330	35.88	139,025	131,500	128,400	5,046,500	39.30
New York irrigation district	17,380	15,150	15,060	383,855	25.49					
Nampa-Meridian irrigation district	40,410	38,710	37,070	1,296,740	34.98					
Boise-Kuna irrigation district	48,480	47,350	43,330	1,415,665	32.67					
Wilder irrigation district	56,710	55,945	47,600	2,015,630	42.34					
Big Bend irrigation district	1,695	1,315	1,315	51,310	39.02					
Black Canyon irrigation district	6,875	6,300	5,805	226,130	38.93	793,650	689,070	663,750	32,896,800	49.56
King Hill	8,000	6,680	6,375	249,560	39.15					
Minidoka	120,170	106,070	99,340	4,417,910	44.47					
Gravity division	71,240	60,675	56,730	2,478,610	43.69					
Pumping division	48,930	45,395	42,610	1,939,300	45.51					
Montana:										
Huntley	32,540	23,485	23,485	1,037,150	44.12					
Milk River:	184,285	40,200	38,330	975,160	25.44					
Malta division	56,650	13,650	13,210	282,290	21.36					
Glasgow division	22,135	4,390	3,800	77,560	20.42					
Chinook division	55,500	22,220	21,320	615,310	28.86					
Sun River:	55,875	20,360	27,700	426,920	15.41					
Fort Shaw division	13,900	7,190	7,340	153,250	20.88					
Greenfields and Big Coulee division	41,975	13,170	20,360	273,670	13.44					

[1] Data are for calendar year (irrigation season) except on Salt River project, where data are for corresponding "agricultural year," October, 1928, to September, 1929.

[2] Areas for which bureau was prepared to supply water in 1929.

[3] Includes 24,950 acres reported as vacant, 2,414 acres of "home tracts," and 3,548 acres (town site acreage) on which no crop was reported.

[4] Includes dry farmed tracts irrespective of the figures given below under "cropped without irrigation."

Status of construction account repayments, June 30, 1930

State and project	Construction account, June 30, 1930, repayable	Value of repayment contracts	Amounts of repayment contract due on June 30, 1930	Balance of repayment contract conditionally deferred (not due)	Amounts paid on amounts due	Amounts uncollected of amounts due	Per cent repaid of amounts due
Arizona: Salt River	$10,166,021.97	$10,166,021.97	$5,896,292.77	$4,269,729.20	$5,286,331.45	$609,961.32	89.7
Arizona-California: Yuma	9,512,609.94	5,048,073.94	3,583,042.45	1,465,031.49	3,511,170.04	71,872.41	98.0
California: Orland	2,356,448.44	2,482,342.95	703,314.19	1,779,028.76	684,975.64	18,338.55	97.4
Colorado:							
Grand Valley	4,052,535.32	4,074,584.11	59,986.08	4,014,598.03	44,053.45	15,932.63	73.4
Uncompahgre	5,466,773.15	5,510,871.31	707,771.71	4,803,099.60	489,277.64	218,494.07	69.1
Idaho:							
Boise	16,124,392.08	14,698,000.12	3,411,581.39	11,286,418.73	3,407,185.08	4,396.31	99.9
King Hill	1,489,968.94	1,489,968.94	25,800.00	1,464,168.94		25,800.00	0.0
Minidoka	13,732,723.34	11,619,819.82	7,784,653.25	3,835,166.57	7,730,684.34	53,968.91	99.3
Minidoka-Gooding	1,889,818.49	5,257,900.00	258,900.00	4,999,000.00	258,900.00		100.0
Montana:							
Huntley	1,859,806.88	1,803,806.19	532,638.91	1,271,167.28	532,638.91		100.0
Milk River	5,319,200.00	5,012,010.00	3,002.76	5,009,007.24	3,002.76		100.0
Sun River	7,030,361.68	10,012,837.24	194,440.78	9,818,396.46	193,394.54	1,046.24	99.5
Montana-North Dakota: Lower Yellowstone	4,061,076.17	4,134,864.70	218,700.47	3,916,164.23	214,077.18	4,623.29	97.9
Nebraska-Wyoming: North Platte	21,066,939.69	22,202,360.38	2,825,682.40	19,376,677.98	2,650,985.50	174,696.90	93.8
Nevada: Newlands	3,484,999.67	3,260,278.05	967,781.11	2,292,496.94	965,618.56	2,162.55	99.8
New Mexico: Carlsbad	1,421,545.31	1,425,182.75	860,170.59	565,012.16	824,860.59	35,310.00	95.9
New Mexico-Texas: Rio Grande	12,914,178.72	13,669,575.00	2,770,134.36	10,899,440.64	2,699,244.80	70,889.56	97.4
Oregon:							
Umatilla	4,403,415.95	3,818,252.93	453,913.64	3,364,339.29	389,274.93	64,638.71	85.8
Vale	2,632,089.41	4,500,000.00		4,500,000.00			
Oregon-California: Klamath	5,462,827.77	4,066,473.62	1,057,907.27	3,008,566.35	1,004,261.55	53,645.72	95.0
Oregon-Idaho: Owyhee	2,523,468.57	18,000,000.00		18,000,000.00			
South Dakota: Belle Fourche	4,461,956.64	5,416,493.23	586,010.86	4,830,482.37	586,010.86		100.0
Utah:							
Salt Lake Basin	2,317,689.04	3,000,000.00		3,000,000.00			
Strawberry Valley	3,331,243.04	3,212,135.57	1,102,641.85	2,109,493.72	1,092,267.85	10,374.00	99.1
Washington:							
Okanogan	424,198.97	424,198.97	130,791.45	293,407.52	130,791.45		100.0
Yakima	14,148,888.45	11,652,641.76	6,151,593.49	5,501,048.27	5,958,511.06	193,082.43	96.9
Yakima-Kittitas	6,562,908.31	9,000,000.00		9,000,000.00			
Wyoming:							
Riverton	3,814,292.47						
Shoshone	8,266,556.08	5,585,614.27	781,232.29	4,804,381.98	780,725.75	506.54	99.9
Total	180,298,935.79	190,544,307.82	41,067,984.07	149,476,323.75	39,438,243.93	1,629,740.14	96.6

Power plants operated on Bureau of Reclamation projects during fiscal year 1929-30

Project	Name of plant	Outgoing line voltage	Plant capacity (kv-a)	Number of units	Head in feet	First cost of plant	Cost of operation and maintenance	Estimated depreciation	Cost per kilowatt-hour, exclusive of depreciation	Distribution of kilowatt-hours generated				Total output kilowatt-hours	Gross power sales
										Sold to consumers	Irrigation and drainage requirements	Used for other purposes	Losses		
Boise	Black Canyon [1]	66,000	10,000	2	82-92	$414,317.21	$13,753.99	$15,290.99	$0.000344	Entire output delivered to Idaho Power Co.				39,922,242	$63,676.42
	Boise River [3]	22,000	1,875	3	25-30	167,905.37		5,000.00						2,250	4,000.00
Minidoka	Minidoka	33,000	10,000	6	47-48	645,921.03	20,188.63	19,470.00	.000370	22,056,423	28,925,875	369,470	3,364,442	54,527,400	157,230.68
	American Falls (2 plants) [3]	33,000	1,540	3	38-45	76,975.00	5,527.04	3,007.04		Not operated during fiscal year.					
Newlands [3]	Lahontan [6]	33,000 / 66,000	1,875	3	105 / 110	141,886.01	5,782.03 [7]	4,260.00	.000655 [5]	2,205,195	238,715	301,040		2,744,950	8,706.68
North Platte	Guernsey	33,000	6,000	2	70-90	672,244.00	12,497.21 [8]	21,000.00	.001607 [5]	23,525,214	46,020	214,954	2,739,402	19,075,340 [4]	235,781.40
	Lingle	33,000	1,750	4	107	206,364.00	11,972.65	9,360.00						7,450,310 [4]	
Okanogan	Power plant No. 1	6,600	187	1	108	11,923.44	Not operated during year.								
	Power plant No. 2	6,600	187	1	105	13,931.42									
Rio Grande	Elephant Butte No. 2	2,300	150	1	18-180	8,440.50	2,801.66	None.	.033	None.	None.	84,900		84,900	None.
Riverton	Pilot Butte	33,000	2,000	2	103	219,735.40	16,839.63	12,600.79	.01002	757,377		724,365	198,608	1,680,350	14,488.18
Salt River	Arizona Falls	11,000 [9]	1,000	2	19	109,500.73	9,716.18	5,475.04	.00377					2,575,675	
	Chandler	11,000 [9]	650	1	40	91,990.84	9,037.65	4,599.54	.00510					1,770,450	
	Crosscut	11,000 [9] / 40,000	5,250	6	111	755,147.29	42,735.73	37,757.36	.00486					8,792,500	
	Roosevelt	110,000	19,250	7	70-240	1,235,894.58	60,026.94	61,794.73	.00293	131,939,645	48,688,803	2,576,222	36,974,403	21,231,000	2,856,862.59
	So. Consolidated	40,000	40,000	5	34	163,139.60	14,654.23	8,156.98	.00277					5,296,000	
	Mormon Flat	110,000	8,750	1	40-150	482,767.80	12,038.42	24,138.39	.00031					39,161,000	
	Horse Mesa	110,000	33,300	3	265	754,885.13	49,808.81	37,744.25	.00064					77,300,000	
	Stewart Moun- tain [10]	45,000	15,000	1	35-114	320,371.98	5,082.39	5,338.91	.00036					13,980,000	
Shoshone	Shoshone	33,000	3,000	2	225	567,698.96	10,301.46	16,914.00	.00136	6,633,124	None.	242,195	724,001	7,599,320 [11]	83,476.81
	Spanish Fork	11,000	1,000	2	123.5	60,904.80	18,739.70	3,045.00	.00821	1,912,377	None.	189,959	247,023	2,349,359 [11]	38,101.40
Strawberry Valley [3]															
Yakima-Sun- nyside [3]	Rocky Ford	6,600	187	1	73	23,000.00	2,398.89	1,056.40	.00361		664,900			664,900	
Yuma [3]	Siphon Drop	33,000	2,000	2	9.29	317,936.09	13,058.82 [4]	13,248.00	.00173	5,485,209	1,581,400	80,665	386,341	7,542,615 [8]	58,080.36

Total area of swamp lands and indemnity for swamp lands granted to the states and territories, in Acres:

Alabama	418,673.61
Arkansas	7,686,455.37
California	2,185,891.18
Florida	20,303,512.13
Illinois	1,459,708.27
Indiana	1,259,190.93
Iowa	1,196,089.61
Louisiana	9,426,674.37
Michigan	5,679,925.83
Minnesota	4,663,007.10
Mississippi	3,343,805.48
Missouri	3,427,952.70
Ohio	26,251.95
Wisconsin	3,356,731.93
Total	64,433,870.46

Areas of the 11 Public Lands States, In Acres

State—	Land Surface	Water Surface	Total Areas
Arizona	72,838,400	93,440	72,931,840
California	99,617,280	1,692,800	101,310,080
Colorado	66,341,120	185,600	66,526,720
Idaho	53,346,560	341,760	63,688,320
Montana	93,568,640	509,440	94,078,080
Nevada	70,285,440	556,160	70,841,600
New Mexico	78,401,920	83,840	78,485,760
Oregon	61,188,480	698,880	61,887,360
Utah	52,597,760	1,795,840	54,393,600
Washington	42,775,040	1,446,240	44,241,280
Wyoming	62,460,160	204,800	62,664,960
Totals	753,420,800	7,628,800	761,049,600

PUBLIC LAND STATISTICS

Status of surface lands in 11 public land States (acres)

	Arizona	California	Colorado	Idaho	Montana	Nevada	New Mexico	Oregon	Utah	Washington	Wyoming	Total
WITHDRAWALS												
Reclamation Bureau	4,327,245	2,219,980	465,480	2,888,400	549,400	2,106,940	303,640	1,294,750	1,357,360	1,346,020	1,740,835	18,000,050
National forests	11,466,626	19,026,819	13,309,549	19,300,773	16,170,658	4,978,198	8,491,831	13,297,938	7,475,762	9,598,372	8,460,755	131,577,281
National Park Service:												
National parks	645,809	1,213,765	293,012	23,040	1,138,481			159,360	91,280	207,782	2,108,800	5,881,329
National monuments	31,125	3,407	13,885	49,565	160		23,593		7,660		1,363	130,758
Geological Survey:												
Power purposes	1,198,875	1,416,160	462,841	412,996	210,962	357,468	261,737	660,663	651,321	363,801	197,728	6,194,552
Reservoir site reserves	23,040	45,264	1,728		9,080			18,603	80	31,797	1,714	131,306
1888 reservoirs		6,547	17,945		20,425	1,440	3,367		11,673			61,397
Public water	19,745	199,231	9,705	15,257	8,857	14,061	10,481	26,221	36,255	920	83,505	424,238
Indian reservations	20,463,020	595,171	478,154	677,206	6,529,436	847,409	3,888,821	1,742,938	452,627	1,991,818	2,243,822	39,910,422
General Land Office:												
Stock driveways	497,042	33,682	210,230	767,861	224,828	3,555,191	1,105,061	428,341	1,224,222	10,919	1,207,293	9,264,670
Carey Act segregation	13,745			77,759	29,212			107,096	37,634		468,360	733,806
Carey Act withdrawals			32,096	156,708								188,804
Game and bird reserves	21,120	44,140		25,600	81,691	248	74,360	180,112	38,760	1,629	49,476	517,136
Naval oil and oil shale		68,249	78,127						91,472		9,481	247,329

Status of surface lands in 11 public-land States (acres)—Continued

	Arizona	California	Colorado	Idaho	Montana	Nevada	New Mexico	Oregon	Utah	Washington	Wyoming	Total
WITHDRAWALS—continued												
(9) Miscellaneous	a 684	a 1,219	a 302	a 2,448	a 6,326	a 534	a 593	a 839	a 360	a 170	a 1,274	
	b 2,560	b 604,242	b 16,493	b 51,840	b 1,134	b 85,760		b 72,624	b 3,401	b 82	b 851,755	
	c 104,127	c 356,924	c 573,178	c 80,628	c 236,270	c 35,480	c 160	c 1,344,201	c 44,501	c 627	c 5,760	
	d 10,651	g 2,680		d 28,427	d 200	g 680	d 192,872	o 40		p 10	e 160	
	e 440	h 451		e 320	j 752	m 30,598	e 53,100			q 40	g 471	
	f 15,080				k 15,776	n 125,724	g 160				m 1,516	
					l 40	l 80					p 400	
											q 295,718	5,262,882
(10) Total	38,840,934	25,837,931	15,962,725	24,558,828	25,233,688	12,139,811	14,409,776	19,333,726	11,524,368	13,553,987	17,730,186	219,125,960
(11) State area	72,838,000	99,617,000	66,401,000	53,324,000	93,397,000	70,520,000	78,396,000	61,192,000	52,599,000	44,241,000	60,542,000	753,067,000
(12) Open public lands	16,911,367	20,209,421	8,218,875	10,734,420	6,900,144	53,410,938	16,282,582	13,227,141	25,147,867	951,903	17,035,537	189,030,195
(13) Unreserved area	33,997,066	73,779,069	50,438,725	28,765,172	68,163,312	58,380,189	63,986,224	41,858,274	41,074,632	30,687,013	42,811,814	533,941,040
(14) Ratio of open public to unreserved land (per cent)	50	27	16	37	10	92	25	32	61	3	40	35

(9) From General Land Office table for period ending Nov. 30, 1929. Includes miscellaneous withdrawals under act of June 25, 1910 (36 Stat. 847), as amended.
 a. Administrative site.
 b. Aid of legislation.
 c. Classifications.
 d. Agricultural experiment stations.
 e. Military purposes.
 f. Public parks.
 g. Aeroplane purposes.
 h. Town-site purpose, harbor development, and lighthouse.
 j. Forest administrative sites.
 k. Sheep experiment station.
 l. Well-drilling reserves.
 m. Game reserves.
 n. Naval ammunition depot.
 o. Lookout station.
 p. Fish-culture purposes.
 q. Elk refuge.
(12) From General Land Office report for year ending June 30, 1929. Includes all vacant, unreserved, unappropriated, public lands of the United States.
(13) Area of State (item 11) less reserved land (item 10) to show acreage in which existing public land laws have been operative.

Withdrawals made under Federal water power act, fiscal year 1929

State	Withdrawals, fiscal year 1929	Area withdrawn	Area of withdrawn lands in national forests	Area of withdrawn lands not in national forests
Alaska	2	1, 261	1, 261	------------
Arizona	3	21, 080	3, 080	18, 000
California	23	37, 638	31, 581	6, 057
Colorado	5	1, 957	1, 957	------------
Idaho	3	4, 182	3, 924	258
Montana	5	295	250	45
Nevada	3	179	120	59
Oregon	15	20, 577	20, 277	300
Utah	2	255	------------	255
Washington	7	6, 062	5, 632	430
Wisconsin	1	40	------------	40
Wyoming	2	300	160	140
Total	71	93, 826	68, 242	25, 584

Withdrawals and restorations during fiscal year ended June 30, 1929, and total

State	Outstanding withdrawn July 1, 1928	Withdrawn, period July 1, 1928, to June 30, 1929	Restored	Outstanding withdrawn June 30, 1929
COAL LANDS	*Acres*	*Acres*	*Acres*	*Acres*
Arizona	139, 415			139, 415
California	17, 603			17, 603
Colorado	1 4, 180, 016		37, 783	4, 142, 233
Idaho	4, 761			4, 761
Montana	1 7, 883, 164		19, 223	7, 863, 941
Nevada	1 83, 673			83, 673
New Mexico	1 5, 084, 069			5, 084, 069
North Dakota	1 5, 954, 364			5, 954, 364
Oregon	4, 361			4, 361
Utah	1 3, 636, 541			3, 636, 541
Washington	1 691, 801			691, 801
Wyoming	1 2, 260, 604			2, 260, 604
Total	1 29, 940, 372		57, 006	29, 883, 366
HELIUM LANDS				
Utah	12, 255			12, 255
MINERAL LANDS				
Arizona	8, 507			8, 507
OIL LANDS				
Arizona	92, 496		92, 140	356
California	1, 178, 392			1, 178, 392
Colorado	218, 997			218, 997
Louisiana	466, 990			466, 990
Montana	1 1, 350, 426			1, 350, 426
North Dakota	84, 894			84, 894
Utah	1 1, 341, 264			1, 341, 264
Wyoming	1 541, 777			541, 777
Total	1 5, 275, 236		92, 140	5, 183, 096
OIL SHALE				
Colorado	1 64, 560			64, 560
Nevada	123			123
Utah	91, 464			91, 464
Total	1 156, 147			156, 147
PHOSPHATE LANDS				
Florida	1 68, 596		1, 520	67, 076
Idaho	1 391, 532			391, 532
Montana	1 279, 944			279, 944
Utah	301, 945		24, 601	277, 344
Wyoming	1 989, 289		2 140	989, 149
Total	1 2, 031, 306		26, 261	2, 005, 045
POTASH LANDS				
California	1 90, 357			90, 357
Nevada	1 39, 422			39, 422
New Mexico	7, 418, 437	1, 863, 723		9, 282, 160
Total	1 7, 548, 216	1, 863, 723		9, 411, 939

1 Revised to accord with Geological Survey report.
2 Withdrawn area reduced by reason of interpretation of withdrawal in terms of new survey.

Report of withdrawals made under the act of June 25, 1910 (36 Stat. 847), as amended by the act of August 24, 1912 A37 Stat. 497), also restorations therefrom, from July 1, 1928, to June 30, 1929.

WITHDRAWALS FOR AND RESTORATION FROM POWER SITE RESERVES

State	Withdrawals			Restorations				
	Number	Date of approval	Area	Number	Date of approval	Area	Outstanding July 1, 1928	Outstanding June 30, 1929
			Acres			Acres	Acres	Acres
Alabama							120	120
Alaska							93,415	93,415
Arkansas							[1] 21,994	21,994
Arizona				430	June 8, 1929	15	433,034	433,019
California				425	Nov. 10, 1928	400	291,056	290,656
Colorado				429	May 13, 1929	5,210	225,641	220,431
Idaho							201,694	201,694
Michigan							1,240	1,240
Minnesota							12,309	12,309
Montana	[2] 128	Dec. 6, 1928	393				127,772	128,165
Nebraska							761	761
Nevada							27,492	27,492
New Mexico	[2] 107	May 14, 1929	960				61,449	62,409
Oregon				424	Aug. 26, 1928	80		
				427	Feb. 26, 1929	4,437		
				428	Apr. 9, 1929	1,200	379,058	373,341
						5,717		
Utah				[2] 133	May 27, 1929	3,720	441,304	437,584
Washington				[2] 131	Mar. 30, 1929	49	98,994	98,945
Wyoming							80,325	80,325
Total			1,353			15,111	2,497,658	2,483,900

WITHDRAWALS FOR AND RESTORATION FROM PUBLIC WATER RESERVES

Arizona				56	Nov. 27, 1928	445	18,335	17,890
California	[2] 85	Mar. 15, 1929	600				187,688	188,288
Colorado	[2] 73	July 3, 1928	80					
	[1] 76	Dec. 4, 1928	640					
	[2] 88	Mar. 15, 1929	480				4,948	6,148
			1,200					
Idaho	[2] 83	Feb. 16, 1929	440				13,905	14,345
Montana	[2] 75	Nov. 10, 1928	160					
	[2] 89	Mar. 25, 1929	80				8,176	8,416
			240					
Nevada	[2] 79	Feb. 2, 1929	320					
	[2] 84	Feb. 21, 1929	120					
	120	Feb. 25, 1929	640					
	[2] 94	Apr. 22, 1929	40					
	[2] 97	May 3, 1929	120				11,406	12,646
			1,240					
New Mexico	[2] 88	Mar. 15, 1929	80					
	[2] 102	June 5, 1929	160				9,811	10,051
			240					

Aggregate cash receipts from the disposal of public and Indian lands from May
20, 1785, to June 30, 1929

Fiscal year	Cash sale	Amount of fees and commissions	Receipts, leasing act, Feb. 25, 1920	Receipts from sales of Indian lands	Miscellaneous receipts	Aggregate receipts from all sources
May 20, 1785, to June 30, 1880						$208, 059, 657. 14
1881	$3, 534, 550. 98	$860, 833. 65		$1, 006, 691. 63	$6, 727. 90	5, 408, 804. 16
1882	6, 628, 775. 92	1, 124, 531. 15		634, 617. 22	6, 591. 75	8, 394, 516. 04
1883	9, 657, 032. 28	1, 423, 329. 10		625, 404. 27	8, 118. 05	11, 713, 883. 70
1884	10, 304, 582. 49	1, 536, 410. 58		938, 137. 26	10, 274. 76	12, 789, 405. 09
1885	6, 223, 926. 74	1, 462, 188. 06		933, 483. 52	8, 821. 86	8, 628, 420. 18
1886	5, 757, 891. 06	1, 654, 876. 25		1, 607, 729. 63	10, 587. 40	9, 031, 084. 34
1887	9, 246, 321. 33	1, 537, 600. 39		1, 484, 302. 30	20, 784. 85	12, 289, 008. 87
1888	11, 203, 071. 95	1, 498, 000. 05		821, 113. 77	24, 951. 65	13, 547, 137. 42
1889	8, 018, 254. 50	1, 251, 971. 23		389, 524. 72	26, 150. 89	9, 685, 901. 34
1890	6, 349, 174. 24	1, 121, 696. 07		293, 062. 30	16, 585. 00	7, 780, 517. 61
1891	4, 160, 099. 07	944, 938. 65		318, 333. 42	5, 849. 00	5, 429, 220. 14
1892	3, 322, 865. 01	1, 064, 805. 26		456, 681. 84	15, 757. 58	4, 860. 109. 69
1893	3, 193, 280. 64	998, 184. 65		284, 752. 65	3, 516. 20	4, 479, 734. 14
1894	1, 653, 080. 71	1, 021, 205. 08		91, 981. 03	1, 557. 50	2, 767, 824. 32
1895	1, 116, 090. 07	750, 710. 59		149, 879. 48	16, 773. 89	2, 033, 454. 03
1896	1, 053, 905. 59	793, 557. 82		214, 700. 42	44, 197. 84	2, 106, 361 67
1897	917, 911. 19	678, 469. 55		438, 716. 31	52, 834. 23	2, 087, 931. 28
1898	1, 291, 076. 10	853, 265. 50		100, 317. 49	33, 336. 09	2, 277, 995. 18
1899	1, 703, 988. 32	890, 702. 17		442, 913. 73	32, 533. 12	3, 070, 137. 34
1900	2, 899, 731. 83	1, 157, 081. 03		239, 769. 39	83, 175. 85	4, 379, 758. 10
1901	2, 966, 542. 86	1, 340, 894. 29		585, 661. 27	79, 062. 37	4, 972, 160. 79
1902	4, 139, 268. 47	1, 740, 820. 18		288. 666. 68	93, 171. 85	6, 261, 927. 18
1903	8, 960, 471. 18	1, 597, 147. 48		308, 939. 14	158, 185. 85	11, 024, 743. 65
1904	7, 445, 902. 84	1, 349, 990. 89		333, 757. 62	153, 690. 63	9, 283, 341. 98
1905	4, 849, 766. 06	1, 286, 621. 93		791, 807. 67	89, 615. 72	7, 017, 811. 38
1906	4, 885, 988. 82	1, 642, 488. 56		967, 532. 50	89, 514. 02	7, 585, 523. 90
1907	7, 728, 114. 30	1, 819, 159. 21		1, 892, 805. 70	113, 098. 79	11, 553, 178. 00
1908	9, 760, 520. 19	1, 731, 883. 57		997, 972. 52	225, 283. 18	12, 715, 709. 46
1909	7, 698, 337. 03	1, 536, 890. 67		2, 651, 051. 08	330, 136. 61	12, 216, 415. 39
1910	6, 342, 744. 75	2, 028, 892. 35		2, 037, 551. 68	1, 054, 735. 28	11, 463, 924. 06
1911	5, 783, 693. 39	1, 461, 514. 30		2, 822, 600. 71	[1] 1, 022, 119. 20	11, 089, 927. 60
1912	5, 437, 502. 07	1, 234, 216. 47		2, 284, 538. 37	[1] 1, 016, 791. 09	9, 973, 048. 00
1913	2, 746, 546. 52	1, 540, 994. 15		2, 118, 469. 34	[1] 549, 494. 80	6, 955, 504. 81
1914	2, 650, 761. 84	1, 654, 085. 02		1, 844, 802. 77	47, 677. 90	6, 148, 367. 63
1915	2, 331, 368. 44	1, 581, 805. 48		1, 556, 630. 97	28, 386. 01	5, 394, 948. 20
1916	1, 769, 860. 33	1, 660, 933. 33		1, 972, 299. 49	41, 468. 44	5, 444, 561. 59
1917	1, 935, 954. 53	1, 641, 860. 14		2, 445, 429. 64	126, 386. 23	6, 149, 630. 54
1918	2, 050, 575. 58	1, 160, 350. 88		1, 935, 773. 73	285, 127. 47	5, 431, 827. 66
1919	1, 464, 718. 99	1, 194, 472. 10		1, 387, 781. 74	256, 701. 33	4, 303, 674. 16
1920	1, 990, 764. 16	1, 587, 060. 79		2, 063, 186. 06	490, 765. 40	6, 131, 776. 41
1921	1, 546, 705. 72	1, 715, 190. 52	$9, 725, 977. 31	903, 371. 93	616, 951. 88	14, 508, 197. 36
1922	906, 544. 59	1, 125, 547. 93	8, 799, 468. 17	545, 711. 91	407, 423. 12	11, 784, 695. 72
1923	645, 505. 61	828, 897. 84	7, 580, 035. 57	473, 001. 63	1, 173, 007. 02	10, 700, 447. 72
1924	551, 339. 06	684, 650. 98	13, 631, 840. 72	359, 088. 97	1, 146, 084. 31	16, 373, 004. 04
1925	638, 396. 13	563, 767. 14	8, 278, 708. 62	337, 090. 46	948, 232. 24	10, 766, 194. 59
1926	733, 648. 39	434, 585. 65	8, 384, 718. 76	805, 983. 75	1, 055, 103. 91	11, 414, 040. 46
1927	612, 132. 72	495, 604. 90	6, 669, 585. 81	620, 694. 66	803, 679. 36	9, 201, 697. 25
1928	389, 569. 57	447, 419. 61	4, 677, 277. 16	372, 031. 95	824, 156. 55	6, 710, 454. 84
1929	312, 144. 45	461, 950. 80	3, 884, 879. 88	428, 105. 77	1, 106, 885. 43	6, 193, 966. 33
Total						599, 518, 251. 05

1 Includes reclamation water-right charges.

Receipts under the mineral leasing act of February 25, 1920, from the passage of the act to June 30, 1929

State	1921–1925	1926	1927	1928	1929	Total
Alabama	$86,380.00	$920.00	$1,564.70	$3,036.10	$8,818.00	$100,718.80
California	13,657,152.02	1,092,492.65	1,194,685.61	1,389,800.40	614,191.22	17,977,721.90
Colorado	131,202.94	94,418.49	109,046.73	96,839.41	101,903.42	533,410.99
Idaho	373.54	923.62	1,963.16	2,482.41	2,995.71	8,738.44
Louisiana	4,067.45	882.73	14,215.85	3,897.63	12,118.40	35,182.06
Montana	911,791.69	249,690.59	188,897.36	119,070.36	113,187.96	1,582,637.96
Nevada	720.00	1,497.15	1,440.00	1,463.05	730.00	5,850.20
New Mexico	11,339.70	17,437.35	15,391.77	25,835.27	45,273.20	115,277.29
North Dakota	25,911.46	8,630.37	7,741.47	32,740.14	30,411.28	105,437.72
South Dakota	290.47	251.66	18.83	40.00	40.00	640.96
Utah	132,017.02	32,749.62	34,870.58	58,081.38	88,886.62	346,605.22
Washington	17,221.42	1,698.98	2,504.28	3,976.86	451.55	25,853.09
Wyoming	33,037,562.68	6,883,125.55	5,097,775.42	2,940,091.00	2,835,871.32	50,794,425.97
Total	48,016,030.39	8,384,718.76	6,669,518.76	4,677,354.01	3,884,878.68	71,632,500.60

Payments to States from receipts under the mineral leasing act of February 25, 1920, from the passage of the act to June 30, 1929

State	1921–1925	1926	1927	1928	1929	Total
Alabama	$32,392.50	$345.00	$586.76	$1,138.54	$3,306.75	$37,769.55
California	2,378,512.53	433,475.44	445,601.48	521,319.18	241,031.71	4,019,940.34
Colorado	49,060.43	31,531.94	40,867.46	34,918.75	36,816.11	193,194.69
Idaho	140.08	370.36	736.19	930.90	1,123.39	3,300.92
Louisiana	1,506.25	350.06	5,330.94	1,461.61	4,544.40	13,193.26
Montana	356,412.67	98,482.97	70,832.76	44,651.39	42,445.49	612,825.28
Nevada	270.00	561.43	540.00	548.64	273.75	2,193.82
New Mexico	4,252.40	6,539.01	5,771.91	9,688.23	16,977.45	43,229.00
North Dakota	9,357.68	3,453.05	2,904.18	12,277.55	11,404.23	39,396.69
South Dakota	108.93	94.37	7.06	15.00	15.00	240.36
Utah	49,748.94	12,311,93	12,905.95	21,705.52	33,332.48	130,004.82
Washington	6,586.84	939.11	939.11	1,491.32	169.33	9,823.72
Wyoming	12,120,637.66	2,584,388.31	1,911,665.78	1,102,534.13	996,590.99	18,715,816.87
Total	15,008,986.91	3,172,540.99	2,498,689.58	1,752,680.76	1,388,031.08	23,820,929.32

FISCAL YEAR 1929

Source of receipts	Disposition in the Treasury			
	General fund	Reclamation fund	State funds	Total
Sales of public lands	$46, 304. 12	$255, 598. 08	$10, 242. 25	$312, 144. 45
Fees and commissions	96, 856. 69	365, 094. 11		461, 950. 80
Bonuses, rentals, and royalties from mineral leases	431, 054. 94	2, 038, 805. 94	1, 456, 289. 95	3, 926, 150. 83
Sales of land and timber in Oregon and California railroad grant	104, 018. 88		[1] 580, 000. 00	684, 018. 88
Sales of land and timber in Coos Bay wagon-road grant	131, 151. 16		[2] 43, 717. 05	174, 868. 21
Sales of reclamation town sites and camp sites		8, 152. 44		8, 152. 44
Sales of timber in Alaska	7, 464. 28			7, 464. 28
Royalties on coal leases in Alaska	6, 661. 80			6, 661. 80
Rentals from fur farms in Alaska	1, 280. 00			1, 280. 00
Royalties and rentals from potash depoits		11, 448. 75		11, 448. 75
Power permits	12, 302. 16			12, 302. 16
Miscellaneous (copies of records, survey fees, sales of Government property, etc.)	47, 992. 40			47, 992. 40
Total	885, 086. 43	2, 679, 099. 32	2, 090, 249. 25	5, 654, 435. 00
Sales and leases of Indian lands				[3] 539, 531. 33
Aggregate				6, 193, 966. 33

1 Estimated amount to be paid certain counties in the State of Oregon in lieu of taxes.
2 Amount payable to Coos County as 25 per cent of proceeds of sales of lands and timber.
3 Of the amount received as royalty from oil lands in the bed of the Red River, Okla., 37½ per cent, amounting to $41,784.58, is paid to the State of Oklahoma, and the balance, amounting to $69,640.98, is credited to Kiowa, Comanche, and Apache Indians.

National forest receipts from all sources in the public-land States, the amounts paid therefrom to the States, the amounts transferred to the road and trail fund, and the balance.

FISCAL YEAR 1929

Arizona	$410, 995. 03	$40, 400. 81	$92, 648. 56	$37, 059. 42	$240, 886. 24
California	1, 426, 424. 41		356, 606. 10	142, 642. 44	927, 175. 87
Colorado	498, 861. 16		124, 715. 29	49, 886. 12	324, 259. 75
Idaho	627, 712. 50		156, 928. 12	62, 771. 25	408, 013. 13
Montana	263, 875. 57		65, 968. 89	26, 387. 56	171, 519. 12
Nevada	92, 523. 09		23, 130. 77	9, 252. 31	60, 140. 01
New Mexico	140, 349. 59	842. 10	34, 876. 87	13, 950. 75	90, 679. 87
Oregon	1, 060, 103. 88		265, 025. 97	106, 010. 39	689, 067. 52
South Dakota	171, 953. 08		42, 988. 27	17, 195. 31	111, 769. 50
Utah	205, 148. 21		51, 287. 05	20, 514. 82	133, 346. 34
Washington	671, 117. 14		167, 779. 28	67, 111. 71	436, 226. 15
Wyoming	297, 837. 61		74, 459. 40	29, 783. 76	193, 594. 45
Total	5, 866, 901. 27	41, 242. 91	1, 456, 414. 57	582, 565. 84	3, 786, 677. 95

Grazing receipts by States, the amounts paid therefrom to the States, and the amounts transferred to the general fund in the Treasury

FISCAL YEAR 1929

State	Grazing receipts	Paid States under act of May 23, 1908	Paid school fund, Arizona and New Mexico, act of June 20, 1910	Transferred to general fund in Treasury
Alabama	$9.60	$2.40		$7.21
Arizona	149,106.96	33,612.44	$14,657.21	100,837.30
Arkansas	176.40	44.10		132.30
California	190,904.34	47,726.08		143,178.26
Colorado	322,296.90	80,574.22		241,722.68
Florida	227.41	56.88		170.53
Georgia	138.36	34.59		103.77
Idaho	225,076.81	56,269.20		168,807.61
Maine	15.69	3.92		11.77
Montana	139,817.64	34,954.41		104,863.23
Nebraska	9,411.98	2,352.99		7,058.99
Nevada	84,007.72	21,001.93		63,005.79
New Hampshire	216.35	54.09		162.26
New Mexico	91,881.33	22,832.51	551.29	68,497.53
North Carolina	266.30	66.57		199.73
Oklahoma	3,137.19	784.30		2,352.89
Oregon	156,970.60	39,242.65		117,727.95
South Carolina	31.14	7.78		23.36
South Dakota	18,185.71	4,546.43		13,639.28
Tennessee	162.43	40.61		121.82
Utah	174,606.51	43,651.62		130,954.89
Virginia	509.78	127.44		382.34
Washington	42,716.98	10,679.24		32,037.74
West Virginia	382.98	95.74		287.24
Wyoming	130,032.70	32,508.17		97,524.53
Total	1,740,289.81	431,270.31	15,208.50	1,293,811.00

Class, number, and area of patents issued during fiscal year ended June 30, 1929

Class	Number	Acres	Class	Number	Acres
Abandoned military reservation	39	6,691.55	Private land claim	32	17,780.33
Agricultural college scrip	1	(¹)	Public sale	370	29,653.03
Cemetery site	3	120.64	Railroad	39	230,106.97
Coal deposits	1	(²)	Railroad lieu	11	746.66
Commuted homesteads	157	13,634.45	Reclamation homestead	181	*13,489.29
Desert land	302	49,956.62	Reclamation desert land	1	120.00
Desert land segregation	4	2,264.50	Reissue	526	(²)
Forest exchange	53	56,630.19	Sioux half-breed scrip	4	440.49
Forest homesteads	171	16,999.90	Small holding claim	16	219.18
Forest lieu	39	6,311.61	Soldiers' additional	64	2,856.66
Homesteads, final	1,583	190,068.93	Special act	97	25,055.66
Homesteads, enlarged	1,229	305,368.39	Supplemental (act Apr. 14, 1914)	1	(²)
Homesteads, stock raising	3,271	1,350,384.64	Swamp	34	12,836.72
Indian fee	1,208	(²)	Timber culture	9	1,281.59
Indian homestead, act July 4, 1884	1	80.00	Timber and stone	140	11,709.20
Indian homestead reservation	24	2,828.04	Timber sales	119	(²)
Indian trust	862	92,896.34	To complete record	153	(³)
Military bounty land warrant	7	519.30	Town lots	588	366.42
Mineral	359	46,931.17	Valentine scrip	9	326.07
Miscellaneous cash	57	5,972.93			
				11,765	2,494,647.47

	Acres
Patented area under the Kinkaid Act	1,480
Patented area under coal reserved	69,606
Patented area under act July 17, 1914 (oil, gas, phosphate, etc., reserved)	59,958

¹ Supplemental; no area reported.
² Patented area not included in above report.

	Acres
Indian fee	177,644
Timber sales	13,037
Coal deposits	80
Under act Apr. 14, 1914	40
Reissues	65,971

³ No area to be reported

Land and Scrip Granted to States and Territories for Educational and Other Purposes

State or Territory	Purpose of Grant	Amount Granted Acres	Total by States
Alabama—			
	Tuskegee Normal and Industrial Institute	25,000.00	
	Industrial School for Girls	25,000.00	
	Seminary of Learning	46,080.00	
	Internal Improvements, including Rivers and Shoals	500,000.00	
	Agricultural College Scrip	240,000.00	
	Common Schools, Sec. 16	911,627.00	
	Salt Springs and contiguous land	23,040.00	
	Seat of Government	1,620.00	
	University	46,080.00	
	Searcy Hospital for colored insane	181.41	
	Swamp	418,715.56	
	Swamp land indemnity	20,920.08	2,258,264.05
Alaska Territory—			
	Common schools, Secs. 16 and 36, reserved (estimated)	21,009,209.00	
	Agricultural College and School of Mines, certain Secs. 33, reserved (estimated)	436,000.00	21,445,209.00
Arizona—			
	University	246,080.00	
	Public buildings	100,000.00	
	Penitentiaries	100,000.00	
	Insane asylums	100,000.00	
	Deaf, dumb and blind asylum	100,000.00	
	Miners' hospital	50,000.00	
	Normal schools	200,000.00	
	Charitable, penal, etc.	100,000.00	
	Agricultural and mechanical colleges	150,000.00	
	School of Mines	150,000.00	
	Military institutes	100,000.00	
	Payment of bonds issued to Maricopa, Pima, Yavapai and Coconimo counties	1,000,000.00	
	Common schools, secs. 2 and 32, 16 and 36	8,093,156.00	
	Miners' Hospital	50,000.00	10,539,236.00
Arkansas—			
	Internal improvements	500,000.00	

State or Territory	Purpose of Grant	Amount Granted Acres	Total by States
Arkansas—(Continued)			
	University	46,080.00	
	Public buildings	10,600.00	
	Agricultural college scrip	150,000.00	
	Common schools, sec. 16	933,778.00	
	Salt springs and contiguous lands	46,080.00	
	Swamp	7,686,455.37	9,372,993.37
California—			
	Internal improvements	500,000.00	
	University	46,080.00	
	Public buildings	6,400.00	
	Agricultural and mechanical colleges	150,000.00	
	Common schools, secs. 16 and 36	5,534,293.00	
	Swamp	2,185,891.18	8,425,581.52
Colorado—			
	Internal improvements	500,000.00	
	University	46,080.00	
	Public buildings	32,000.00	
	Penitentiaries	32,000.00	
	Agricultural college	90,000.00	
	Common schools, secs. 16 and 36	3,685,618,00	
	Salt Springs and contiguous lands	46,080.00	
	State Agricultural college	1,600.00	
	Biological Station	160.00	4,433,538.00
Connecticut—			
	Agricultural college scrip	180,000.00	180,000.00
Delaware—			
	Agricultural college scrip	90,000.00	90,000.00
Florida—			
	Internal improvements	500,000.00	
	Seminaries of learning	92,160.00	
	Seat of government	5,120.00	
	Agricultural college scrip	90,000.00	
	Common schools, sec. 16	975,307.00	
	Swamp	20,212,380.29	
	Swamp land indemnity	94,782.80	21,969,750.19
Georgia—			
	Agricultural college scrip	270,000.00	270,000.00
Idaho—			
	Lava hot springs	187.30	
	University	46,080.00	
	University, Moscow	50,000.00	

State or Territory	Purpose of Grant	Amount Granted Acres	Total by States
Idaho—(Continued)			
	Agricultural college	90,000.00	
	Penitentiary	50,000.00	
	Public buildings	32,000.00	
	Insane asylum	50,000.00	
	Educational, charitable, etc.	150,000.00	
	Normal schools	100,000.00	
	Scientific schools	100,000.00	
	Common schools, secs. 16 and 36	2,963,698.00	
	Fish culture	191.95	3,632,157.25
Illinois—			
	Internal improvements, including canals	533,368.24	
	Seminary of learning	46,080.00	
	Seat of government	2,560.00	
	Agricultural college scrip	480,000.00	
	Common schools, sec. 16	996,320.00	
	Salt Springs and contiguous lands	121,029.00	
	Swamp	1,457,559.20	
	Swamp land indemnity	2,309.07	3,639,225.51
Indiana—			
	Internal improvements (canals and and roads)	1,916,804.56	
	Seminary of learning	46,080.00	
	Seat of government	2,560.00	
	Agricultural college scrip	390,000.00	
	Common schools, sec. 16	668,578.00	
	Salt springs and contiguous lands	23,040.00	
	Swamp	1,254,310.73	
	Swamp land indemnity	4,880.20	4,306,253.49
Iowa—			
	Internal improvements	500,000.00	
	University	46,080.00	
	Public buildings	3,200.00	
	Agricultural college	240,000.00	
	Common schools, sec. 16	988,196.00	
	Salt springs and contiguous lands	46,080.00	
	Swamp	874,152.63	
	Swamp land indemnity	321,976.98	3,019,685.61
Kansas—			
	Internal improvements	500,000.00	
	University	46,080.00	
	Public buildings	6,400.00	
	Agricultural college	90,000.00	
	Agricultural college	7,682.00	

State or Territory	Purpose of Grant	Amount Granted Acres	Total by States
Kansas—(Continued)			
	Common schools, secs. 16 and 36	2,907,520.00	
	Salt springs and contiguous lands	46,080.00	
	Game preserve	3,021.20	3,606,783.20
Kentucky—			
	Deaf and dumb asylum	22,508.65	
	Agricultural college scrip	330,000.00	352,508.65
Louisiana—			
	Internal improvements	500,000.00	
	Seminary of learning	46,080.00	
	Agricultural college scrip	210,000.00	
	Common schools, sec. 16	807,271,00	
	Swamp	9,424,545.60	
	Swamp land indemnity	32,630.97	11,020,739.13
Maine—			
	Agricultural college scrip	210,000.00	210,000.00
Maryland—			
	Agricultural college scrip	210,000,00	210,000.00
Massachusetts—			
	Agricultural college scrip	360,000.00	360,000.00
Michigan—			
	Internal improvements	500,000.00	
	University	46,080.00	
	Public buildings	3,200.00	
	Agricultural college	240,000.00	
	Common schools, sec. 16	1,021,867.00	
	Salt springs and contiguous lands	46,080.00	
	Swamp	5,656,071.73	
	Swamp land indemnity	24,038.69	
	Canals	1,250,235.85	8,787,523.27
Minnesota—			
	Internal improvements	500,000.00	
	University	92,160.00	
	Public buildings	6,400.00	
	Agricultural college	120,000.00	
	Experimental forestry	20,000.00	
	Public park	8,392.51	
	Common schols, secs. 16 and 36	2,874,951.00	
	Salt springs and contigious lands	46,080.00	
	Swamp	4,701,543.34	8,369,526.85
Mississippi—			
	Internal improvements	500,000.00	

State or Territory	Purpose of Grant	Amount Granted Acres	Total by States
Mississippi—(Continued)			
	Seminary of learning	69,120.00	
	Seat of government	1,253.16	
	Agricultural college scrip	210,000.00	
	Common schools, sec. 16	824,213,00	
	Swamp	3,289,638.73	
	Swamp land indemnity	56,781.76	4,951,006.65
Missouri—			
	Internal improvements	500,000.00	
	Seminary of learning	46,080.00	
	Seat of government	2,560.00	
	Agricultural college	330,000.00	
	Common schools, sec. 16	1,221,813.00	
	Salt springs and contiguous lands	46,080.00	
	Swamp	3,346,936.01	
	Swamp land indemnity	81,016.69	5,574,485.70
Montana—			
	University	46,080.00	
	Agricultural college	140,000.00	
	Public buildings	182,000.00	
	Deaf and dumb asylum	50,000.00	
	Reform school	50,000.00	
	School of mines	100,000.00	
	Normal schools	100,000.00	
	Militia camp	640.00	
	Observatory for university	480.00	
	Biological station	160.00	
	Common schools, secs. 16 and 36	5,198,258,00	
	Fort Assinniboine, for educational institutions	2,000.00	5,869,618.00
Nebraska—			
	Penitentiary	32,000.00	
	Internal improvements	500,000.00	
	University	46,080.00	
	Public Buildings	12,800.00	
	Agricultural college	90,000.00	
	Common schools, Secs. 16 and 36	2,730,951.00	
	Salt Springs and contiguous lands	46,000.00	
	Dry-land agricultural experiments	800.00	3,458,711.00
Nevada—			
	Internal improvements	500,000.00	
	University	46,080.00	
	Penitentiary	12,800.00	
	Public buildings	12,800.00	
	Mining and mechanic arts	90,000.00	

State or Territory Purpose of Grant	Amount Granted Acres	Total by States
Nevada—(Continued)		
Public buildings	12,800.00	
Mining and mechanic arts	90,000.00	
Common schools, Secs. 16 and 36, and lieu lands, act June 16, 1880	2,061,967.00	2,723,647.00
New Hampshire—		
Agricultural college scrip	150,000.00	150,000.00
New Jersey—		
Agricultural college scrip		210,000.00
New Mexico, (Act June 21, 1898)—		
University	111,080.00	
Saline land (University)	1,622.86	
Agricultural college	100,000.00	
Improvement of Rio Grande	100,000.00	
Penitentiary	50,000.00	
Public buildings	32,000.00	
Insane asylum	50,000.00	
Deaf and dumb asylum	50,000.00	
Reform school	50,000.00	
Normal schools	100,000.00	
School of Mines	50,000.00	
Blind asylum	50,000.00	
Reservoirs	500,000.00	
Miners' hospital	50,000.00	
Military institute	50,000.00	
Common schools, Secs. 16 and 36	4,355,662.00	
New Mexico, (Act June 20, 1910)—		
University	200,000.00	
Public buildings	100,000.00	
Insane asylums	100,000.00	
Penitentiaries	100,000.00	
Deaf, dumb and blind asylum	100,000.00	
Miners' hospitals	50,000.00	
Normal schools	200,000.00	
Charitable, penal and reformatory	100,000.00	
Agricultural and mechanical colleges	150,000.00	
School of Mines	150,000.00	
Military institutes	100,000.00	
Payment of bonds issued by Grant and Sante Fe counties	1,000,000.00	
Common schools, Secs. 2 and 32	4,355,662.00	
Reimbursements:	250,000.00	12,656,026.86
New York—		
Agricultural college Scrip	990,000.00	990,000.00

State or Territory	Purpose of Grant	Amount Granted Acres	Total by States
North Carolina—			
	Agricultural college scrip	270,000.00	270,000.00
North Dakota—			
	State Historical Society	75.50	
	University	86,080.00	
	Agricultural college	130,000.00	
	Public buildings	82,000.00	
	Educational, charitable, etc.	170,000.00	
	Deaf and dumb asylum	40,000.00	
	Reform school	40,000.00	
	School of mines	40,000.00	
	Normal school	80,000.00	
	Common schools, Secs. 16 and 36	2,495,396.00	3,163,551.50
Ohio—			
	Internal improvements (canals and roads)	1,019,071.98	
	Seminaries of learning	69,120.00	
	Agricultural college scrip	630,000.00	
	Common schools, Sec. 16	724,266.00	
	Salt Springs and contiguous lands	24,216.00	
	Swamp	26,251.95	2,492,925.93
Oklahoma—			
	Normal schools	300,000.00	
	Oklahoma university	250,000.00	
	University preparatory school	150,000.00	
	Agricultural and mechanical college	250,000.00	
	Colored agricultural and normal university	100,000.00	
	Common schools, Secs. 16 and 36	1,375,000.00	
	Certain Secs. 13 and 33	669,000.00	
	Insane asylum	1,760.25	3,095,760.25
Oregon—			
	Internal improvements	500,000.00	
	University	46,080.00	
	Public buildings	6,400.00	
	Agricultural college	90,000.00	
	Common schools, Secs. 16 and 36	3,399,360.00	
	Salt Springs and contiguous lands	46,080.00	
	Public Park	1,401.96	
	Swamp	264,212.66	4,352,534.62
Pennsylvania—			
	Agricultural college scrip	780,000.00	780,000.00

State or Territory	Purpose of Grant	Amount Granted Acres	Total by States
Rhode Island—			
	Agricultural college scrip	120,000.00	120,000.00
South Carolina—			
	Agricultural college scrip	180,000.00	180,000.00
South Dakota—			
	University	86,080.00	
	Agricultural college	160,000.00	
	Public buildings	82,000.00	
	Educational and charitable	170,000.00	
	Deaf and dumb asylum	40,000.00	
	Reform school	40,000.00	
	School of mines	40,000.00	
	Normal schools	80,000.00	
	Missionary work	160.00	
	Military camp ground	640.00	
	Insane asylum	640.00	
	Common schools, Secs. 16 and 36	2,733,084.00	
	Public Park	1,599.39	3,434,203.39
Tennessee—			
	Agricultural college scrip	300,000.00	300,000.00
Texas—			
	Agricultural college scrip	180,000.00	180,000.00
Utah—			
	University	156,080.00	
	Agricultural college	200,000.00	
	Public buildings	64,000.00	
	Insane asylum	100,000.00	
	Deaf and dumb asylum	100,000.00	
	Reform school	100,000.00	
	School of mines	100,000.00	
	Normal schools	100,000.00	
	Blind asylum	100,000.00	
	Reservoirs	500,000.00	
	Miners' hospital	50,000.00	
	Common schools, Secs. 2, 16, 32 and 36	5,844,196.00	
	Miners' hospital	50,000.00	7,464,276.00
Vermont—			
	Agricultural college scrip	150,000.00	150,000.00
Virginia—			
	Agricultural college scrip	300,000.00	300,000.00
Washington—			
	University	46,080.00	

State or Territory	Purpose of Grant	Amount Granted Acres	Total by States
Washington—(Continued)			
	Agricultural college	90,000.00	
	Public buildings	132,000.00	
	Educational and charitable	200,000.00	
	Normal schools	100,000.00	
	Scientific schools	100,000.00	
	Common schools, Secs. 16 and 36	2,376,391.00	3,044,471.00
West Virginia—			
	Agricultural college scrip	150,000.00	150,000.00
Wisconsin—			
	Canal	338,626.97	
	River improvement	683,722.43	
	Internal improvements	500,000.00	
	University	92,160.00	
	Public buildings	6,400.00	
	Agricultural college	240,000.00	
	Forestry	20,000.00	
	Common schools, Sec. 16	982,329.00	
	Swamp	3,251,985.36	
	Swamp land indemnity	105,047.99	6,220,271.25
Wyoming—			
	University	46,080.00	
	Agricultural college	90,000.00	
	Public buildings	107,000.00	
	Penitentiary	30,000.00	
	Insane asylum	30,000.00	
	Educational, penal, etc.	290,000.00	
	Deaf and dumb asylum	30,000.00	
	Miners' hospital	30,000.00	
	Fish hatcheries	5,480.00	
	Poor farm	10,000.00	
	Common schools, Secs. 16 and 36	3,470,009.00	4,138,569.00
GRAND TOTAL			202,920,083.74

INDEX TO STATISTICS IN TEXT

INDEX TO STATISTICS

THE DEVELOPMENT OF PUBLIC LAND IN THE UNITED STATES

An Arno Press Collection

Bartley, Ernest R. **The Tidelands Oil Controversy.** 1953

Bayard, Charles J. **The Development of the Public Land Policy, 1783-1820, With Special Reference to Indiana** (Doctoral Dissertation, Indiana University, 1956). 1979

Bledsoe, S[amuel] T[homas]. **Indian Land Laws.** 1909

Copp, Henry N[orris]. **Manual for the Use of Prospectors on the Mineral Lands of the United States.** 1897

Copp, Henry N[orris]. **Public Land Laws.** 1875

Copp, Henry N[orris]. **United States Mineral Lands.** 1882

Dana, Samuel Trask and Myron Krueger. **California Lands.** 1958

Davison, Stanley R. **The Leadership of the Reclamation Movement, 1875-1902** (Doctoral Dissertation, University of California, Berkeley, 1952). 1979

Gould, Clarence P. **The Land System in Maryland, 1720-1765.** 1913

Ise, John. **Our National Park Policy.** 1961

Johnson, V. Webster and Raleigh Barlowe. **Land Problems and Policies.** 1954

Martz, Clyde O. **Cases and Materials on the Law of Natural Resources.** 1951

Malone, Joseph J. **Pine Trees and Politics.** 1964

Montgomery, Mary and Marion Clawson. **History of Legislation and Policy Formation of the Central Valley Project.** 1946

O'Callaghan, Jerry A. **The Disposition of the Public Domain in Oregon.** 1960

Peters, William E. **Ohio Lands and Their History.** 1930

Rae, John B. **The Development of Railway Land Subsidy Policy in the United States** (Doctoral Dissertation, Brown University, 1936). 1979

Shambaugh, Benjamin F[ranklin]. **Constitution and Records of the Claim Association of Johnson County, Iowa.** 1894

Smathers, George H. **The History of Land Titles in Western North Carolina.** 1938

Stewart, Lowell O. **Public Land Surveys.** 1935

Tatter, Henry W. **The Preferential Treatment of the Actual Settler in the Primary Disposition of the Vacant Lands in the United States** (Doctoral Dissertation, Northwestern University, 1933). 1979

Taylor, Paul S. **Essays on Land, Water, and the Law in California.** 1979

U.S. House of Representatives. **The Existing Laws of the United States of a General and Permanent Character, and Relating to the Survey and Disposition of the Public Domain, December 1, 1880.** 1884

U.S. House of Representatives. **Laws of the United States:** Of a Temporary Character, and Exhibiting the Entire Legislation of Congress Upon Which the Public Land Titles Have Depended. Two vols. 1881

U.S. Senate. **A National Plan for American Forestry.** Two vols. 1933

U.S. Senate. **The Western Range.** 1936

Wiel, Samuel C. **Water Rights in the Western States.** Two vols. 1911

Winter, Charles E. **Four Hundred Million Acres.** 1932

Wirth, Fremont P. **The Discovery and Exploitation of the Minnesota Iron Lands.** 1937